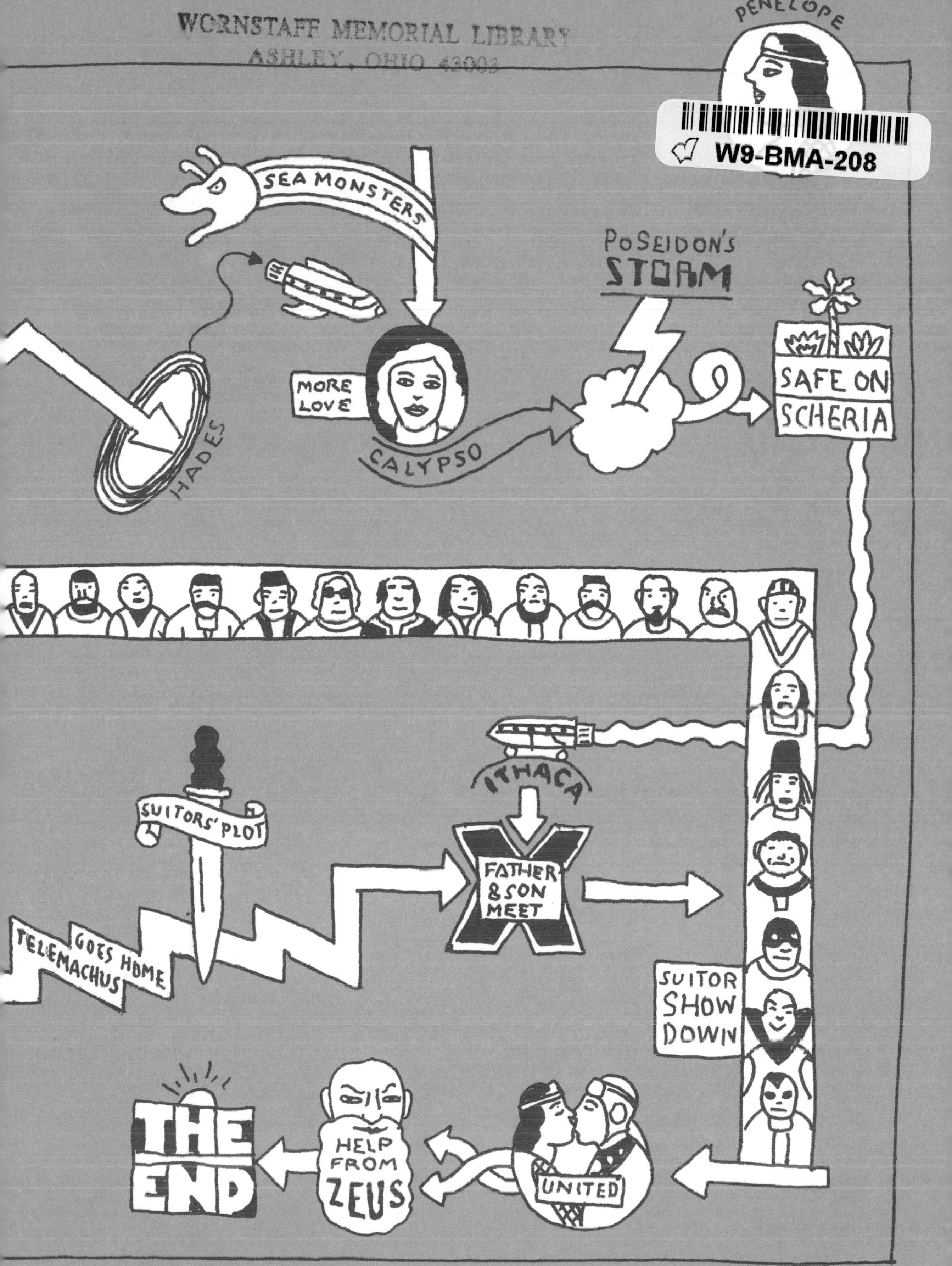
PENELOPE
SEA MONSTERS
HADES
MORE LOVE
CALYPSO
POSEIDON'S STORM
SAFE ON SCHERIA
ITHACA
FATHER & SON MEET
SUITORS' PLOT
TELEMACHUS GOES HOME
SUITOR SHOW DOWN
UNITED
HELP FROM ZEUS
THE END

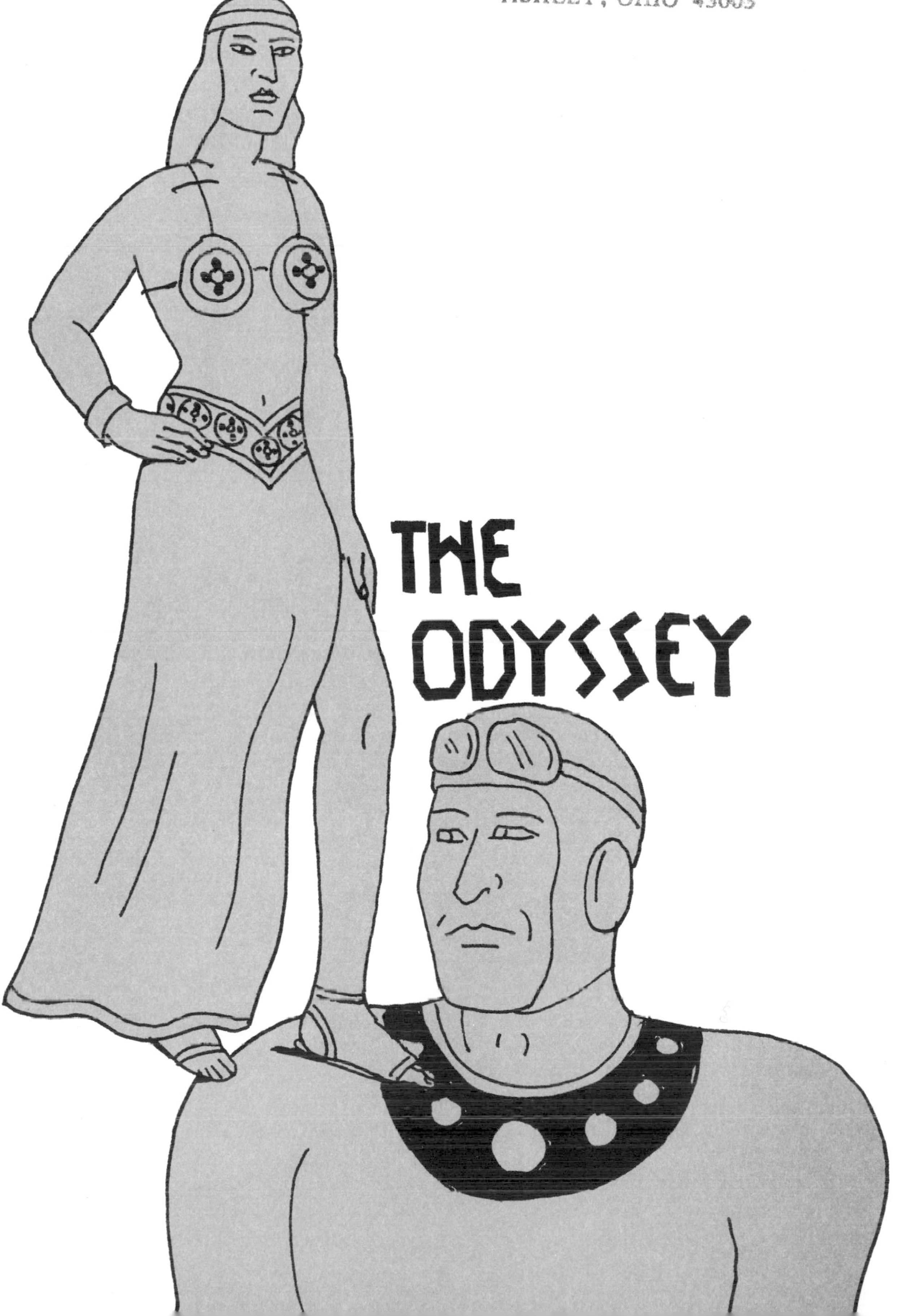
THE
ODYSSEY

BY THE SAME AUTHOR

DANTE'S DIVINE COMEDY
SEYMOUR: THE OBSESSIVE IMAGES OF SEYMOUR CHWAST
THE CANTERBURY TALES
THE PUSH PIN GRAPHIC
MOONRIDE
THE 12 CIRCUS RINGS
THE ALPHABET PARADE
THE LEFT-HANDED DESIGNER

WITH STEVEN HELLER:
GRAPHIC STYLE
ILLUSTRATION: A VISUAL HISTORY

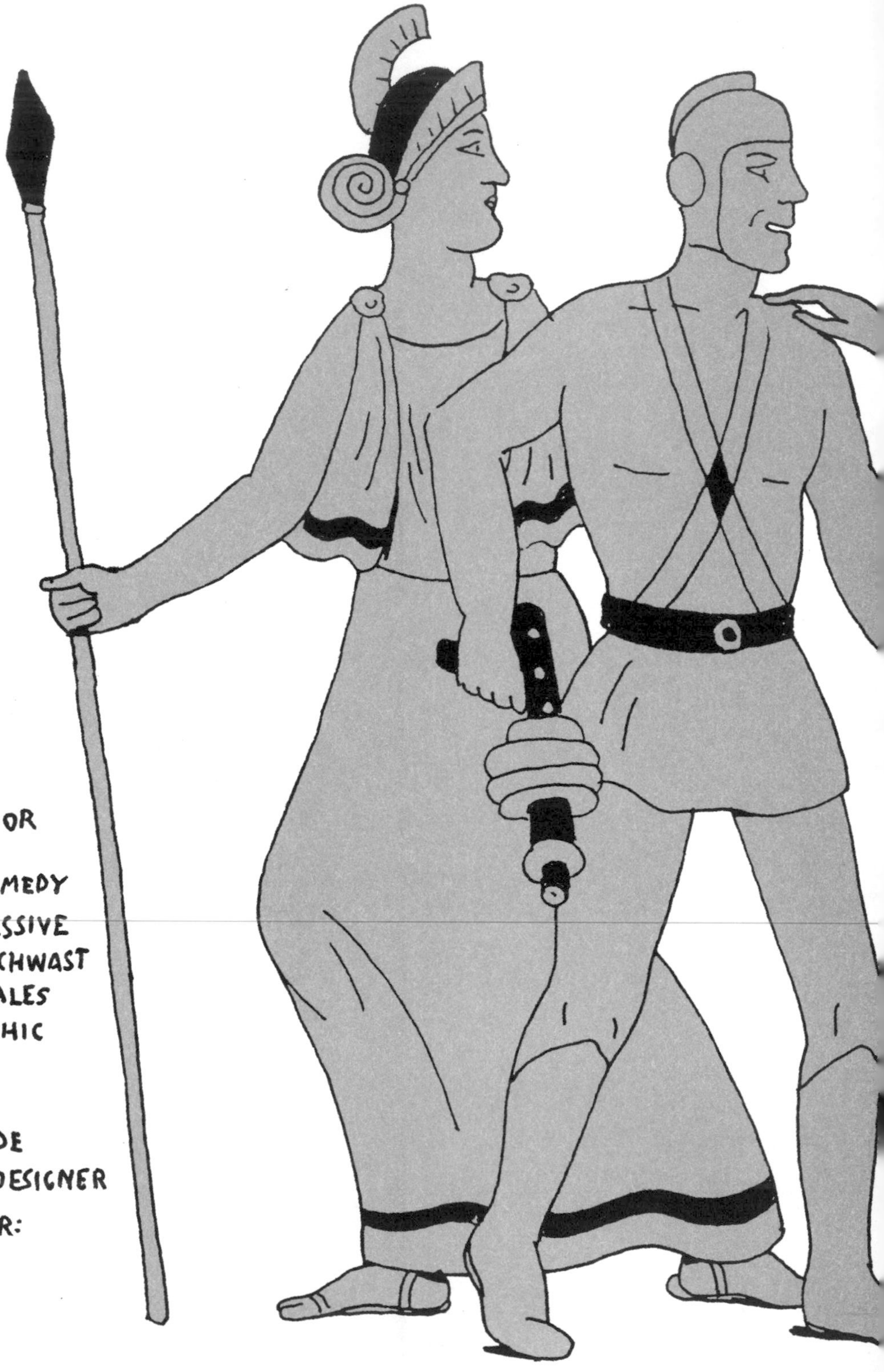

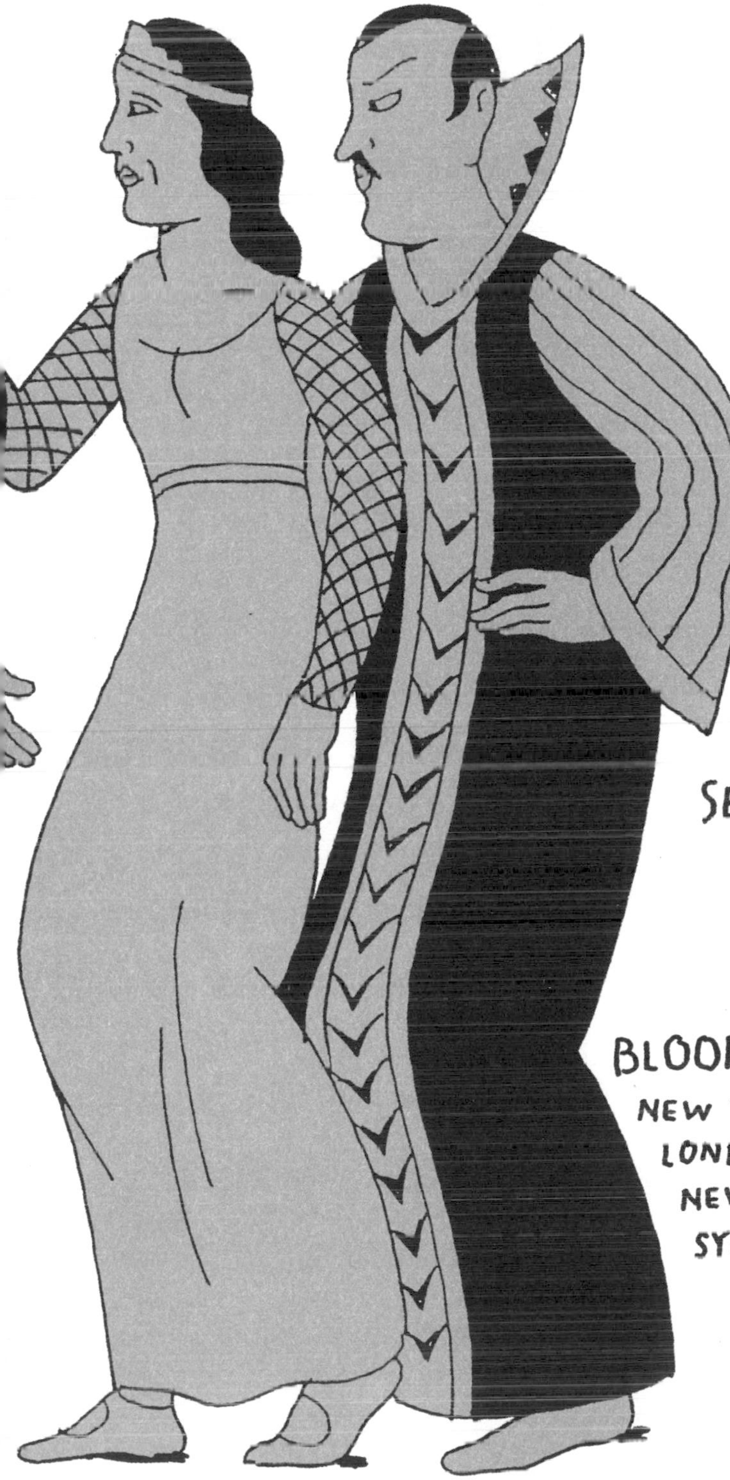

HOMER
THE ODYSSEY

ADAPTED BY
SEYMOUR CHWAST

BLOOMSBURY
NEW YORK
LONDON
NEW DELHI
SYDNEY

FOR

THOSE AGAINST

FUTURE

TROJAN WARS

 FOR INFORMATION ADDRESS BLOOMSBURY USA, 175 FIFTH AVENUE, NEW YORK, NY 10010

PUBLISHED BY BLOOMSBURY USA, NEW YORK

ALL PAPERS USED BY BLOOMSBURY USA ARE NATURAL, RECYCLABLE PRODUCTS MADE FROM WOOD GROWN IN WELL-MANAGED FORESTS. THE MANUFACTURING PROCESSES CONFORM TO THE ENVIRONMENTAL REGULATIONS OF THE COUNTRY OF ORIGIN.

LIBRARY OF CONGRESS CATALOGING-IN-PUBLICATION DATA

CHWAST, SEYMOUR.

THE ODYSSEY / [HOMER]; ADAPTED BY SEYMOUR CHWAST.--1ST U.S. ED.

P. CM.

ISBN 978-1-60819-486-5

1. GRAPHIC NOVELS. I HOMER. ODYSSEY. II. TITLE

PN6727. C499039 2012

741.5'973--DC23

2012010047

FIRST U.S. EDITION 2012

1 3 5 7 9 10 8 6 4 2

ART, DESIGN, AND LETTERING BY SEYMOUR CHWAST

PRINTED IN THE U.S.A. BY QUAD/GRAPHICS TAUNTON

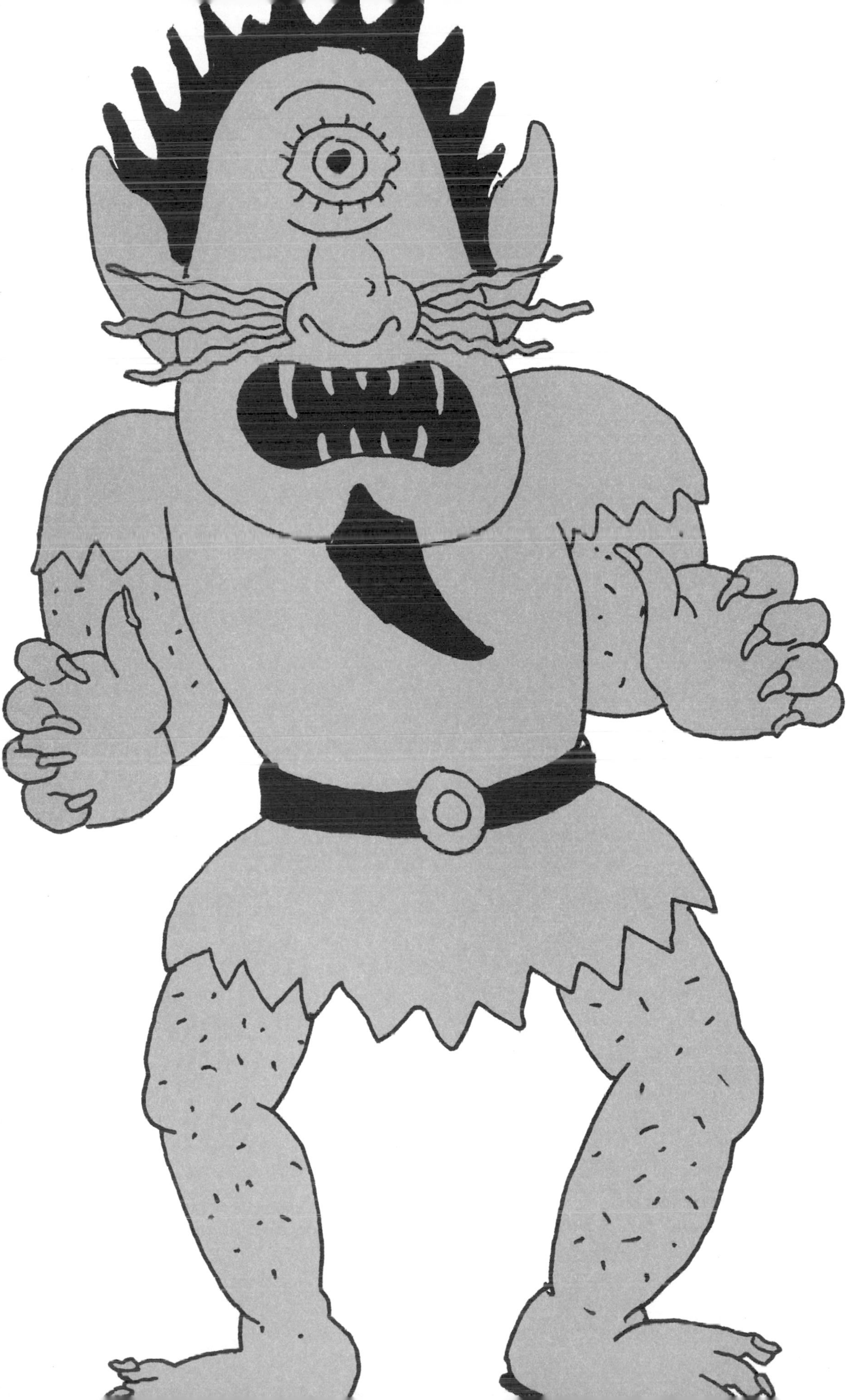

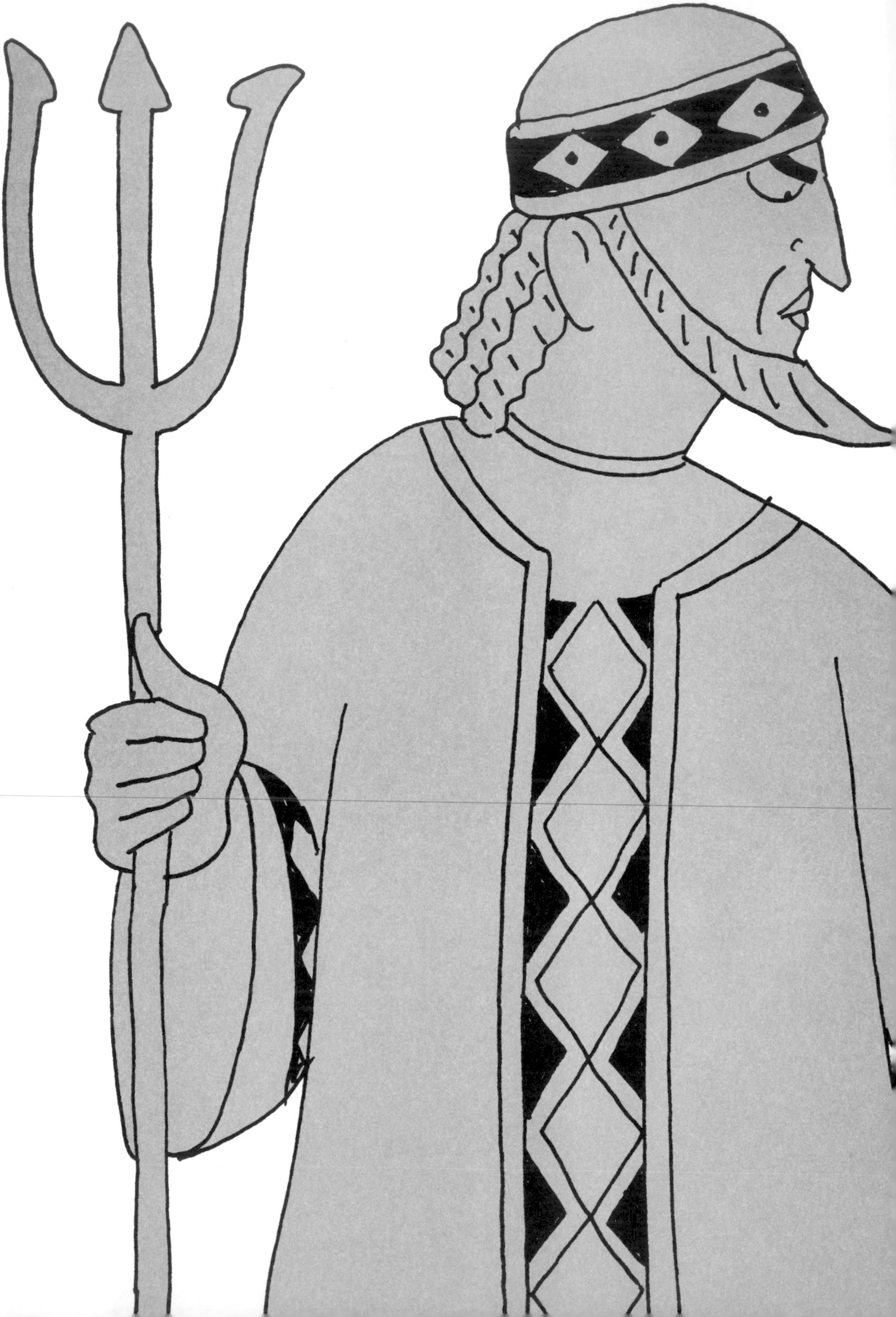

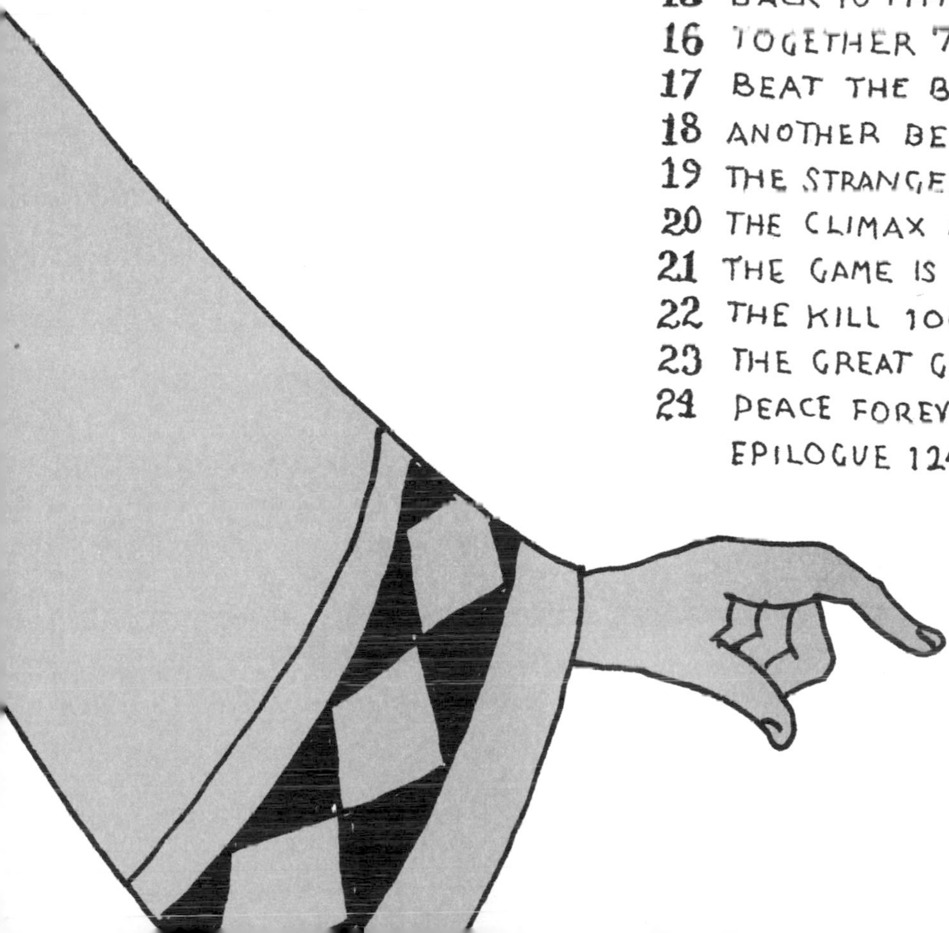

THE ODYSSEY

PROLOGUE

WITH HOMER, THE BLIND POET, AND PRINCE, THE GUIDE DOG

PRINCE HOMER, IS IT TRUE YOU LIVED DURING THE TROJAN WAR?

HOMER IN 1190 B.C.? SOME SCHOLARS SAY SO. BUT I COULD HAVE COME ALONG MUCH LATER, IN THE FIRST CENTURY B.C.

PRINCE BUT YOU DON'T KNOW?

HOMER I'M AN ENIGMA. MAYBE I'M FROM BABYLON, MAYBE I'M FROM ASIA MINOR — MORE THAN SIX CITIES CLAIM ME. WAS I A WOMAN OR A BEGGAR, OR A MINSTREL? WAS I BLIND? THE ONLY THINGS THAT ARE CERTAIN ARE THE STORIES I LEFT BEHIND.

PRINCE LIKE THE STORY OF THE TROJAN WAR? I'VE HEARD THAT ONE.

HOMER YES, THE ILIAD. HAVE YOU HEARD THE ONE THAT COMES LATER, THE ODYSSEY?

PRINCE NO, BUT I'VE HEARD THAT YOU MIGHT NOT HAVE WRITTEN THE WHOLE THING, AND THAT THE LAST TWO BOOKS WERE WRITTEN BY A LESSER POET.

HOMER WELL, YOU CAN JUDGE FOR YOURSELF. DO YOU WANT TO HEAR IT?

PRINCE ONLY IF IT'S NOT BORING.

HOMER HOW COULD IT BE BORING? MEN WERE STRONG AND ARTICULATE THEN, AND WOMEN WERE BEAUTIFUL AND SMART.

PRINCE HEY! AREN'T WE LIKE THAT NOW?

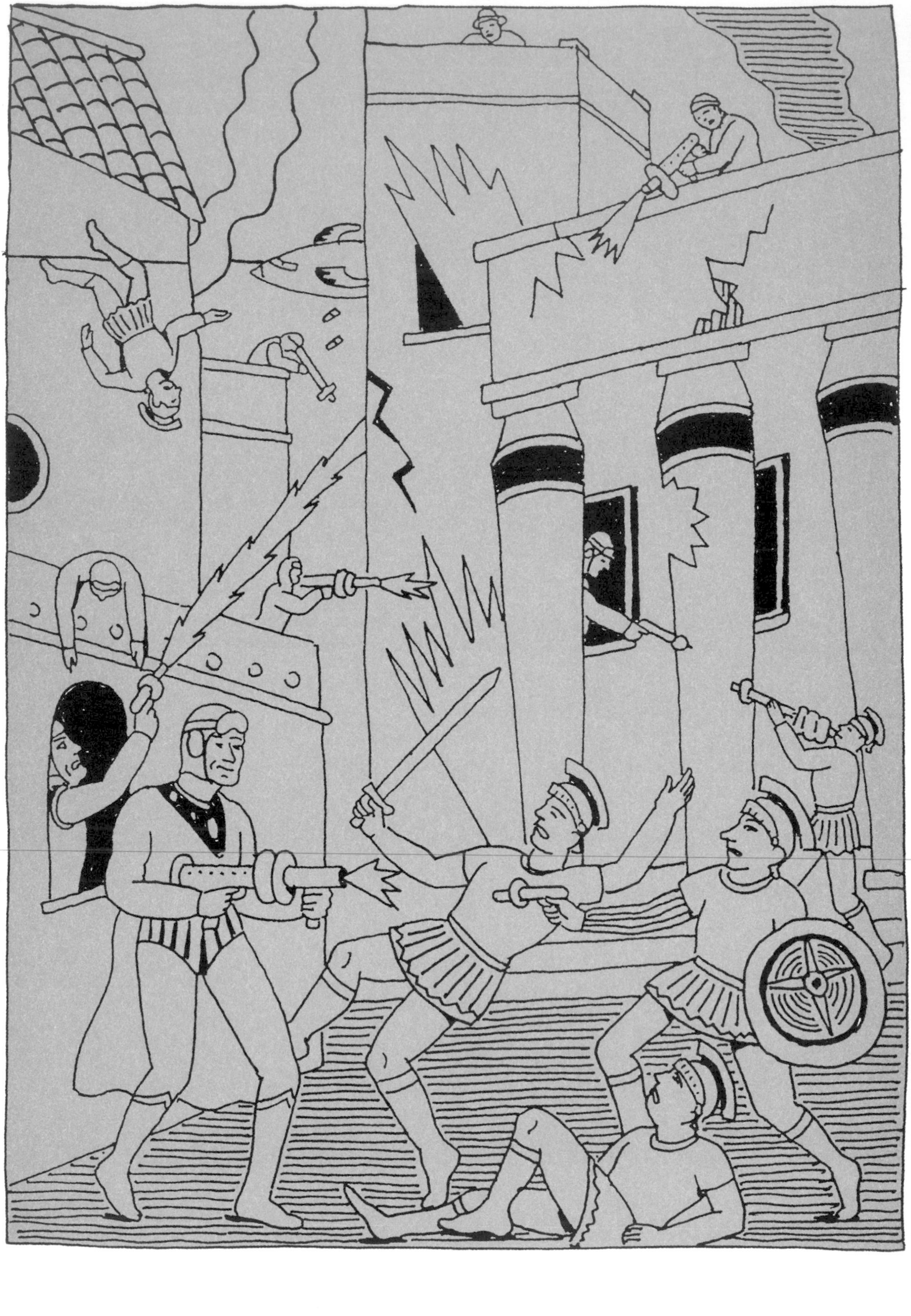

HOMER EVEN IF PEOPLE ARE THE SAME, THE GODS WERE DIFFERENT IN THOSE DAYS. THEY GOT THEMSELVES INVOLVED IN THE LIVES OF MORTALS — EVEN ZEUS, THE KING OF THE GODS.

PRINCE WILL THERE BE LOTS OF EXCITING BATTLES?

HOMER YOU MEAN LIKE THE SCENE OPPOSITE? THE ODYSSEY IS MORE ABOUT WHAT HAPPENS AFTER BATTLES END. IN THOSE DAYS, ONLY MEN FOUGHT IN WARS, BUT THIS STORY SHOWS HOW THEY AFFECTED EVERYONE — WOMEN TOO. MY STORY TELLS YOU A LOT ABOUT HUMAN NATURE.

PRINCE SO HOW DOES IT BEGIN?

HOMER I THOUGHT YOU'D NEVER ASK. MY TALE BEGINS EIGHT YEARS AFTER ODYSSEUS, WHO FOUGHT DURING THE TROJAN WAR, LEFT TROY. HE'S BEEN TRYING TO GET HOME ALL THIS TIME...

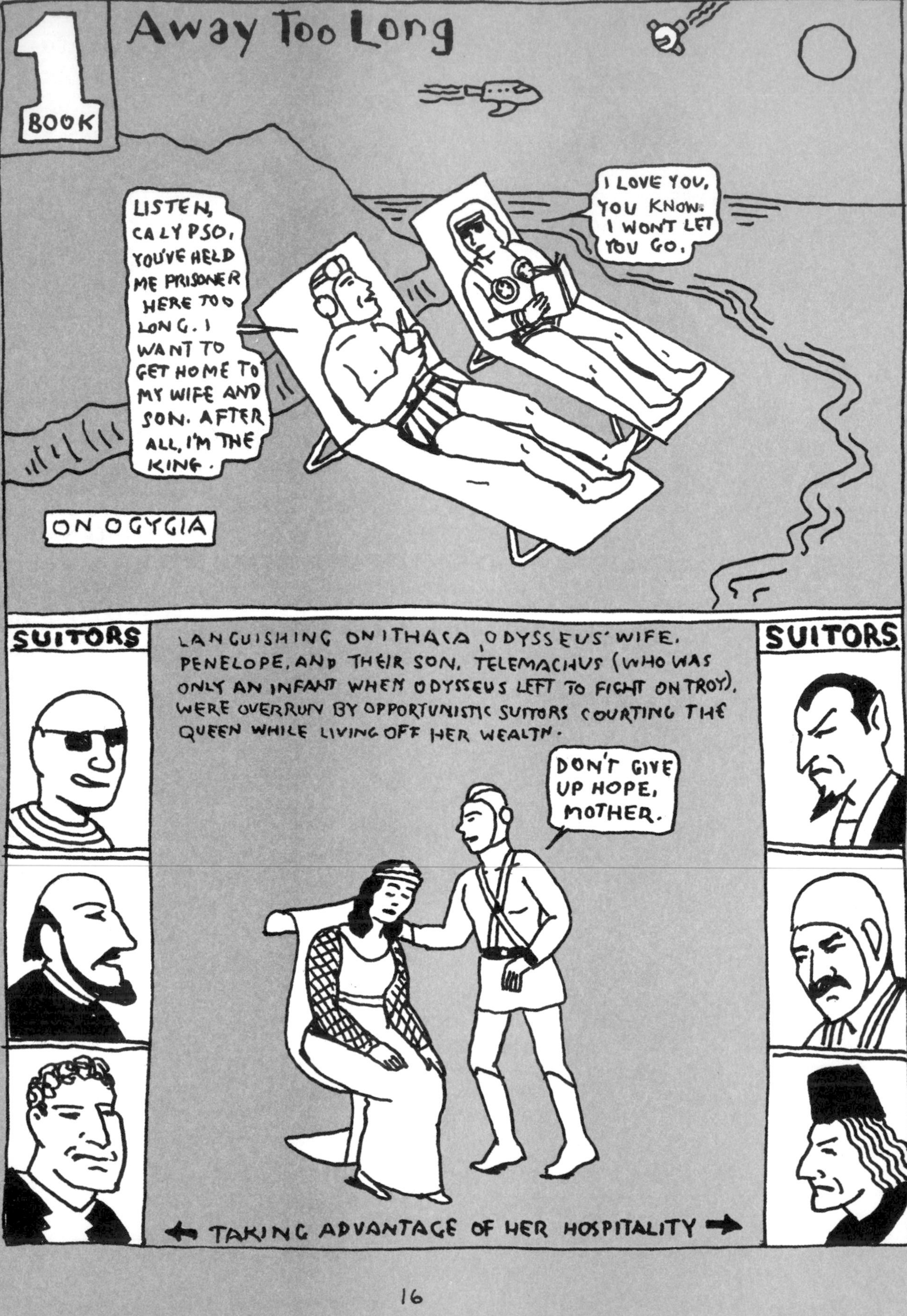
1
BOOK
Away Too Long
LISTEN, CALYPSO, YOU'VE HELD ME PRISONER HERE TOO LONG. I WANT TO GET HOME TO MY WIFE AND SON. AFTER ALL, I'M THE KING.
I LOVE YOU, YOU KNOW. I WONT LET YOU GO.
ON OGYGIA
SUITORS
LANGUISHING ON ITHACA, ODYSSEUS' WIFE, PENELOPE, AND THEIR SON, TELEMACHUS (WHO WAS ONLY AN INFANT WHEN ODYSSEUS LEFT TO FIGHT ON TROY), WERE OVERRUN BY OPPORTUNISTIC SUITORS COURTING THE QUEEN WHILE LIVING OFF HER WEALTH.
DON'T GIVE UP HOPE, MOTHER.
SUITORS
TAKING ADVANTAGE OF HER HOSPITALITY

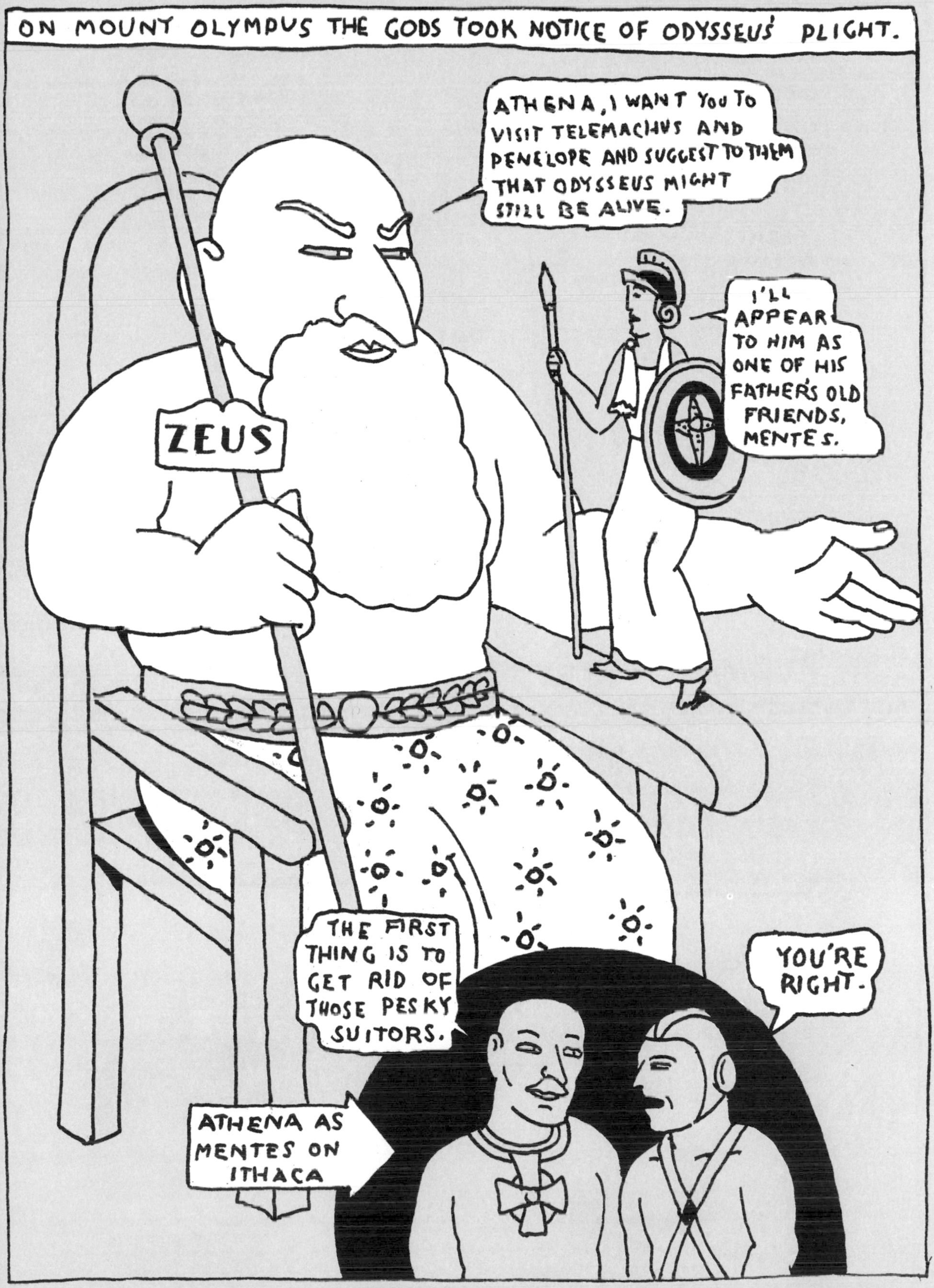
ON MOUNT OLYMPUS THE GODS TOOK NOTICE OF ODYSSEUS' PLIGHT.
ATHENA, I WANT YOU TO VISIT TELEMACHUS AND PENELOPE AND SUGGEST TO THEM THAT ODYSSEUS MIGHT STILL BE ALIVE.
I'LL APPEAR TO HIM AS ONE OF HIS FATHER'S OLD FRIENDS, MENTES.
ZEUS
THE FIRST THING IS TO GET RID OF THOSE PESKY SUITORS.
YOU'RE RIGHT.
ATHENA AS MENTES ON ITHACA

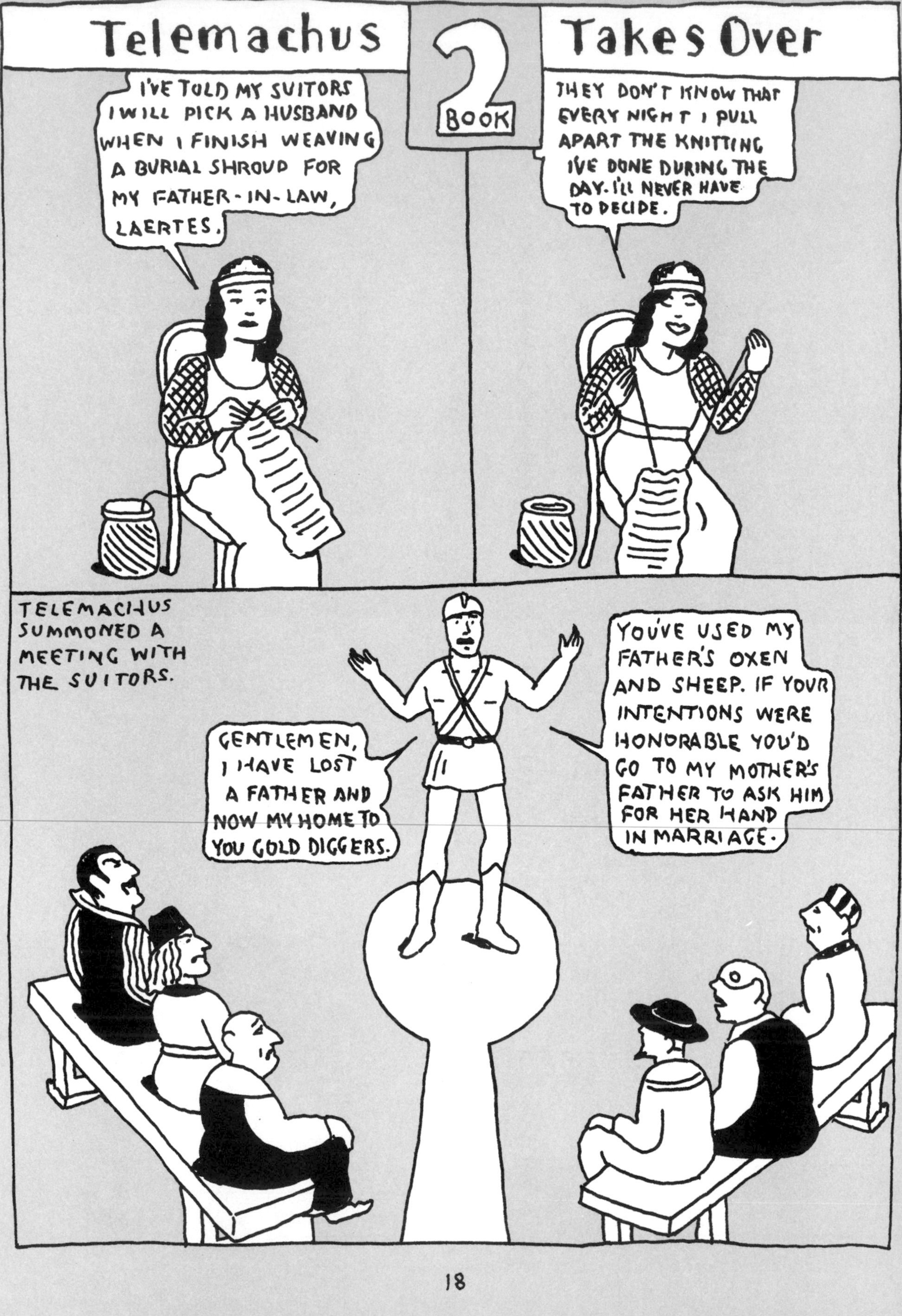
Telemachus
2
BOOK
Takes Over
I'VE TOLD MY SUITORS I WILL PICK A HUSBAND WHEN I FINISH WEAVING A BURIAL SHROUD FOR MY FATHER-IN-LAW, LAERTES.
THEY DON'T KNOW THAT EVERY NIGHT I PULL APART THE KNITTING I'VE DONE DURING THE DAY. I'LL NEVER HAVE TO DECIDE.
TELEMACHUS SUMMONED A MEETING WITH THE SUITORS.
GENTLEMEN, I HAVE LOST A FATHER AND NOW MY HOME TO YOU GOLD DIGGERS.
YOU'VE USED MY FATHER'S OXEN AND SHEEP. IF YOUR INTENTIONS WERE HONORABLE YOU'D GO TO MY MOTHER'S FATHER TO ASK HIM FOR HER HAND IN MARRIAGE.

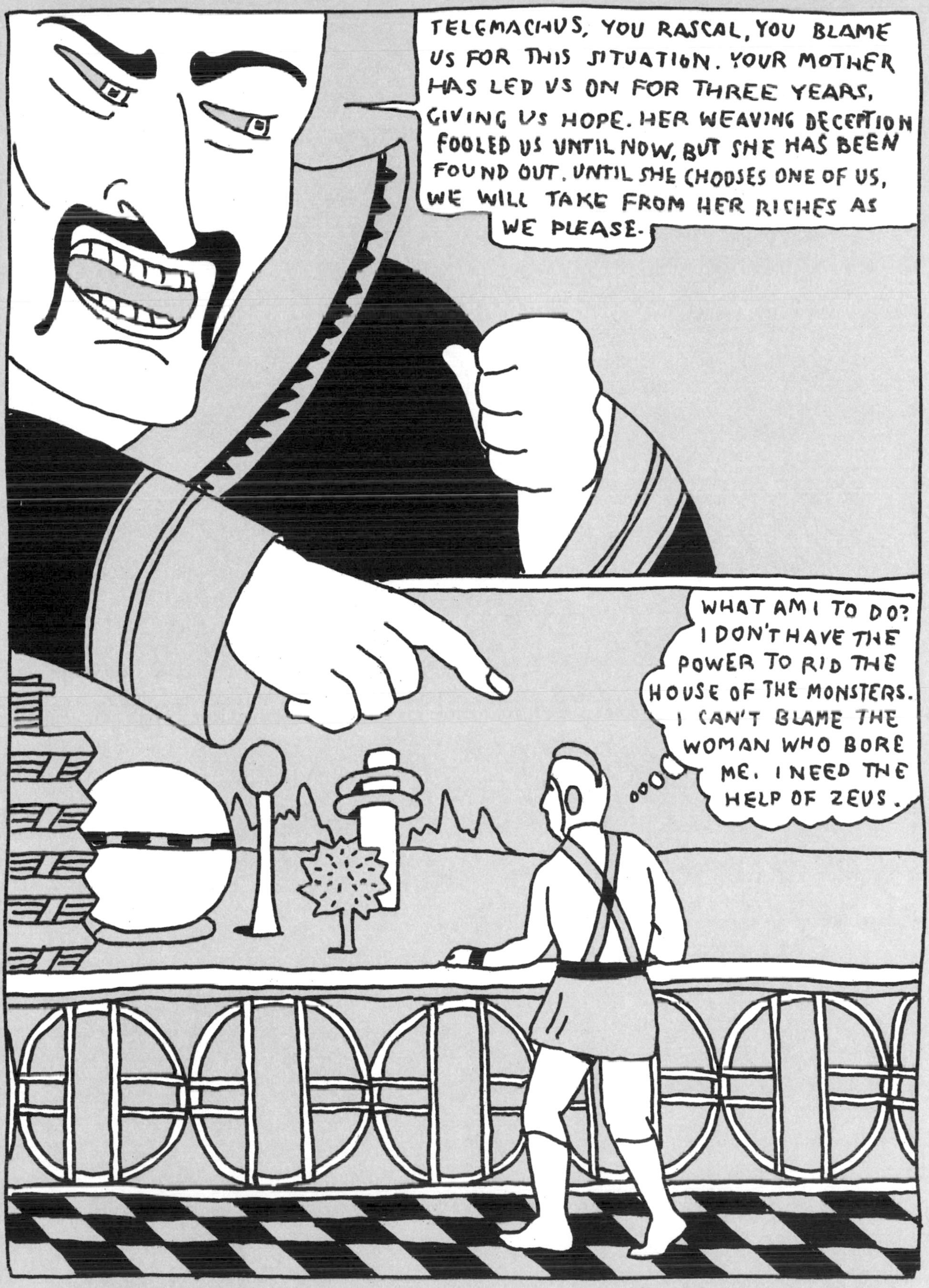
TELEMACHUS, YOU RASCAL, YOU BLAME US FOR THIS SITUATION. YOUR MOTHER HAS LED US ON FOR THREE YEARS, GIVING US HOPE. HER WEAVING DECEPTION FOOLED US UNTIL NOW, BUT SHE HAS BEEN FOUND OUT. UNTIL SHE CHOOSES ONE OF US, WE WILL TAKE FROM HER RICHES AS WE PLEASE.
WHAT AM I TO DO? I DON'T HAVE THE POWER TO RID THE HOUSE OF THE MONSTERS. I CAN'T BLAME THE WOMAN WHO BORE ME. I NEED THE HELP OF ZEUS.

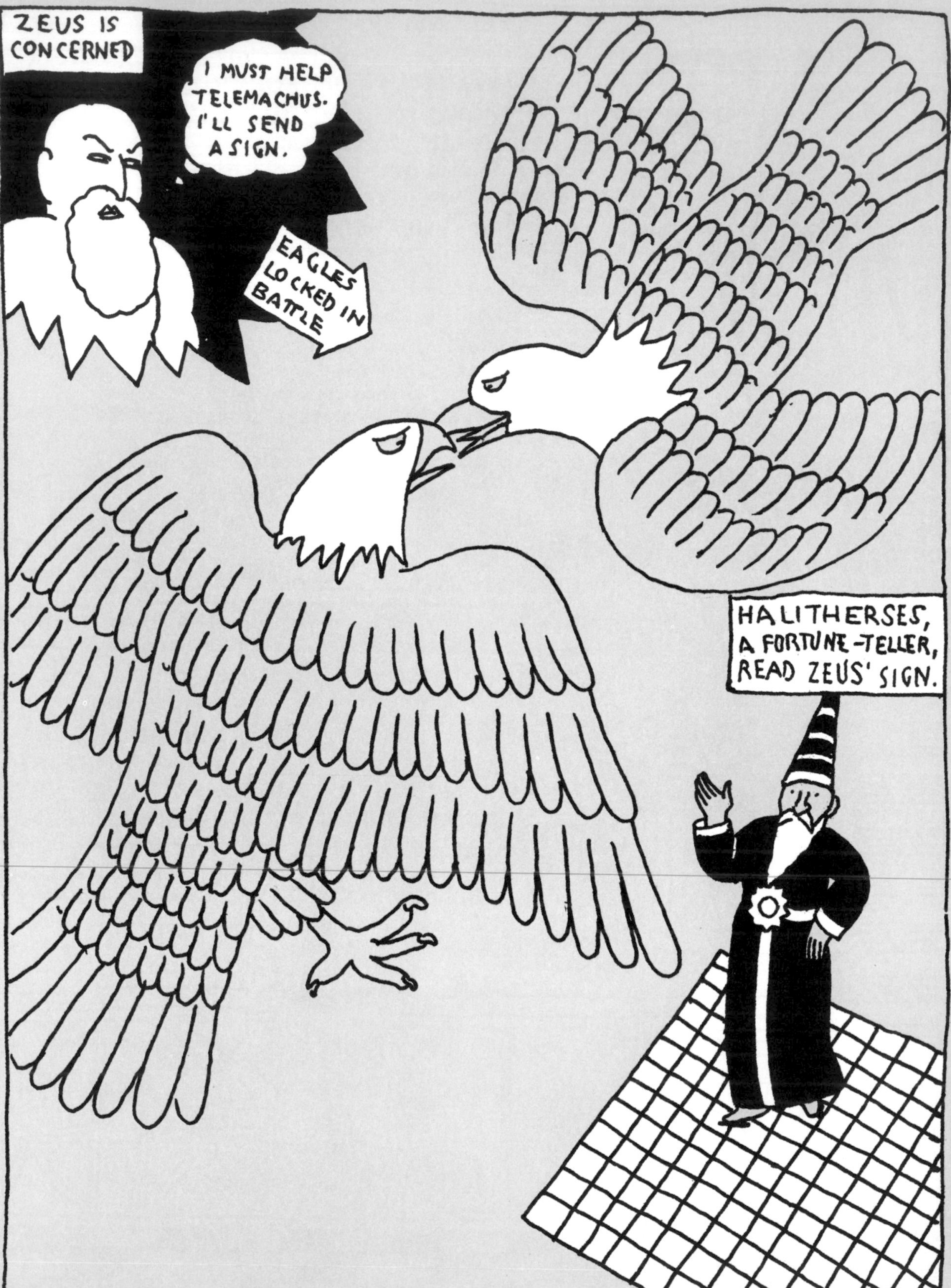
ZEUS IS CONCERNED
I MUST HELP TELEMACHUS. I'LL SEND A SIGN.
EAGLES LOCKED IN BATTLE
HALITHERSES, A FORTUNE-TELLER, READ ZEUS' SIGN.

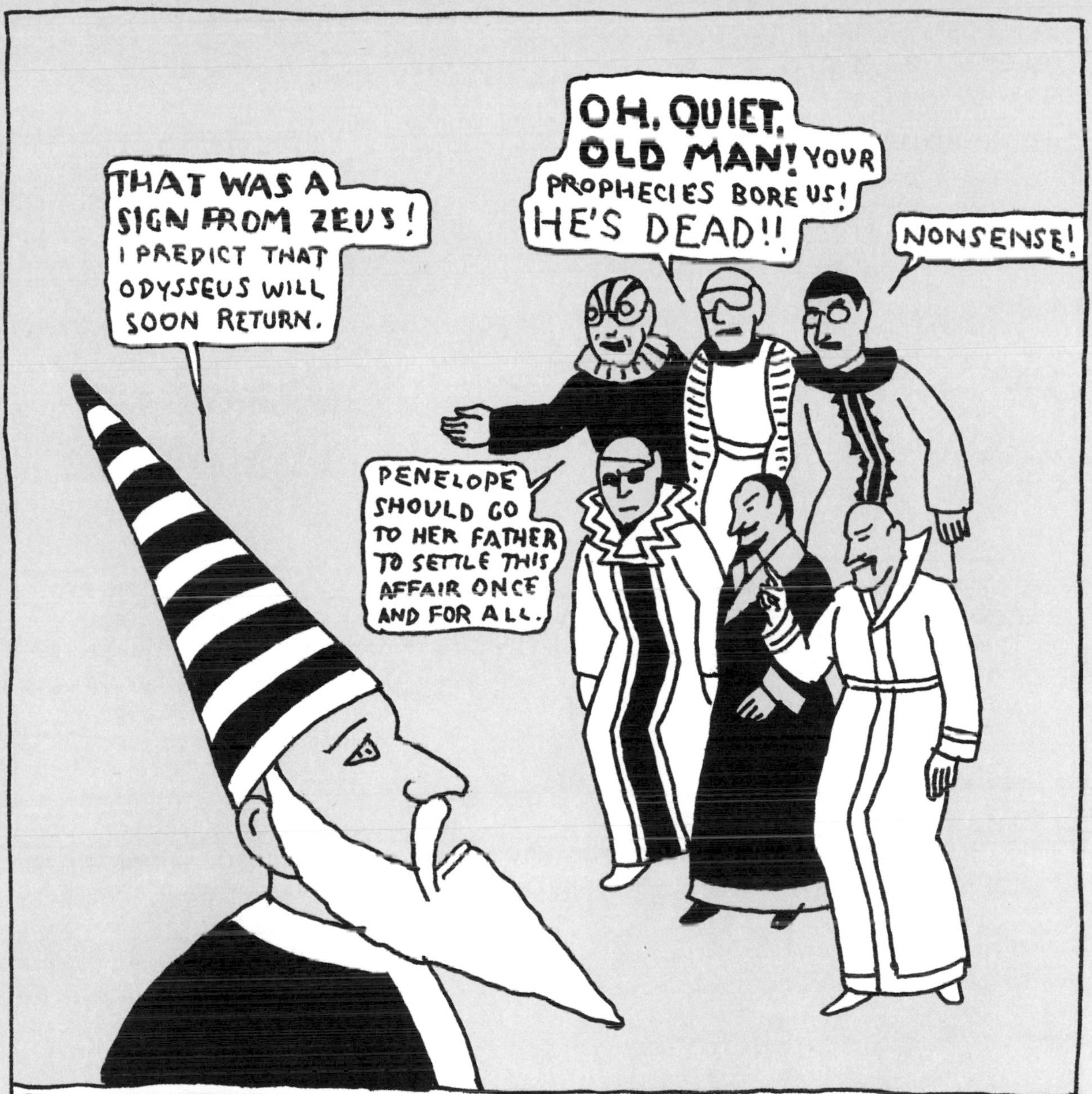
THAT WAS A SIGN FROM ZEUS! I PREDICT THAT ODYSSEUS WILL SOON RETURN.
OH, QUIET, OLD MAN! YOUR PROPHECIES BORE US! HE'S DEAD!!
NONSENSE!
PENELOPE SHOULD GO TO HER FATHER TO SETTLE THIS AFFAIR ONCE AND FOR ALL.

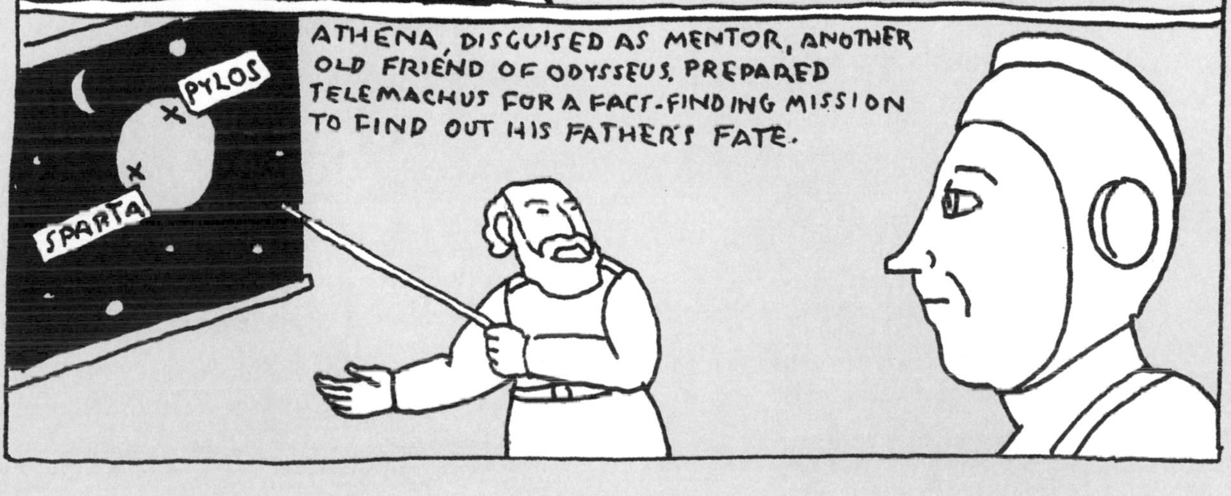
ATHENA, DISGUISED AS MENTOR, ANOTHER OLD FRIEND OF ODYSSEUS, PREPARED TELEMACHUS FOR A FACT-FINDING MISSION TO FIND OUT HIS FATHER'S FATE.
PYLOS
SPARTA

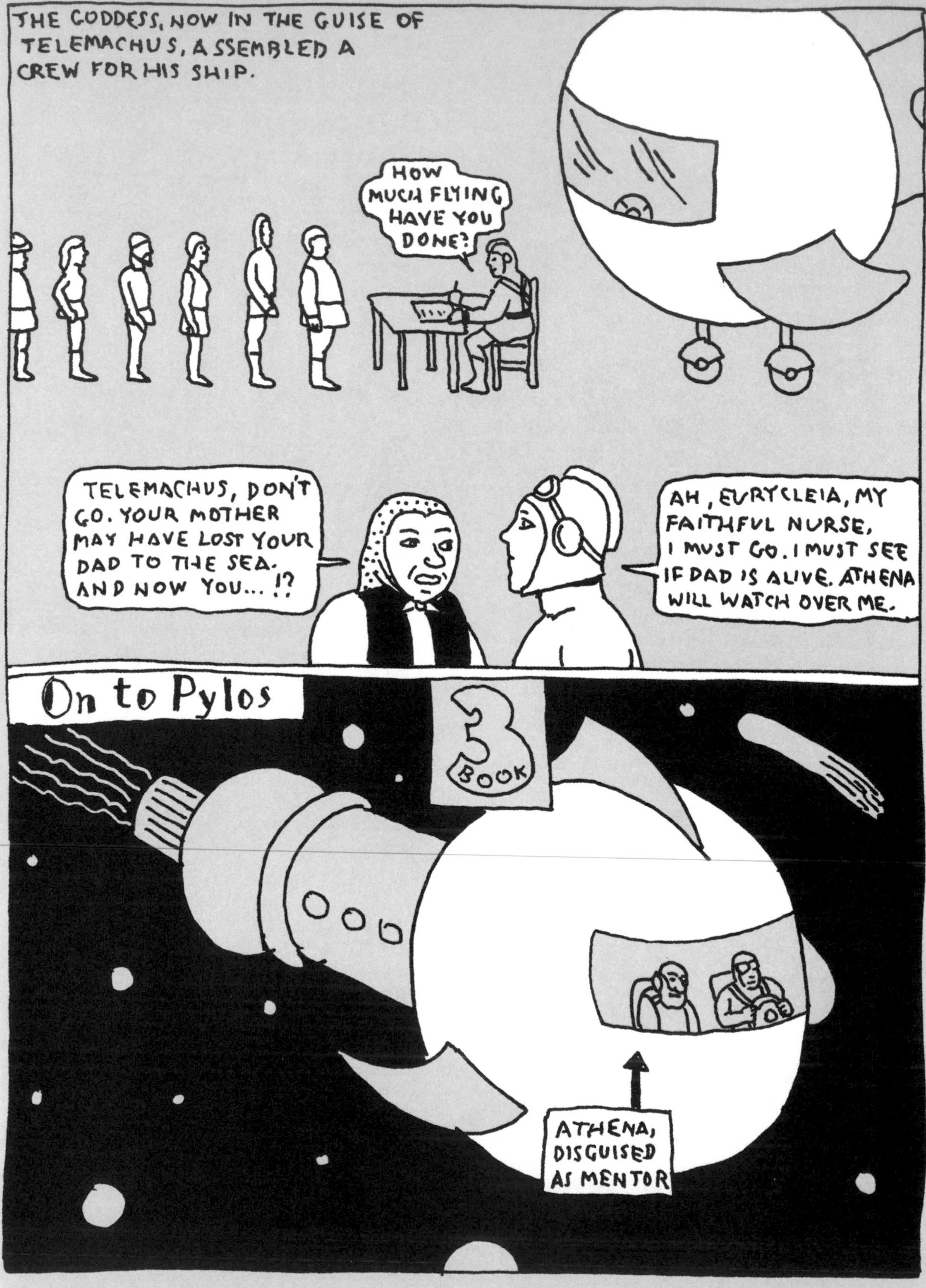
THE GODDESS, NOW IN THE GUISE OF TELEMACHUS, ASSEMBLED A CREW FOR HIS SHIP.
HOW MUCH FLYING HAVE YOU DONE?
TELEMACHUS, DON'T GO. YOUR MOTHER MAY HAVE LOST YOUR DAD TO THE SEA. AND NOW YOU... !?
AH, EURYCLEIA, MY FAITHFUL NURSE, I MUST GO. I MUST SEE IF DAD IS ALIVE. ATHENA WILL WATCH OVER ME.
On to Pylos
3 BOOK
ATHENA, DISGUISED AS MENTOR

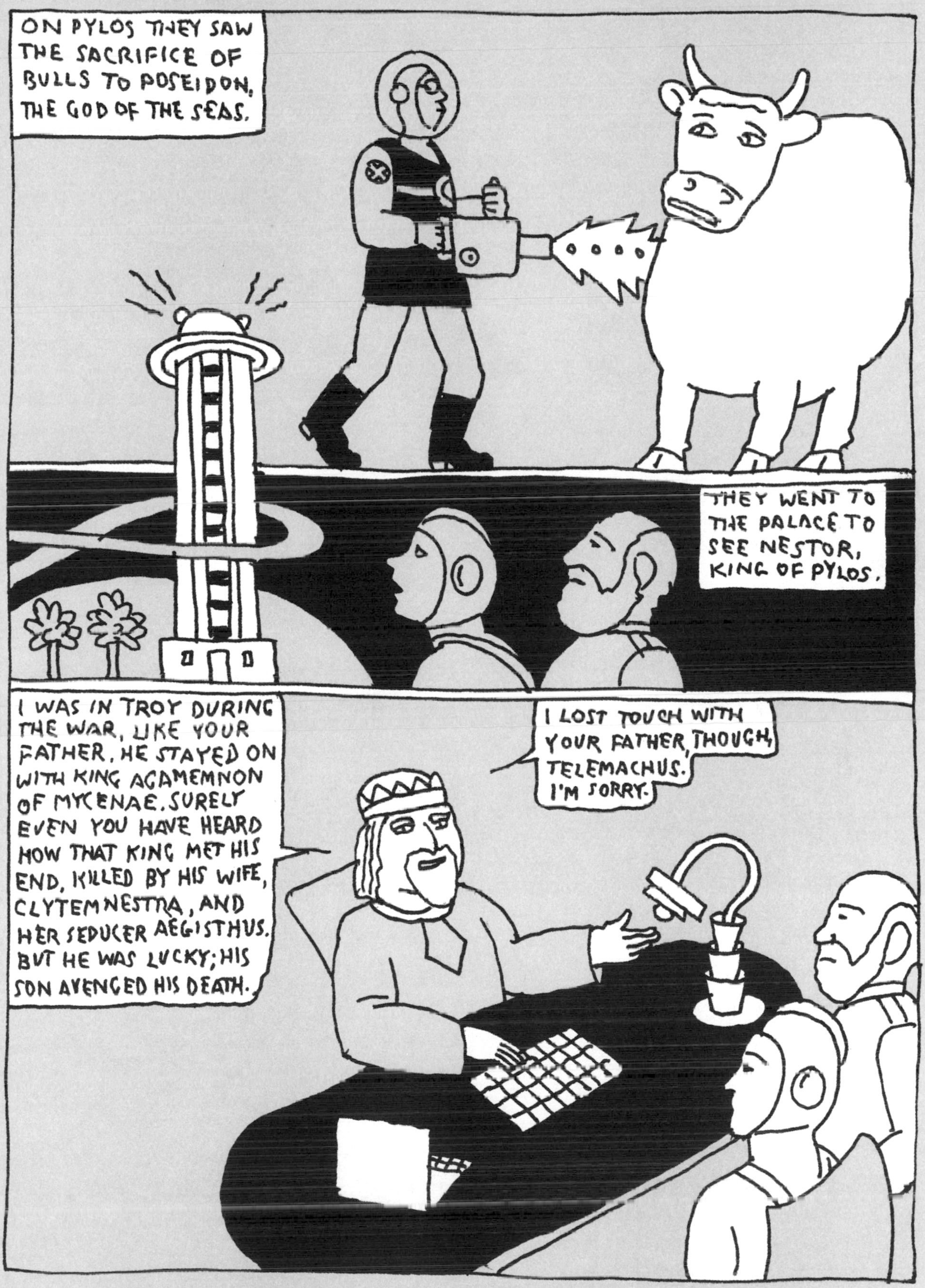
ON PYLOS THEY SAW THE SACRIFICE OF BULLS TO POSEIDON, THE GOD OF THE SEAS.
THEY WENT TO THE PALACE TO SEE NESTOR, KING OF PYLOS.
I WAS IN TROY DURING THE WAR, LIKE YOUR FATHER. HE STAYED ON WITH KING AGAMEMNON OF MYCENAE. SURELY EVEN YOU HAVE HEARD HOW THAT KING MET HIS END, KILLED BY HIS WIFE, CLYTEMNESTRA, AND HER SEDUCER AEGISTHUS. BUT HE WAS LUCKY; HIS SON AVENGED HIS DEATH.
I LOST TOUCH WITH YOUR FATHER, THOUGH, TELEMACHUS. I'M SORRY.

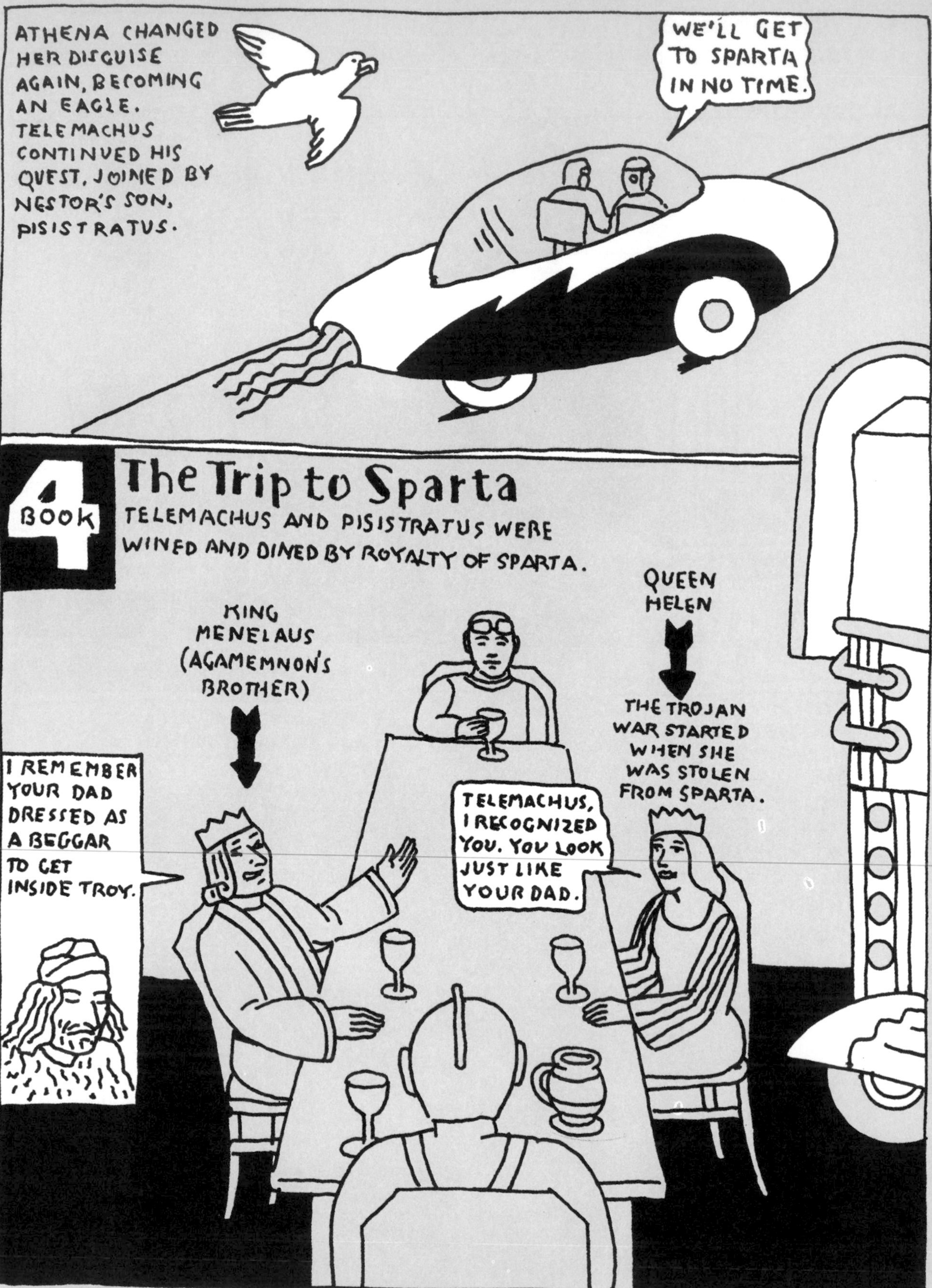
ATHENA CHANGED HER DISGUISE AGAIN, BECOMING AN EAGLE. TELEMACHUS CONTINUED HIS QUEST, JOINED BY NESTOR'S SON, PISISTRATUS.
WE'LL GET TO SPARTA IN NO TIME.
4 BOOK
The Trip to Sparta
TELEMACHUS AND PISISTRATUS WERE WINED AND DINED BY ROYALTY OF SPARTA.
KING MENELAUS (AGAMEMNON'S BROTHER)
QUEEN HELEN
THE TROJAN WAR STARTED WHEN SHE WAS STOLEN FROM SPARTA.
I REMEMBER YOUR DAD DRESSED AS A BEGGAR TO GET INSIDE TROY.
TELEMACHUS, I RECOGNIZED YOU. YOU LOOK JUST LIKE YOUR DAD.

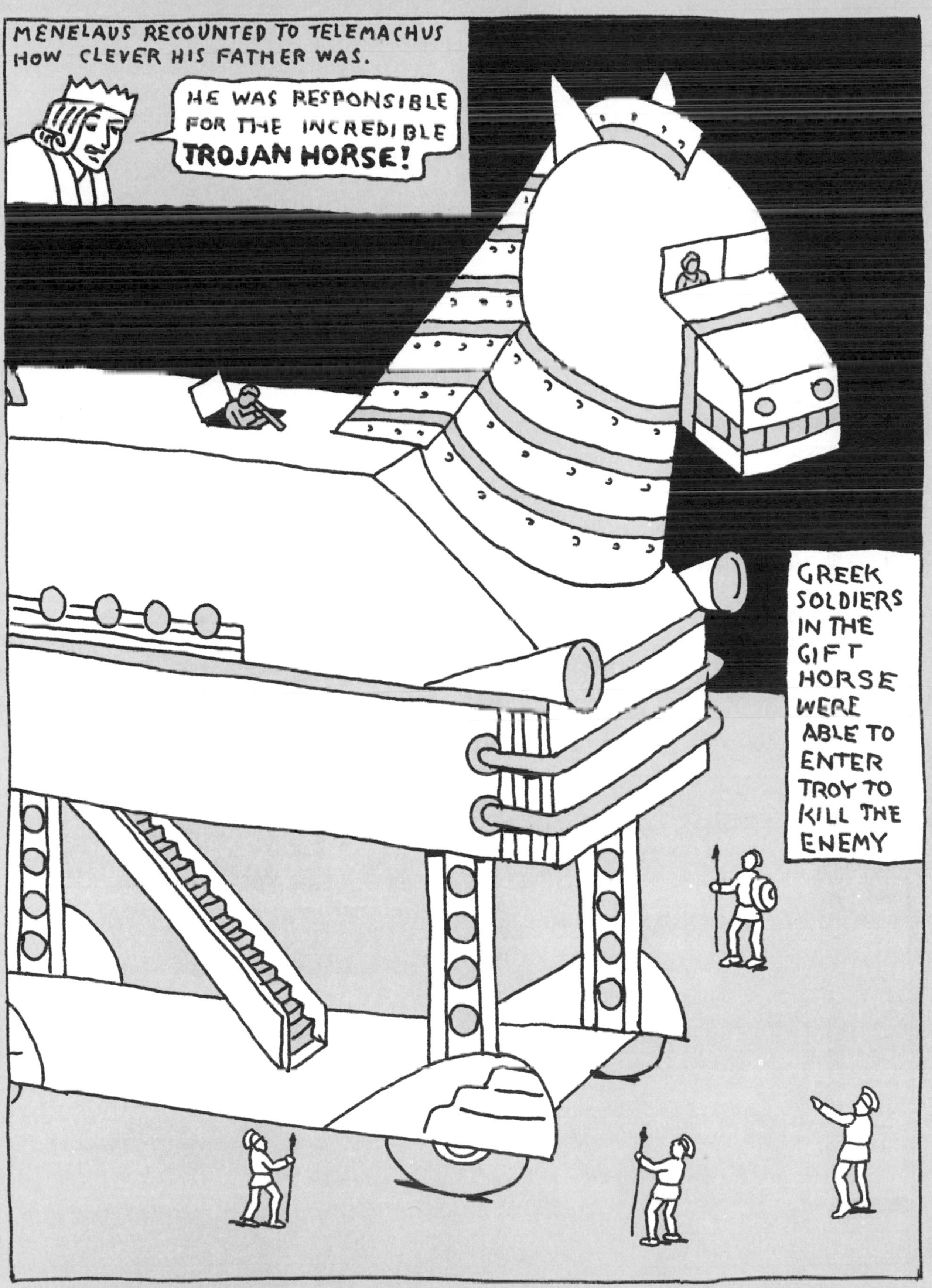
MENELAUS RECOUNTED TO TELEMACHUS HOW CLEVER HIS FATHER WAS.
HE WAS RESPONSIBLE FOR THE INCREDIBLE **TROJAN HORSE!**
GREEK SOLDIERS IN THE GIFT HORSE WERE ABLE TO ENTER TROY TO KILL THE ENEMY

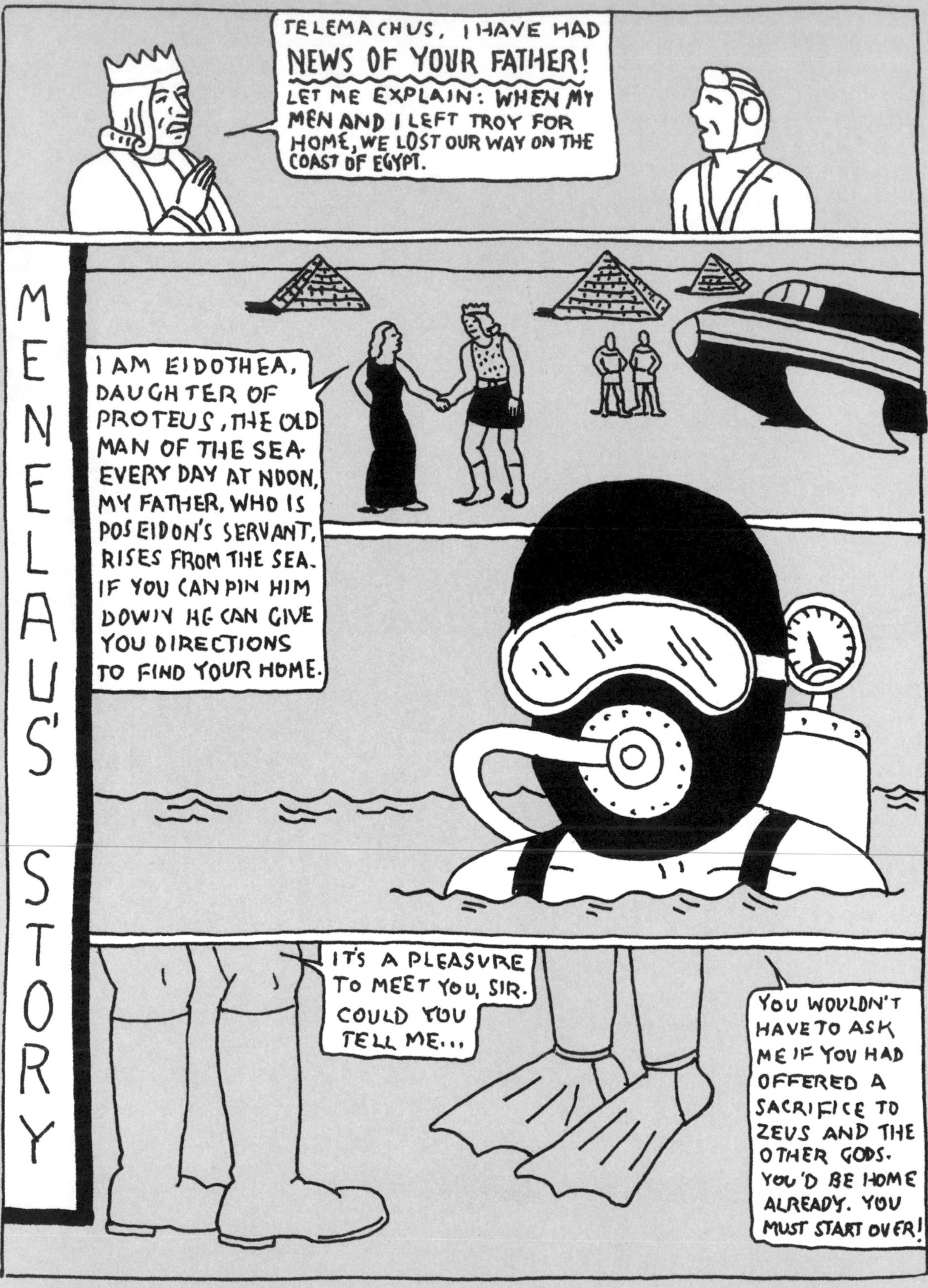
TELEMACHUS, I HAVE HAD NEWS OF YOUR FATHER! LET ME EXPLAIN: WHEN MY MEN AND I LEFT TROY FOR HOME, WE LOST OUR WAY ON THE COAST OF EGYPT.
MENELAUS'S STORY
I AM EIDOTHEA, DAUGHTER OF PROTEUS, THE OLD MAN OF THE SEA. EVERY DAY AT NOON, MY FATHER, WHO IS POSEIDON'S SERVANT, RISES FROM THE SEA. IF YOU CAN PIN HIM DOWN HE CAN GIVE YOU DIRECTIONS TO FIND YOUR HOME.
IT'S A PLEASURE TO MEET YOU, SIR. COULD YOU TELL ME...
YOU WOULDN'T HAVE TO ASK ME IF YOU HAD OFFERED A SACRIFICE TO ZEUS AND THE OTHER GODS. YOU'D BE HOME ALREADY. YOU MUST START OVER!

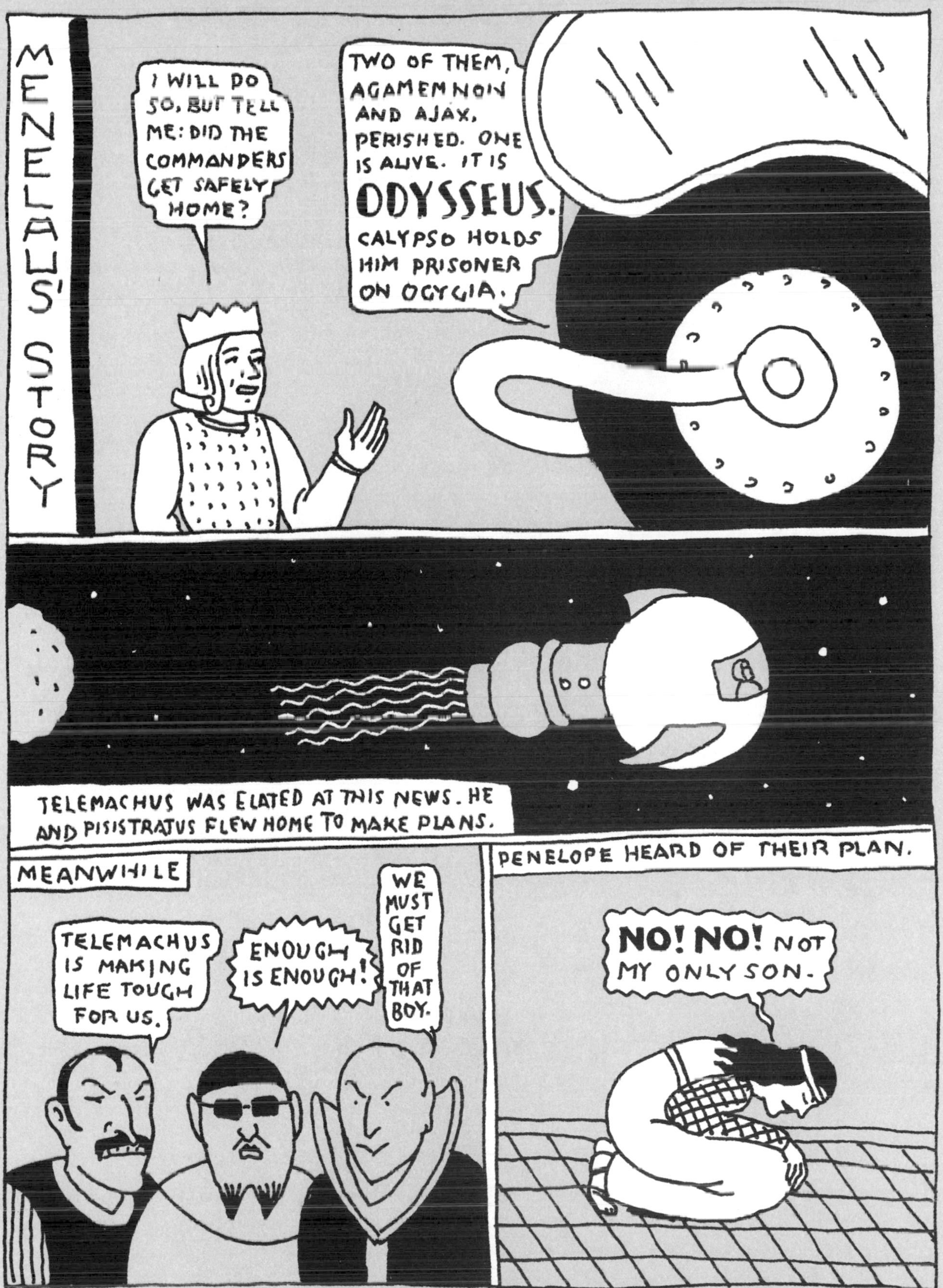

MENELAUS' STORY
I WILL DO SO, BUT TELL ME: DID THE COMMANDERS GET SAFELY HOME?
TWO OF THEM, AGAMEMNON AND AJAX, PERISHED. ONE IS ALIVE. IT IS ODYSSEUS. CALYPSO HOLDS HIM PRISONER ON OGYGIA.
TELEMACHUS WAS ELATED AT THIS NEWS. HE AND PISISTRATUS FLEW HOME TO MAKE PLANS.
MEANWHILE
TELEMACHUS IS MAKING LIFE TOUGH FOR US.
ENOUGH IS ENOUGH!
WE MUST GET RID OF THAT BOY.
PENELOPE HEARD OF THEIR PLAN.
NO! NO! NOT MY ONLY SON.

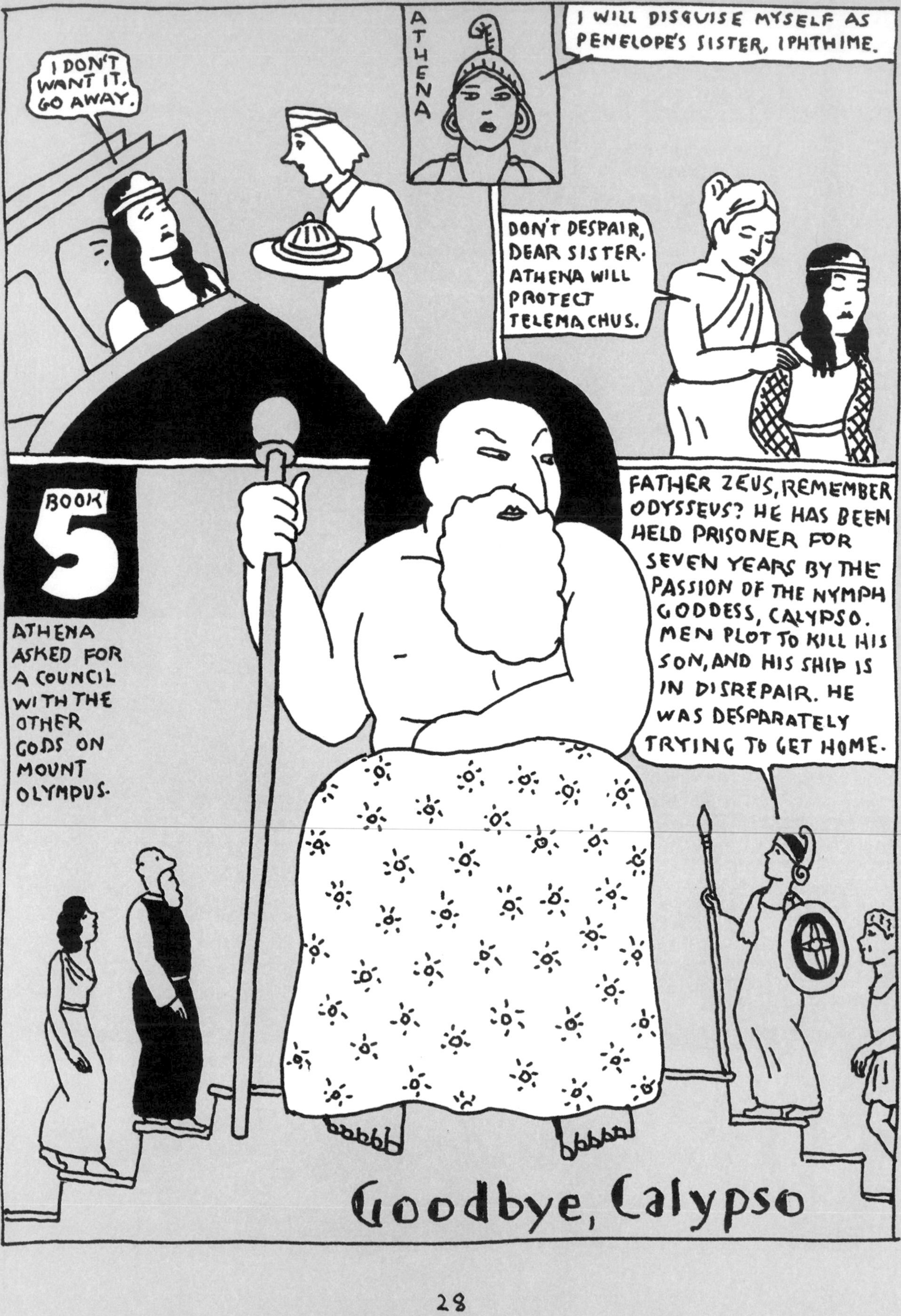
I DON'T WANT IT. GO AWAY.
ATHENA
I WILL DISGUISE MYSELF AS PENELOPE'S SISTER, IPHTHIME.
DON'T DESPAIR, DEAR SISTER. ATHENA WILL PROTECT TELEMACHUS.
BOOK 5
ATHENA ASKED FOR A COUNCIL WITH THE OTHER GODS ON MOUNT OLYMPUS.
FATHER ZEUS, REMEMBER ODYSSEUS? HE HAS BEEN HELD PRISONER FOR SEVEN YEARS BY THE PASSION OF THE NYMPH GODDESS, CALYPSO. MEN PLOT TO KILL HIS SON, AND HIS SHIP IS IN DISREPAIR. HE WAS DESPARATELY TRYING TO GET HOME.
Goodbye, Calypso

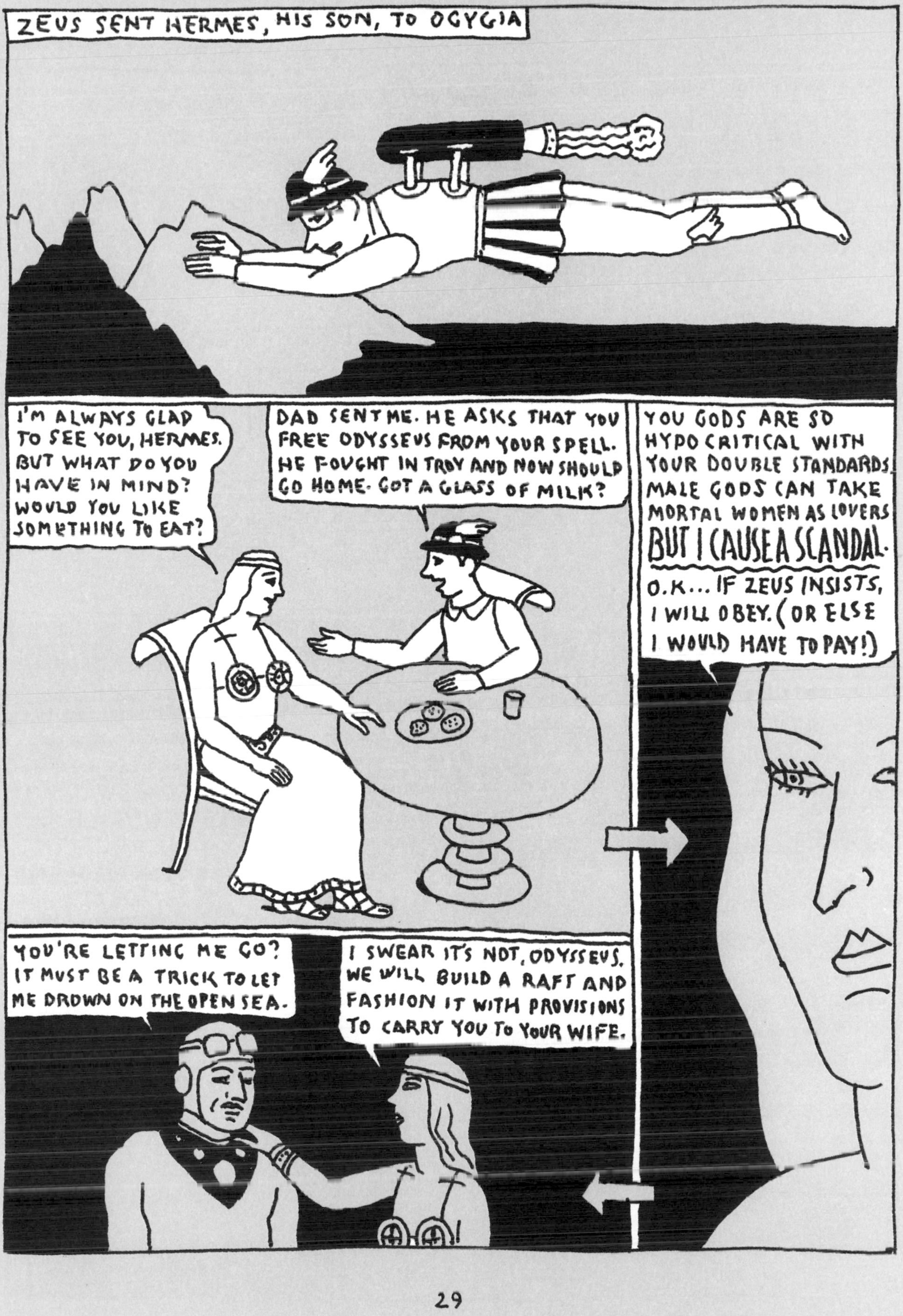
ZEUS SENT HERMES, HIS SON, TO OGYGIA
I'M ALWAYS GLAD TO SEE YOU, HERMES. BUT WHAT DO YOU HAVE IN MIND? WOULD YOU LIKE SOMETHING TO EAT?
DAD SENT ME. HE ASKS THAT YOU FREE ODYSSEUS FROM YOUR SPELL. HE FOUGHT IN TROY AND NOW SHOULD GO HOME. GOT A GLASS OF MILK?
YOU GODS ARE SO HYPOCRITICAL WITH YOUR DOUBLE STANDARDS. MALE GODS CAN TAKE MORTAL WOMEN AS LOVERS BUT I CAUSE A SCANDAL.
O.K... IF ZEUS INSISTS, I WILL OBEY. (OR ELSE I WOULD HAVE TO PAY!)
YOU'RE LETTING ME GO? IT MUST BE A TRICK TO LET ME DROWN ON THE OPEN SEA.
I SWEAR IT'S NOT, ODYSSEUS. WE WILL BUILD A RAFT AND FASHION IT WITH PROVISIONS TO CARRY YOU TO YOUR WIFE.

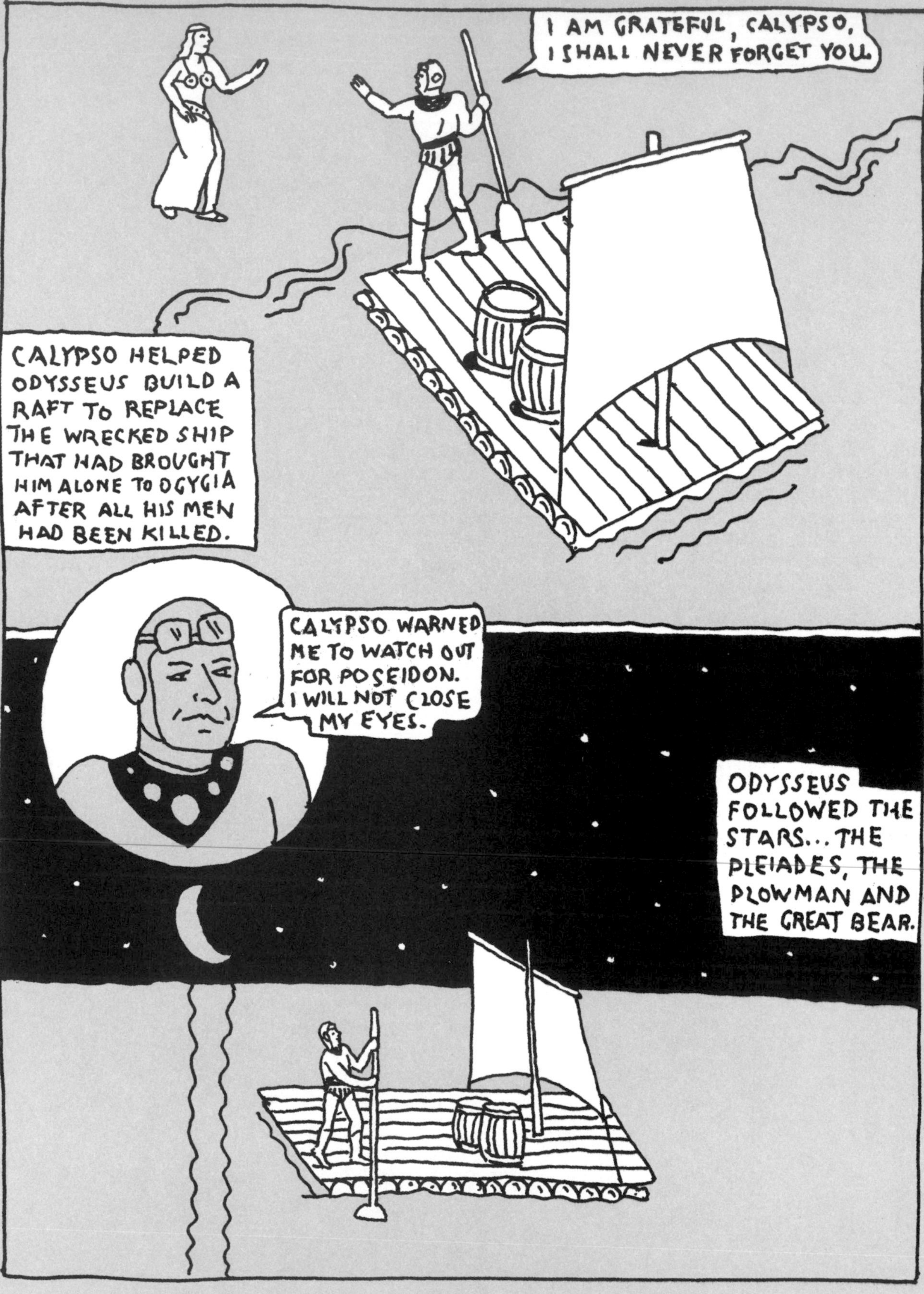
I AM GRATEFUL, CALYPSO, I SHALL NEVER FORGET YOU.
CALYPSO HELPED ODYSSEUS BUILD A RAFT TO REPLACE THE WRECKED SHIP THAT HAD BROUGHT HIM ALONE TO OGYGIA AFTER ALL HIS MEN HAD BEEN KILLED.
CALYPSO WARNED ME TO WATCH OUT FOR POSEIDON. I WILL NOT CLOSE MY EYES.
ODYSSEUS FOLLOWED THE STARS... THE PLEIADES, THE PLOWMAN AND THE GREAT BEAR.

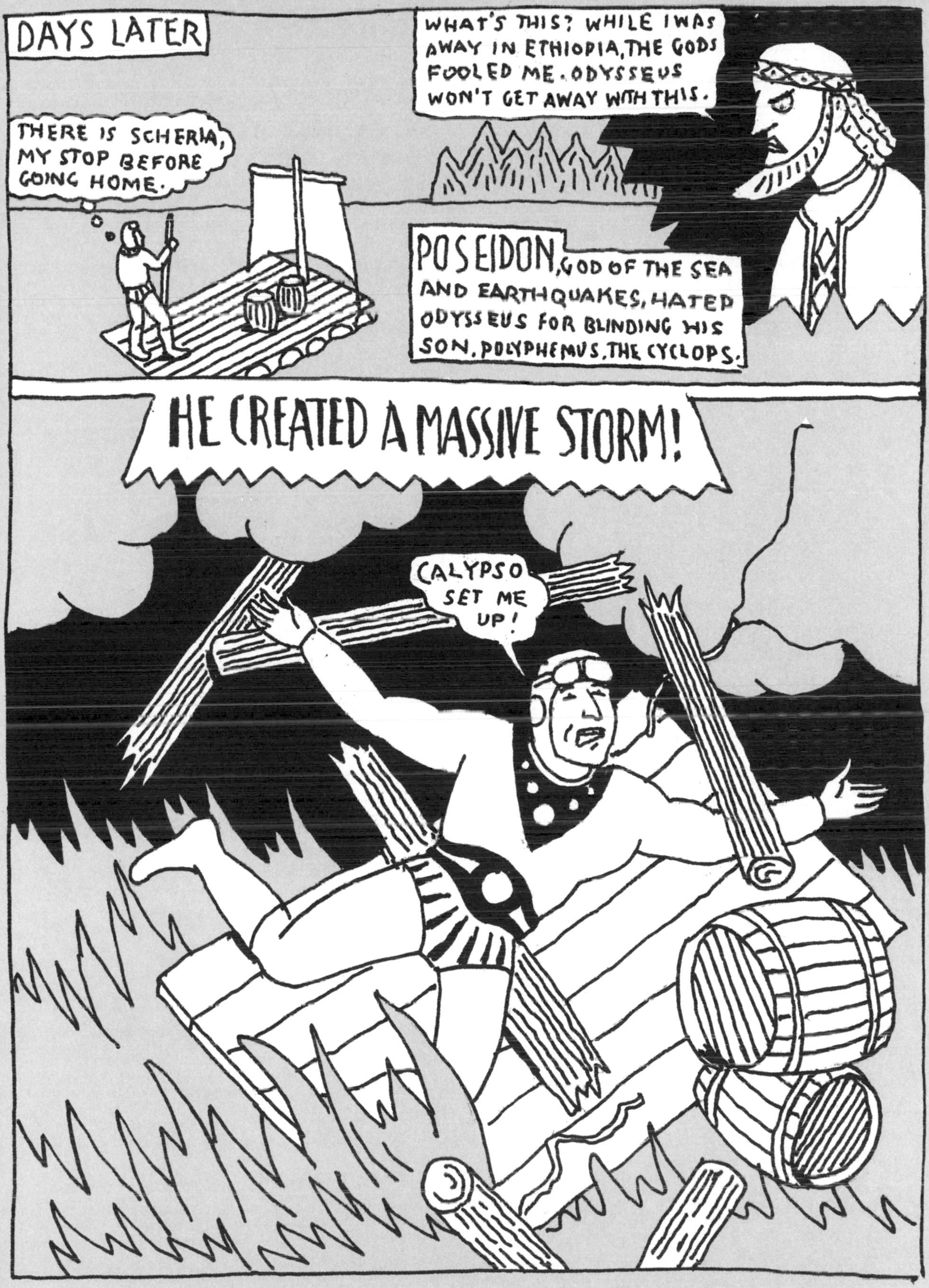
DAYS LATER
THERE IS SCHERIA, MY STOP BEFORE GOING HOME.
WHAT'S THIS? WHILE I WAS AWAY IN ETHIOPIA, THE GODS FOOLED ME. ODYSSEUS WON'T GET AWAY WITH THIS.
POSEIDON, GOD OF THE SEA AND EARTHQUAKES, HATED ODYSSEUS FOR BLINDING HIS SON, POLYPHEMUS, THE CYCLOPS.
HE CREATED A MASSIVE STORM!
CALYPSO SET ME UP!

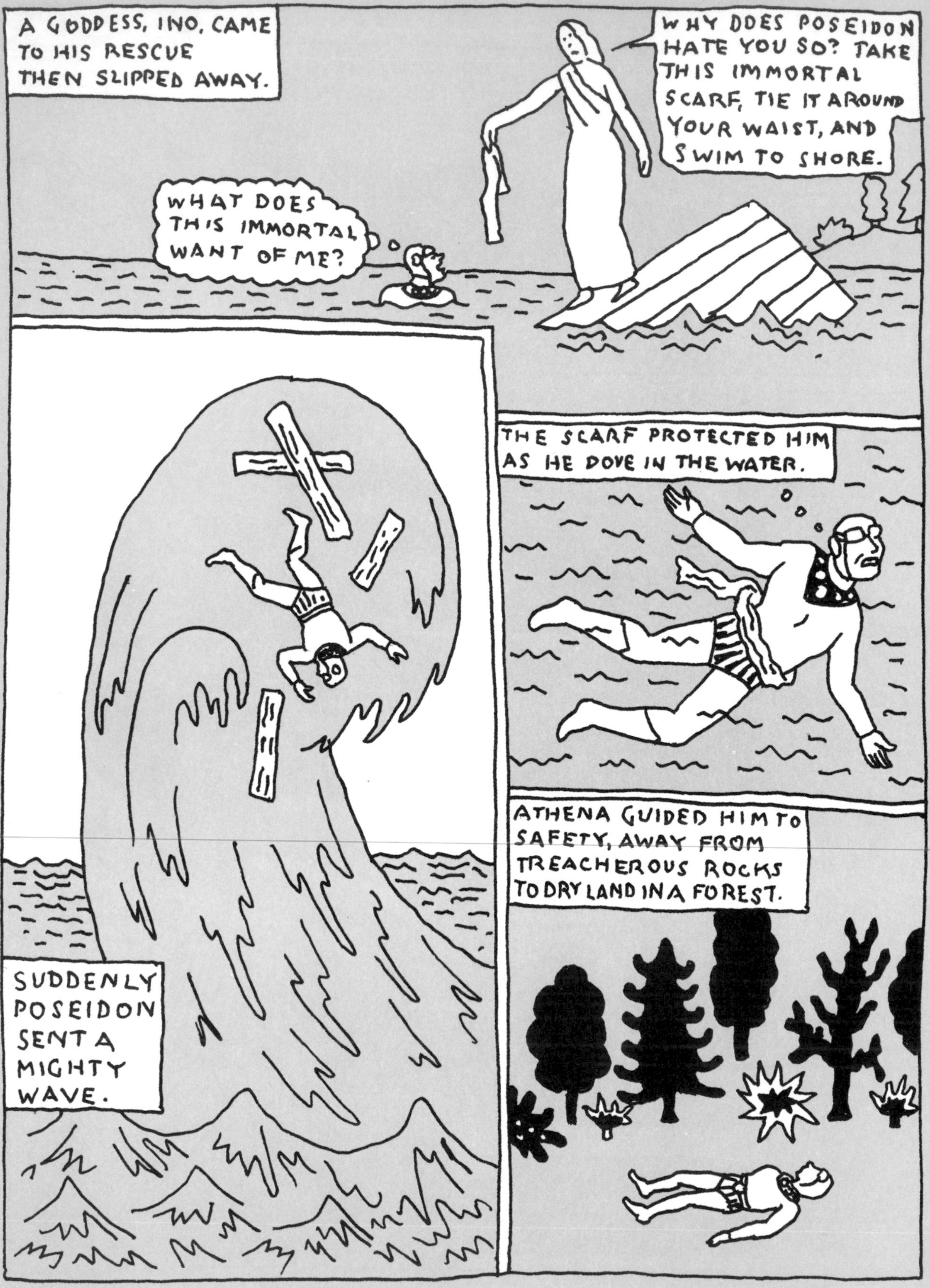

A GODDESS, INO, CAME TO HIS RESCUE THEN SLIPPED AWAY.
WHY DOES POSEIDON HATE YOU SO? TAKE THIS IMMORTAL SCARF, TIE IT AROUND YOUR WAIST, AND SWIM TO SHORE.
WHAT DOES THIS IMMORTAL WANT OF ME?
SUDDENLY POSEIDON SENT A MIGHTY WAVE.
THE SCARF PROTECTED HIM AS HE DOVE IN THE WATER.
ATHENA GUIDED HIM TO SAFETY, AWAY FROM TREACHEROUS ROCKS TO DRY LAND IN A FOREST.

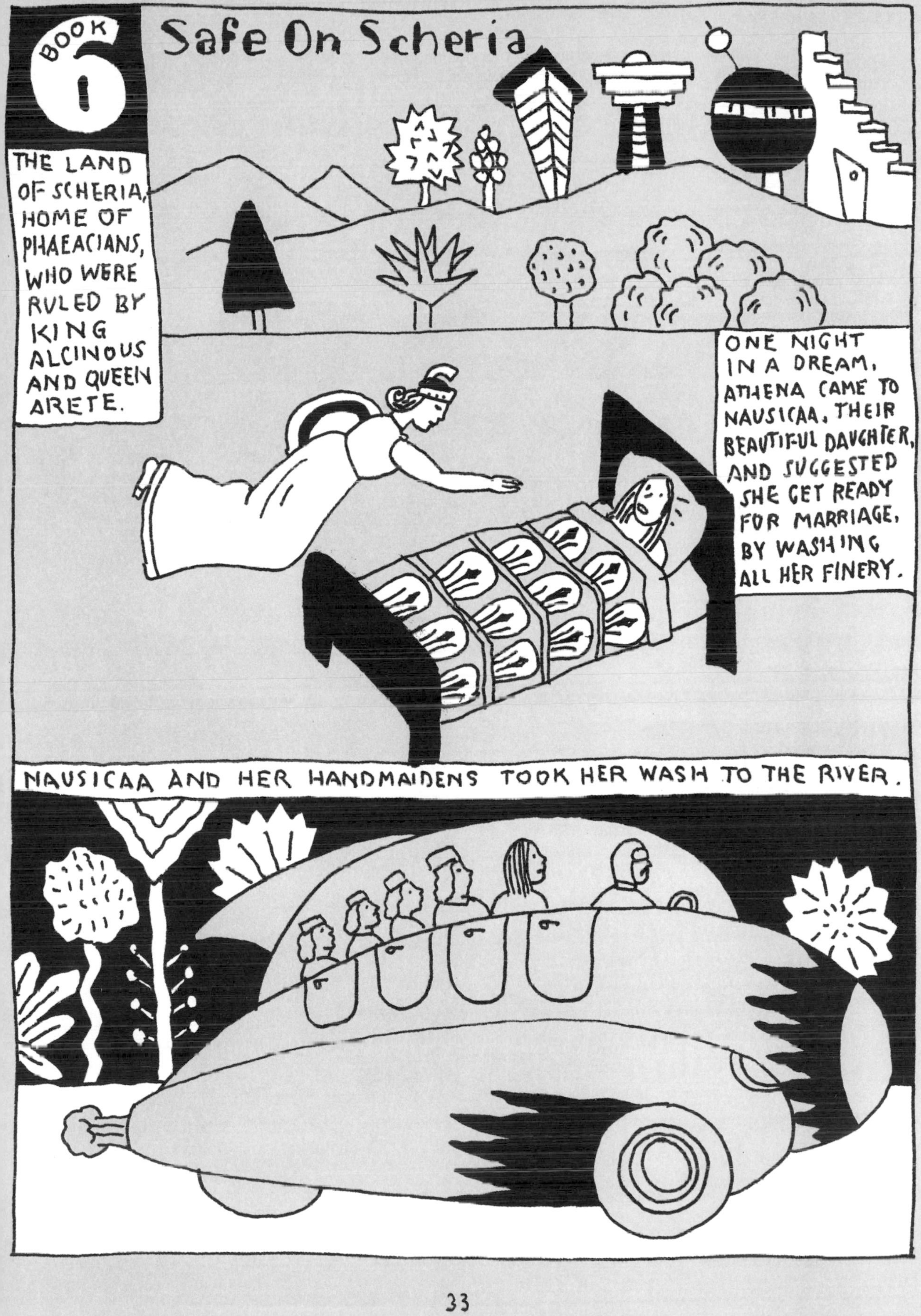
BOOK 6
Safe On Scheria
THE LAND OF SCHERIA, HOME OF PHAEACIANS, WHO WERE RULED BY KING ALCINOUS AND QUEEN ARETE.
ONE NIGHT IN A DREAM, ATHENA CAME TO NAUSICAA, THEIR BEAUTIFUL DAUGHTER, AND SUGGESTED SHE GET READY FOR MARRIAGE, BY WASHING ALL HER FINERY.
NAUSICAA AND HER HANDMAIDENS TOOK HER WASH TO THE RIVER.

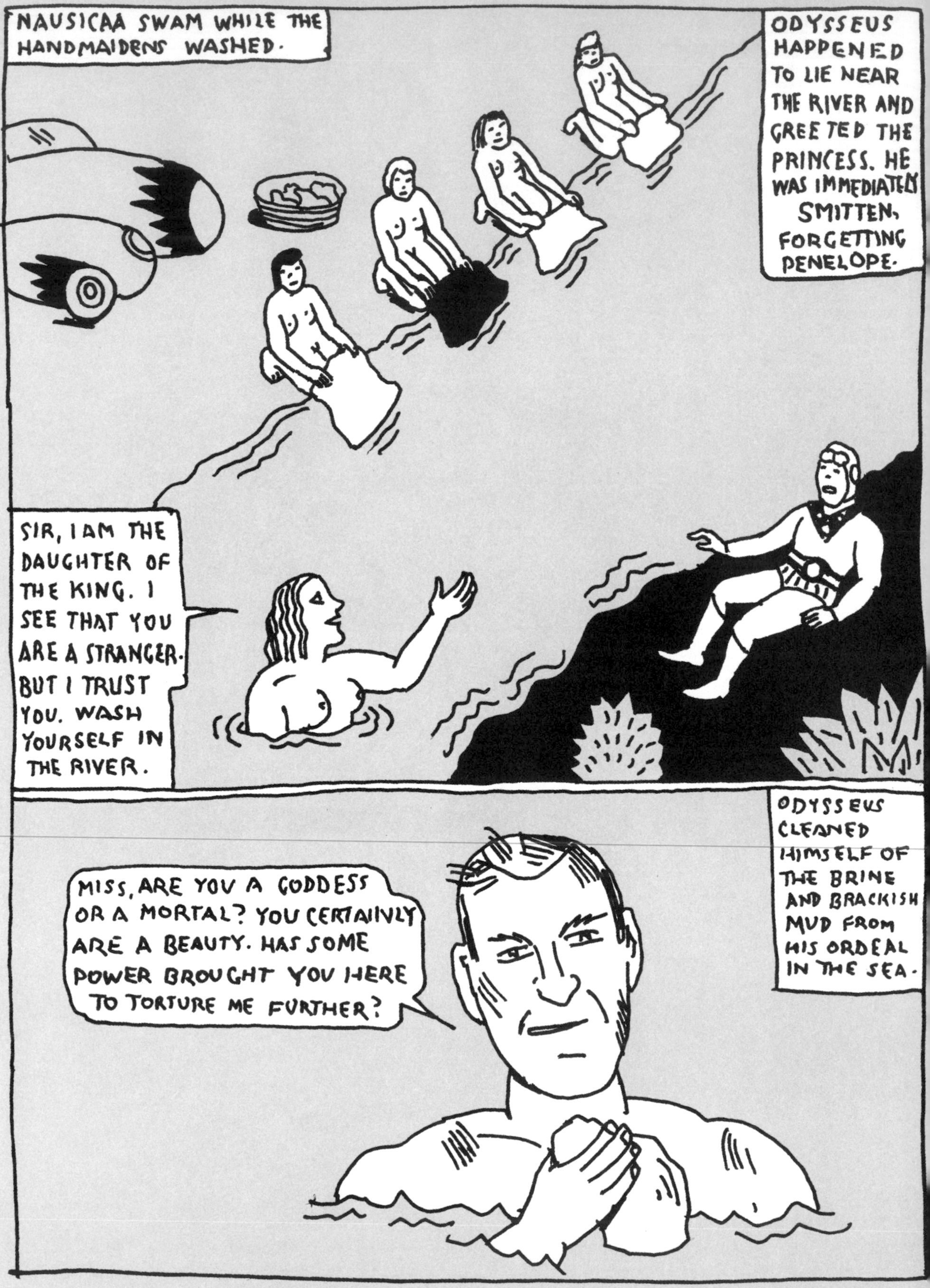
NAUSICAA SWAM WHILE THE HANDMAIDENS WASHED.
ODYSSEUS HAPPENED TO LIE NEAR THE RIVER AND GREETED THE PRINCESS. HE WAS IMMEDIATELY SMITTEN, FORGETTING PENELOPE.
SIR, I AM THE DAUGHTER OF THE KING. I SEE THAT YOU ARE A STRANGER. BUT I TRUST YOU. WASH YOURSELF IN THE RIVER.
ODYSSEUS CLEANED HIMSELF OF THE BRINE AND BRACKISH MUD FROM HIS ORDEAL IN THE SEA.
MISS, ARE YOU A GODDESS OR A MORTAL? YOU CERTAINLY ARE A BEAUTY. HAS SOME POWER BROUGHT YOU HERE TO TORTURE ME FURTHER?

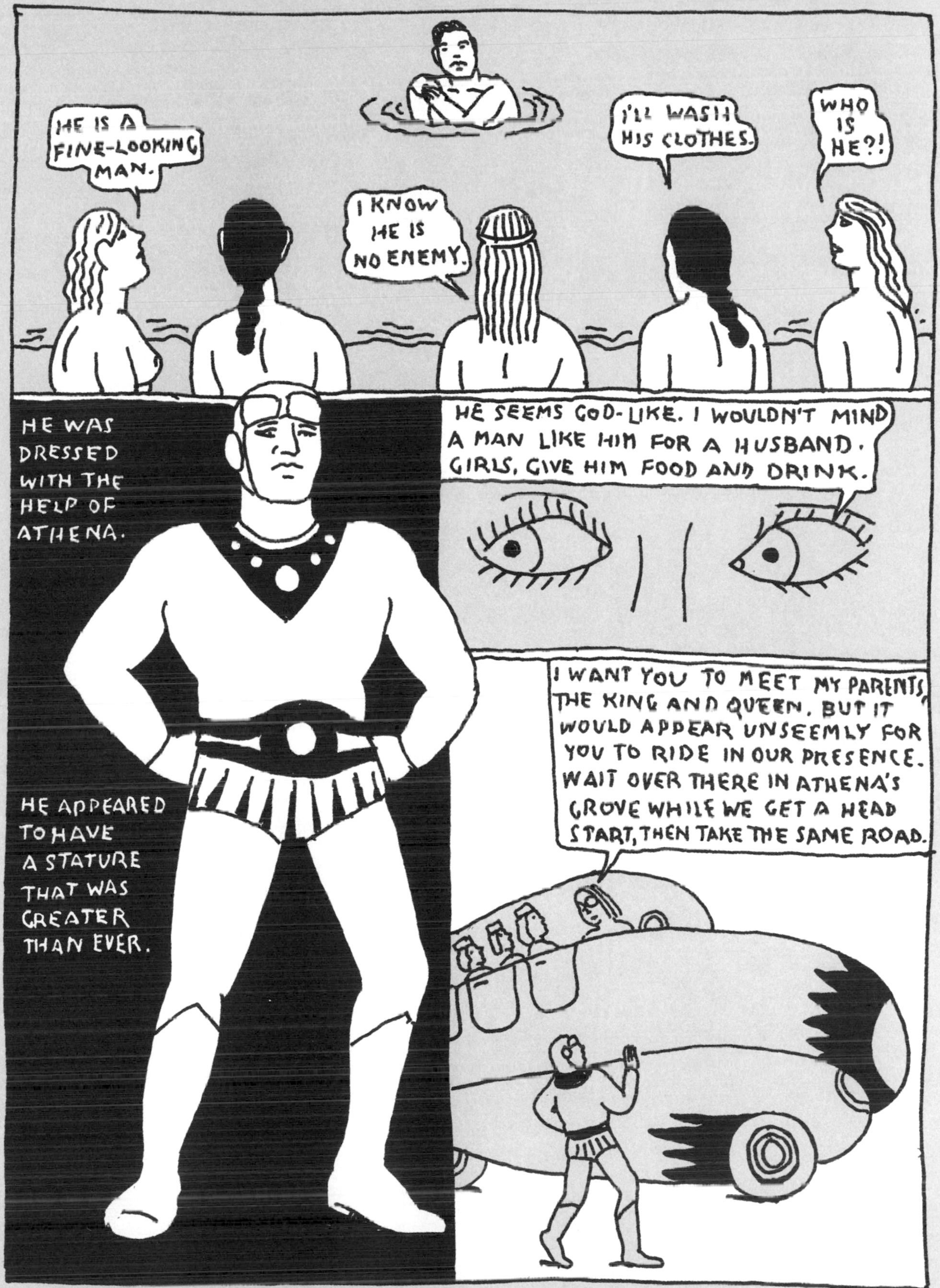
HE IS A FINE-LOOKING MAN.
I KNOW HE IS NO ENEMY.
I'LL WASH HIS CLOTHES.
WHO IS HE?!
HE WAS DRESSED WITH THE HELP OF ATHENA.
HE APPEARED TO HAVE A STATURE THAT WAS GREATER THAN EVER.
HE SEEMS GOD-LIKE. I WOULDN'T MIND A MAN LIKE HIM FOR A HUSBAND. GIRLS, GIVE HIM FOOD AND DRINK.
I WANT YOU TO MEET MY PARENTS, THE KING AND QUEEN. BUT IT WOULD APPEAR UNSEEMLY FOR YOU TO RIDE IN OUR PRESENCE. WAIT OVER THERE IN ATHENA'S GROVE WHILE WE GET A HEAD START, THEN TAKE THE SAME ROAD.

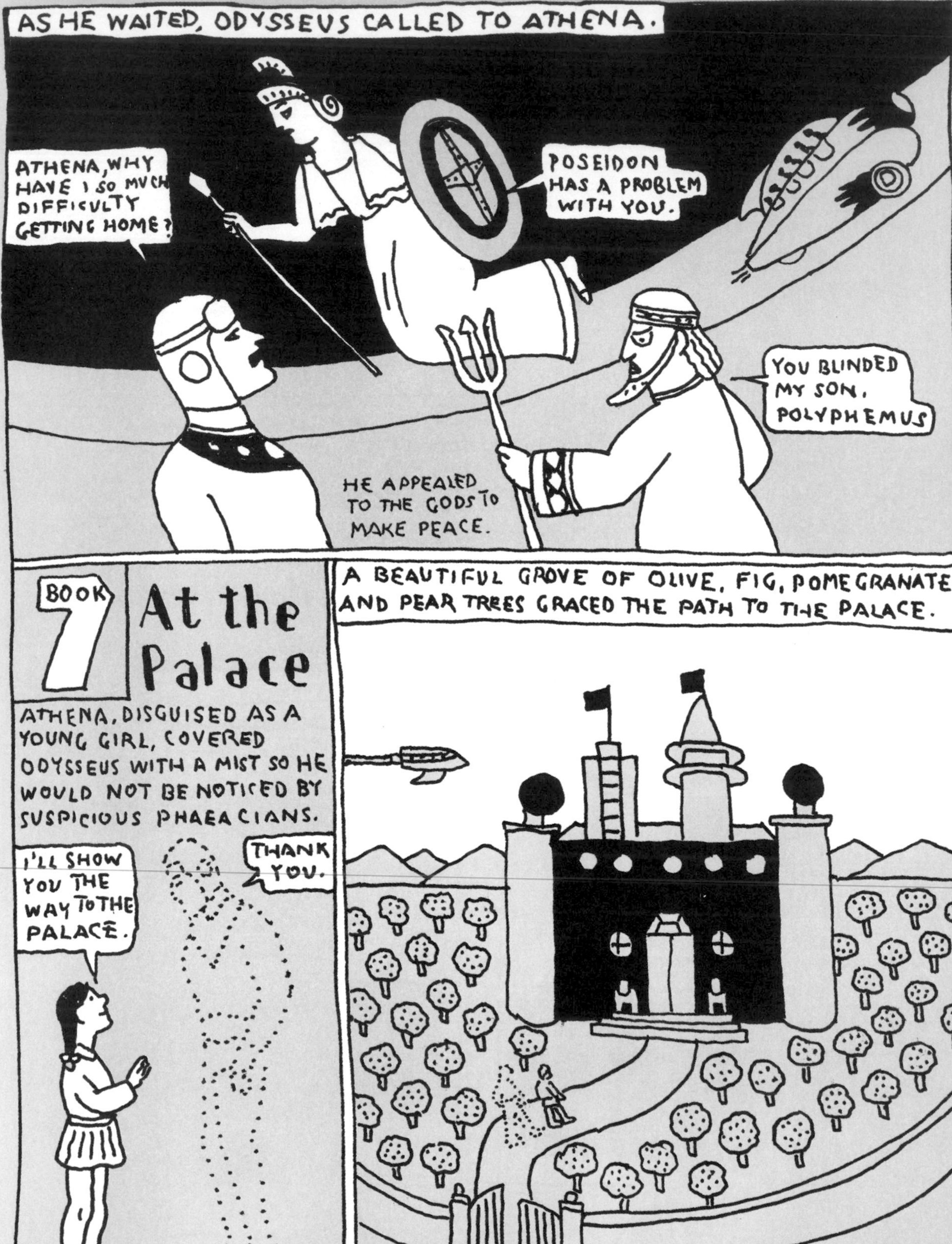
AS HE WAITED, ODYSSEUS CALLED TO ATHENA.
ATHENA, WHY HAVE I SO MUCH DIFFICULTY GETTING HOME?
POSEIDON HAS A PROBLEM WITH YOU.
YOU BLINDED MY SON, POLYPHEMUS
HE APPEALED TO THE GODS TO MAKE PEACE.
BOOK 7 At the Palace
ATHENA, DISGUISED AS A YOUNG GIRL, COVERED ODYSSEUS WITH A MIST SO HE WOULD NOT BE NOTICED BY SUSPICIOUS PHAEACIANS.
I'LL SHOW YOU THE WAY TO THE PALACE.
THANK YOU.
A BEAUTIFUL GROVE OF OLIVE, FIG, POMEGRANATE AND PEAR TREES GRACED THE PATH TO THE PALACE.

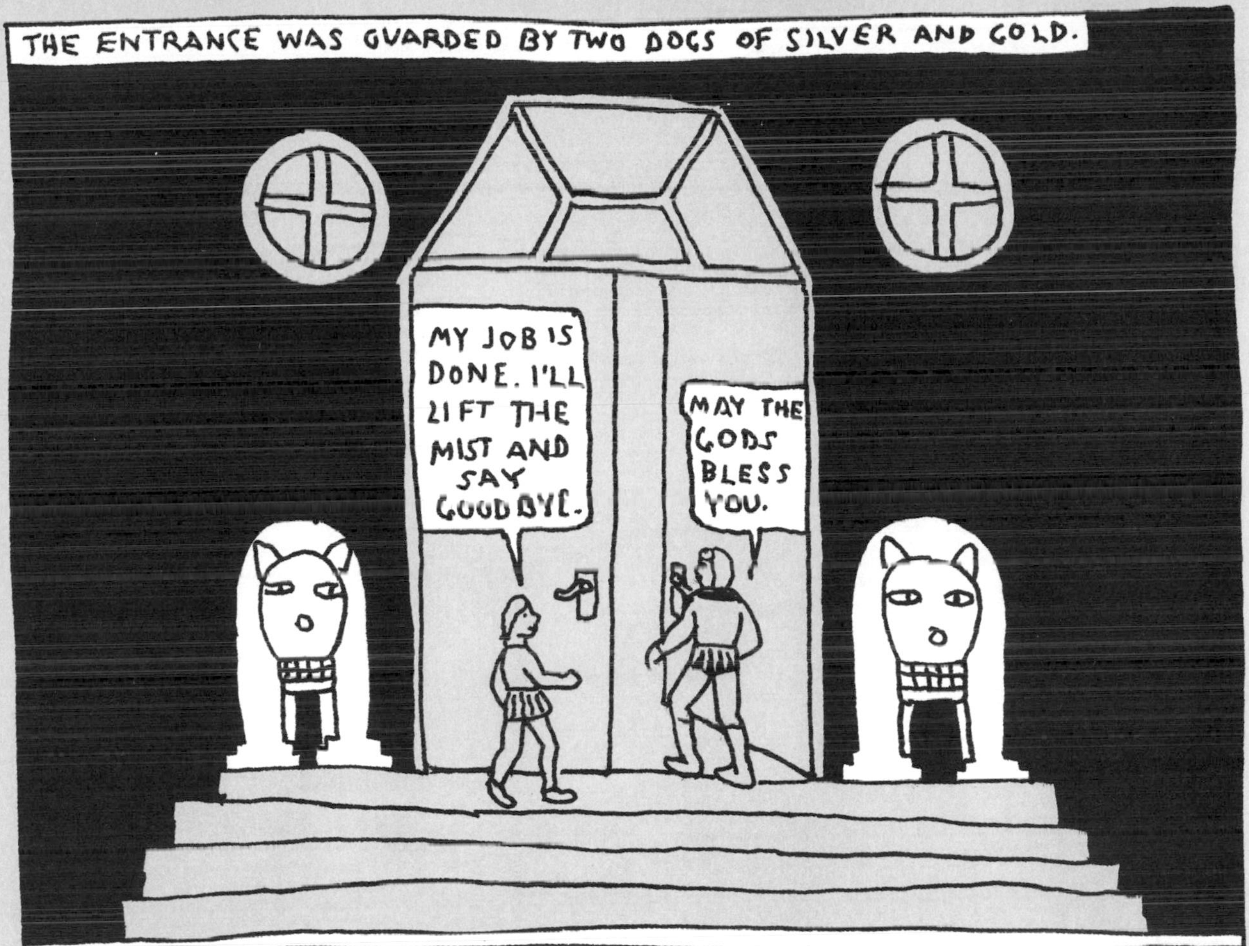
THE ENTRANCE WAS GUARDED BY TWO DOGS OF SILVER AND GOLD.
MY JOB IS DONE. I'LL LIFT THE MIST AND SAY GOODBYE.
MAY THE GODS BLESS YOU.

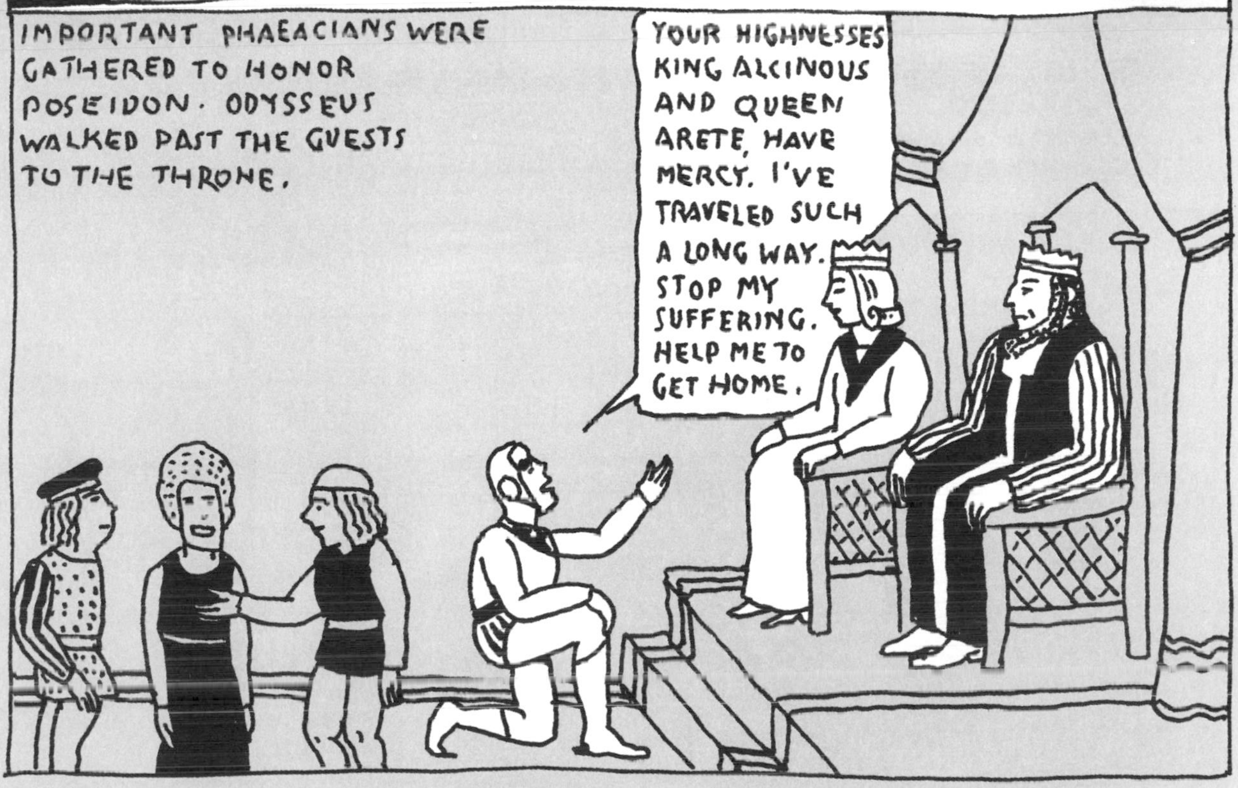
IMPORTANT PHAEACIANS WERE GATHERED TO HONOR POSEIDON. ODYSSEUS WALKED PAST THE GUESTS TO THE THRONE.
YOUR HIGHNESSES KING ALCINOUS AND QUEEN ARETE, HAVE MERCY. I'VE TRAVELED SUCH A LONG WAY. STOP MY SUFFERING. HELP ME TO GET HOME.

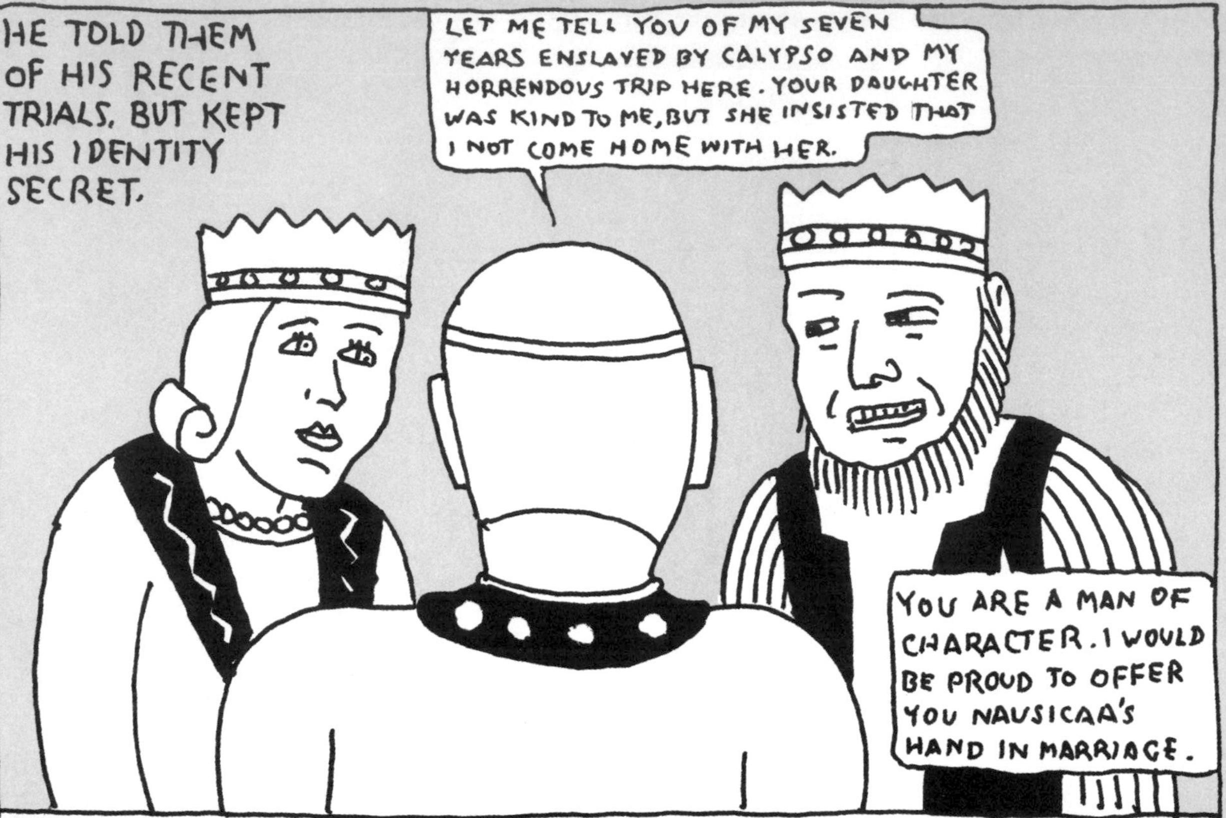
HE TOLD THEM OF HIS RECENT TRIALS, BUT KEPT HIS IDENTITY SECRET.
LET ME TELL YOU OF MY SEVEN YEARS ENSLAVED BY CALYPSO AND MY HORRENDOUS TRIP HERE. YOUR DAUGHTER WAS KIND TO ME, BUT SHE INSISTED THAT I NOT COME HOME WITH HER.
YOU ARE A MAN OF CHARACTER. I WOULD BE PROUD TO OFFER YOU NAUSICAA'S HAND IN MARRIAGE.

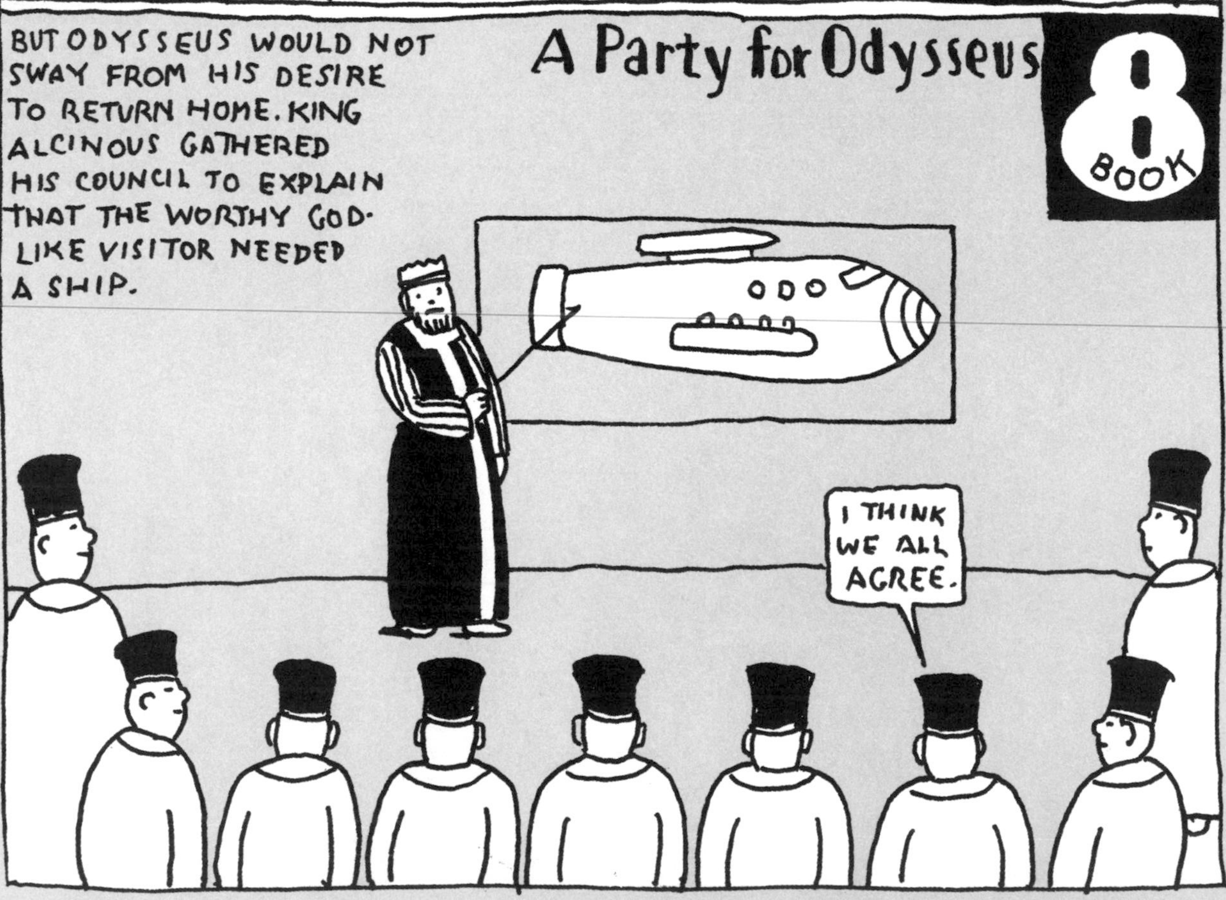
A Party for Odysseus
8
BOOK
BUT ODYSSEUS WOULD NOT SWAY FROM HIS DESIRE TO RETURN HOME. KING ALCINOUS GATHERED HIS COUNCIL TO EXPLAIN THAT THE WORTHY GOD-LIKE VISITOR NEEDED A SHIP.
I THINK WE ALL AGREE.

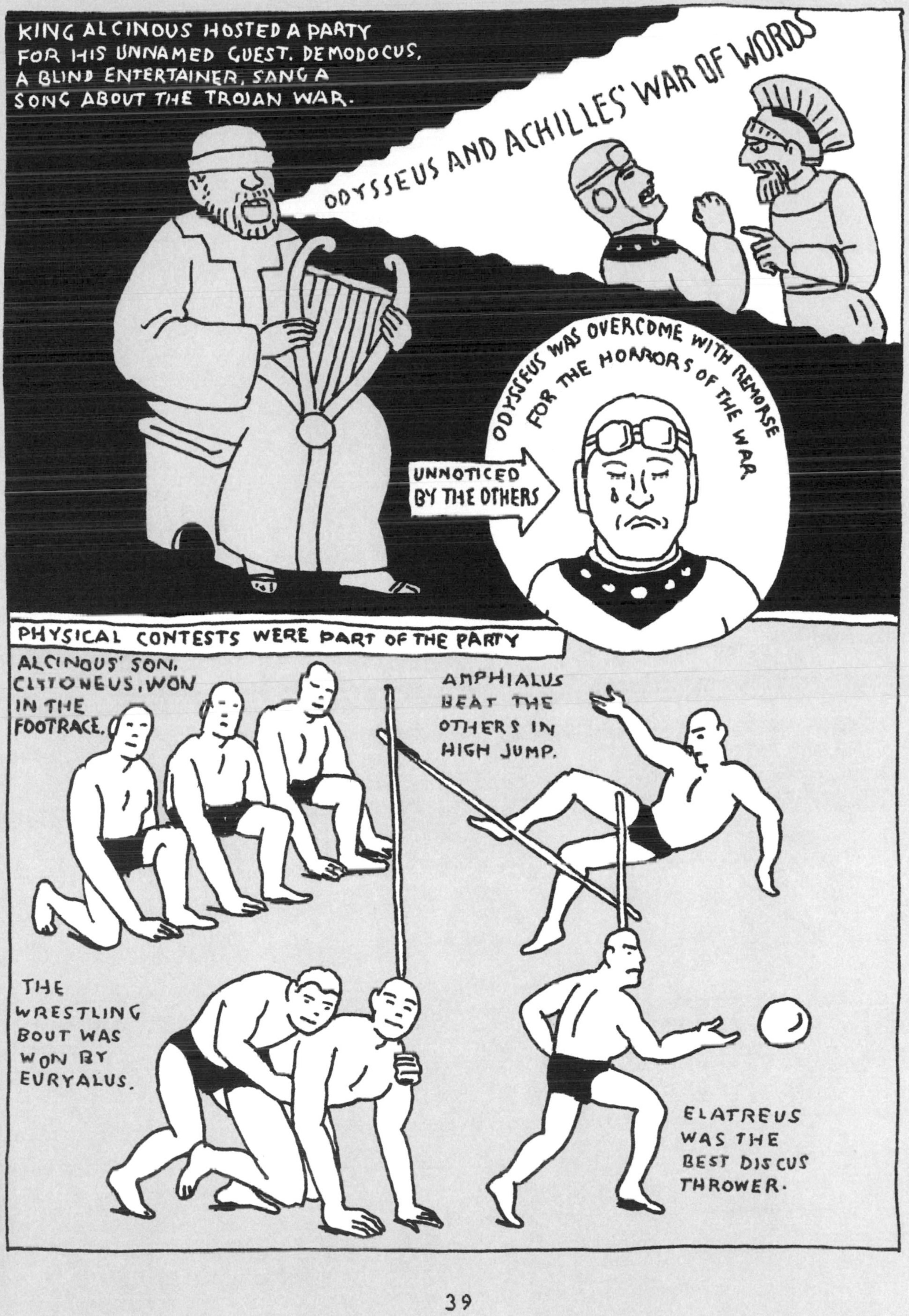
KING ALCINOUS HOSTED A PARTY FOR HIS UNNAMED GUEST. DEMODOCUS, A BLIND ENTERTAINER, SANG A SONG ABOUT THE TROJAN WAR.
ODYSSEUS AND ACHILLES' WAR OF WORDS
ODYSSEUS WAS OVERCOME WITH REMORSE FOR THE HORRORS OF THE WAR.
UNNOTICED BY THE OTHERS
PHYSICAL CONTESTS WERE PART OF THE PARTY
ALCINOUS' SON, CLYTONEUS, WON IN THE FOOTRACE.
AMPHIALUS BEAT THE OTHERS IN HIGH JUMP.
THE WRESTLING BOUT WAS WON BY EURYALUS.
ELATREUS WAS THE BEST DISCUS THROWER.

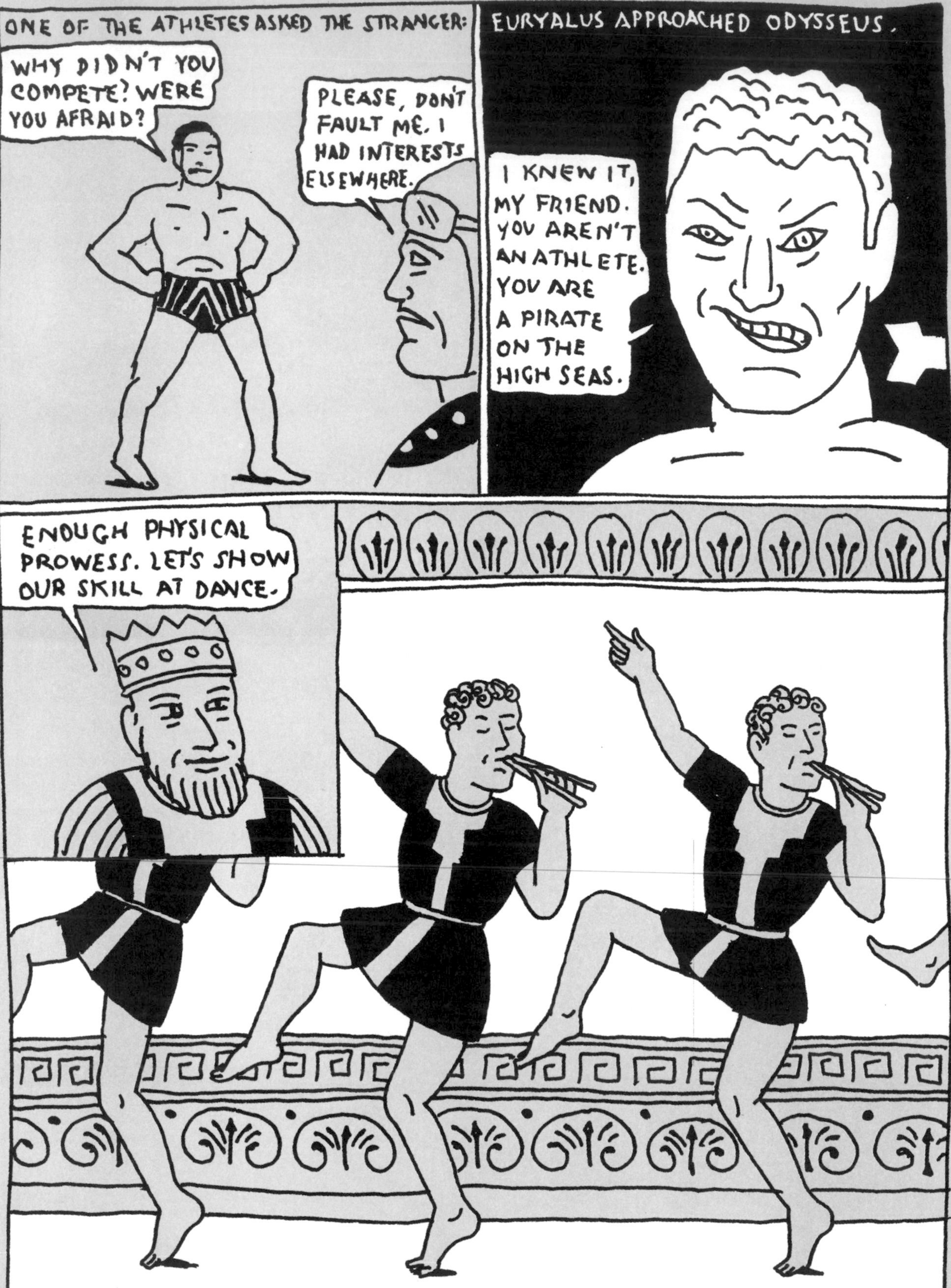
ONE OF THE ATHLETES ASKED THE STRANGER:
WHY DIDN'T YOU COMPETE? WERE YOU AFRAID?
PLEASE, DON'T FAULT ME. I HAD INTERESTS ELSEWHERE.
EURYALUS APPROACHED ODYSSEUS.
I KNEW IT, MY FRIEND. YOU AREN'T AN ATHLETE. YOU ARE A PIRATE ON THE HIGH SEAS.
ENOUGH PHYSICAL PROWESS. LET'S SHOW OUR SKILL AT DANCE.

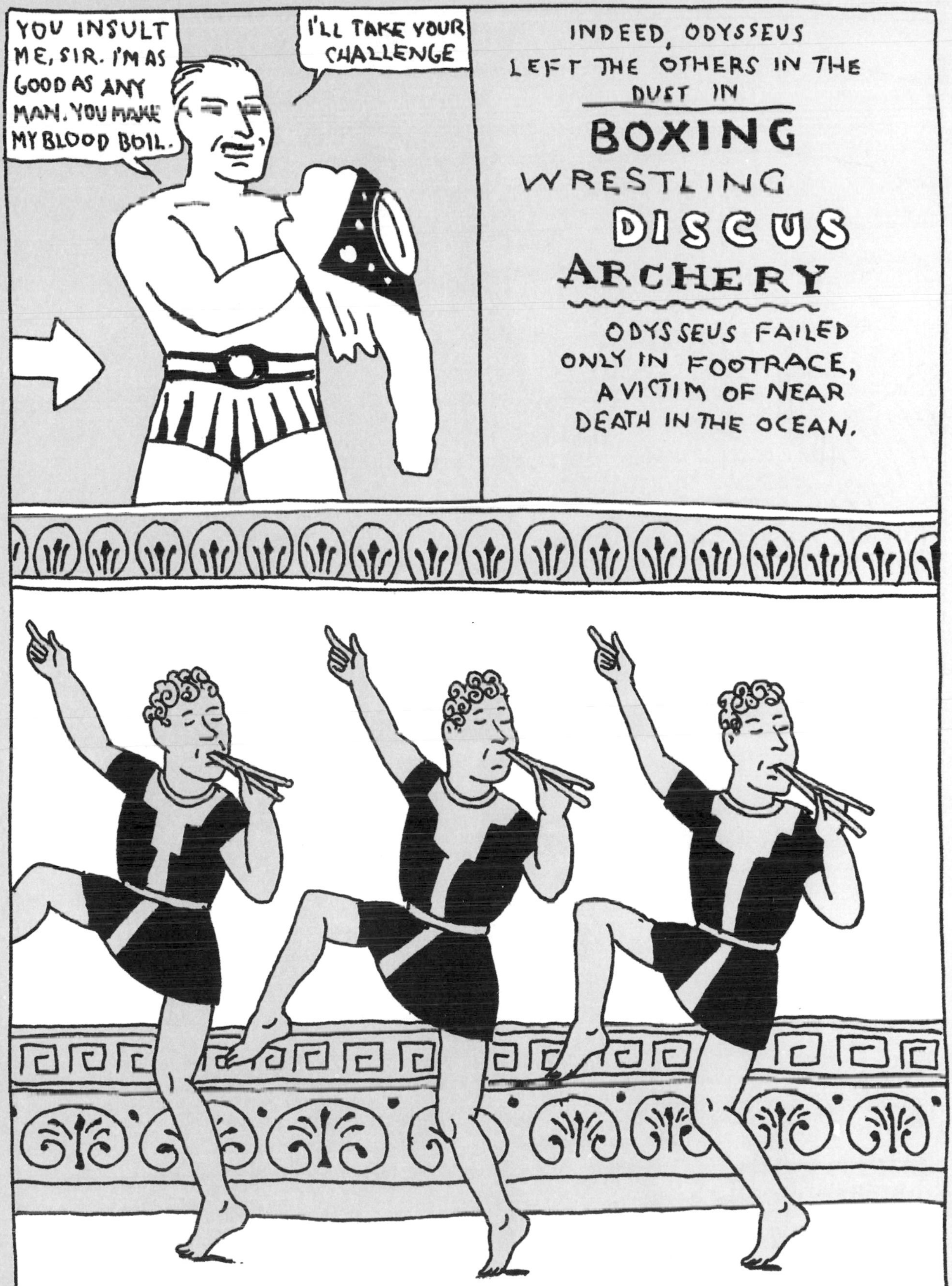
YOU INSULT ME, SIR. I'M AS GOOD AS ANY MAN. YOU MAKE MY BLOOD BOIL.
I'LL TAKE YOUR CHALLENGE
INDEED, ODYSSEUS LEFT THE OTHERS IN THE DUST IN
BOXING
WRESTLING
DISCUS
ARCHERY
ODYSSEUS FAILED ONLY IN FOOTRACE, A VICTIM OF NEAR DEATH IN THE OCEAN.

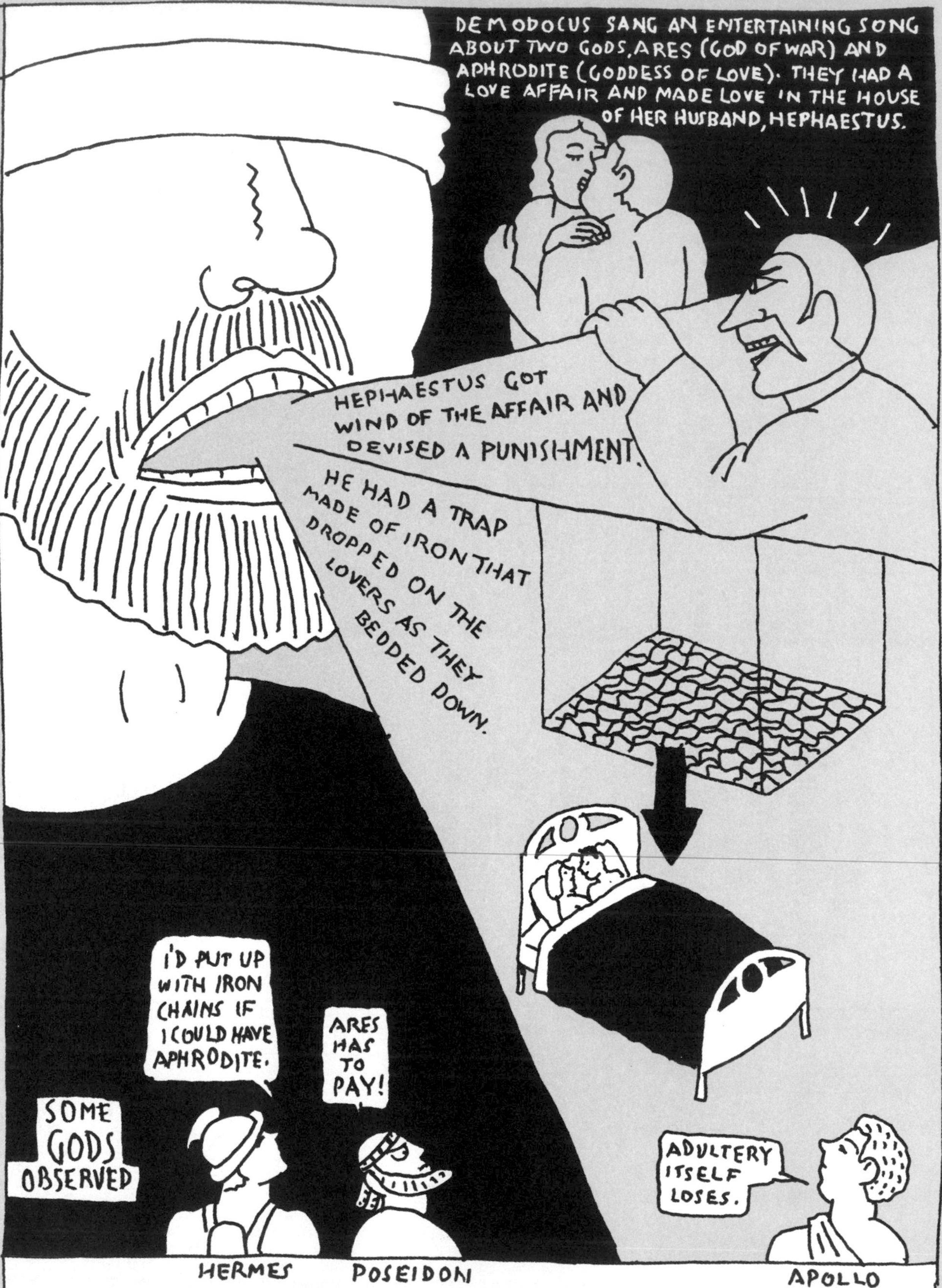
DEMODOCUS SANG AN ENTERTAINING SONG ABOUT TWO GODS, ARES (GOD OF WAR) AND APHRODITE (GODDESS OF LOVE). THEY HAD A LOVE AFFAIR AND MADE LOVE IN THE HOUSE OF HER HUSBAND, HEPHAESTUS.
HEPHAESTUS GOT WIND OF THE AFFAIR AND DEVISED A PUNISHMENT.
HE HAD A TRAP MADE OF IRON THAT DROPPED ON THE LOVERS AS THEY BEDDED DOWN.
SOME GODS OBSERVED
I'D PUT UP WITH IRON CHAINS IF I COULD HAVE APHRODITE.
ARES HAS TO PAY!
ADULTERY ITSELF LOSES.
HERMES
POSEIDON
APOLLO

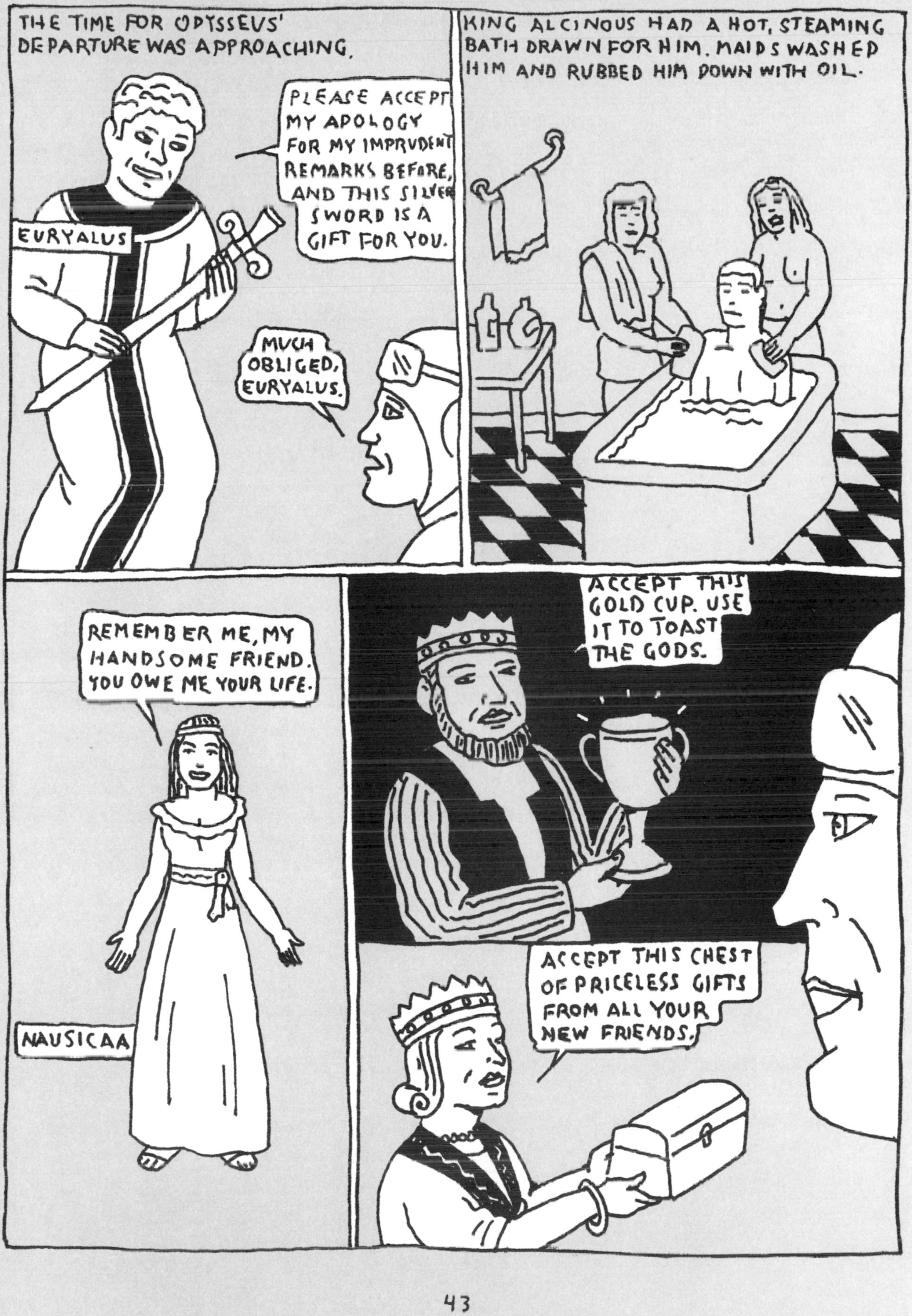
THE TIME FOR ODYSSEUS' DEPARTURE WAS APPROACHING.
EURYALUS
PLEASE ACCEPT MY APOLOGY FOR MY IMPRUDENT REMARKS BEFORE, AND THIS SILVER SWORD IS A GIFT FOR YOU.
MUCH OBLIGED, EURYALUS.
KING ALCINOUS HAD A HOT, STEAMING BATH DRAWN FOR HIM. MAIDS WASHED HIM AND RUBBED HIM DOWN WITH OIL.
REMEMBER ME, MY HANDSOME FRIEND. YOU OWE ME YOUR LIFE.
NAUSICAA
ACCEPT THIS GOLD CUP. USE IT TO TOAST THE GODS.
ACCEPT THIS CHEST OF PRICELESS GIFTS FROM ALL YOUR NEW FRIENDS.

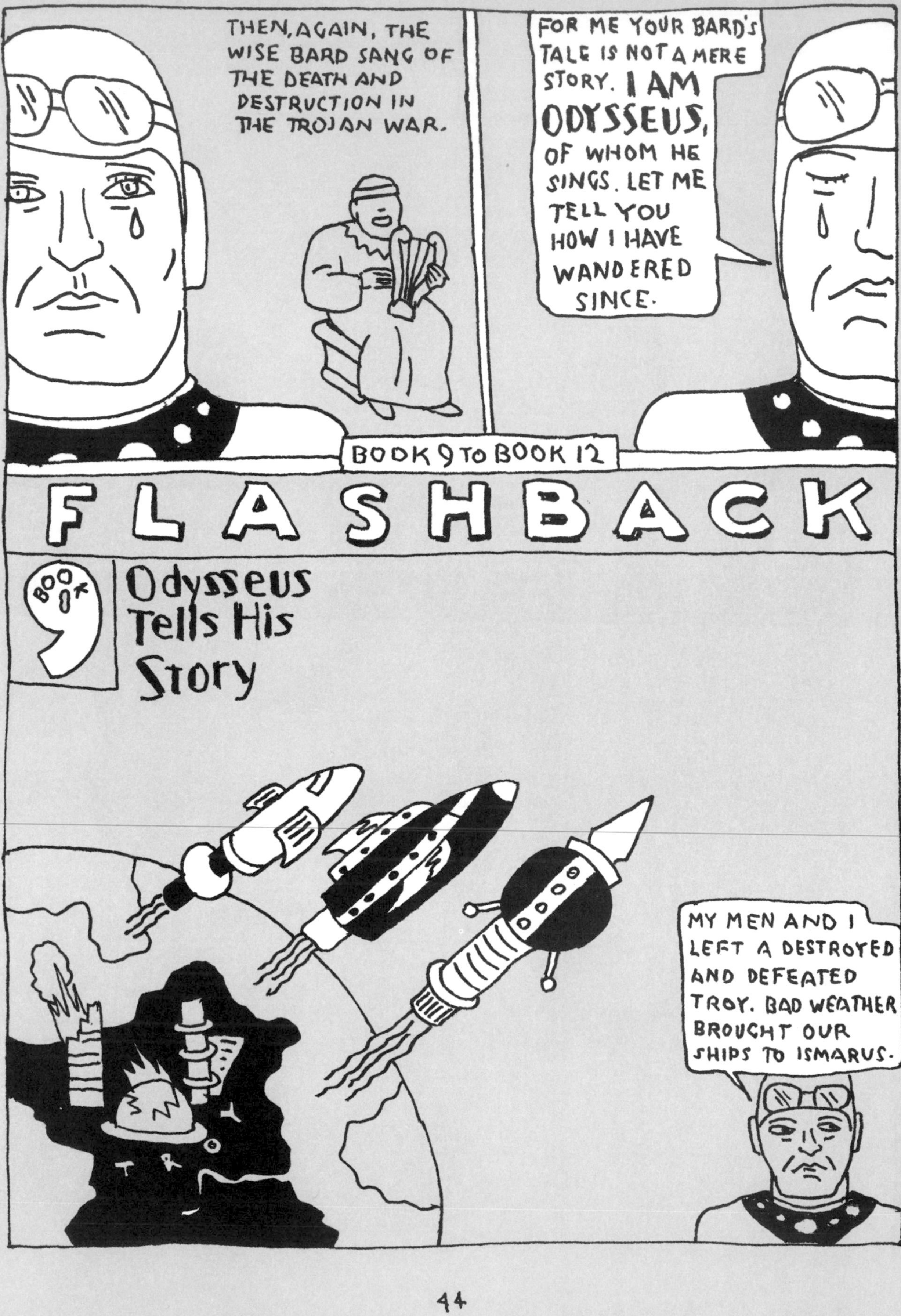
THEN, AGAIN, THE WISE BARD SANG OF THE DEATH AND DESTRUCTION IN THE TROJAN WAR.
FOR ME YOUR BARD'S TALE IS NOT A MERE STORY. I AM ODYSSEUS, OF WHOM HE SINGS. LET ME TELL YOU HOW I HAVE WANDERED SINCE.
BOOK 9 TO BOOK 12
FLASHBACK
BOOK 9
Odysseus Tells His Story
TROY
MY MEN AND I LEFT A DESTROYED AND DEFEATED TROY. BAD WEATHER BROUGHT OUR SHIPS TO ISMARUS.

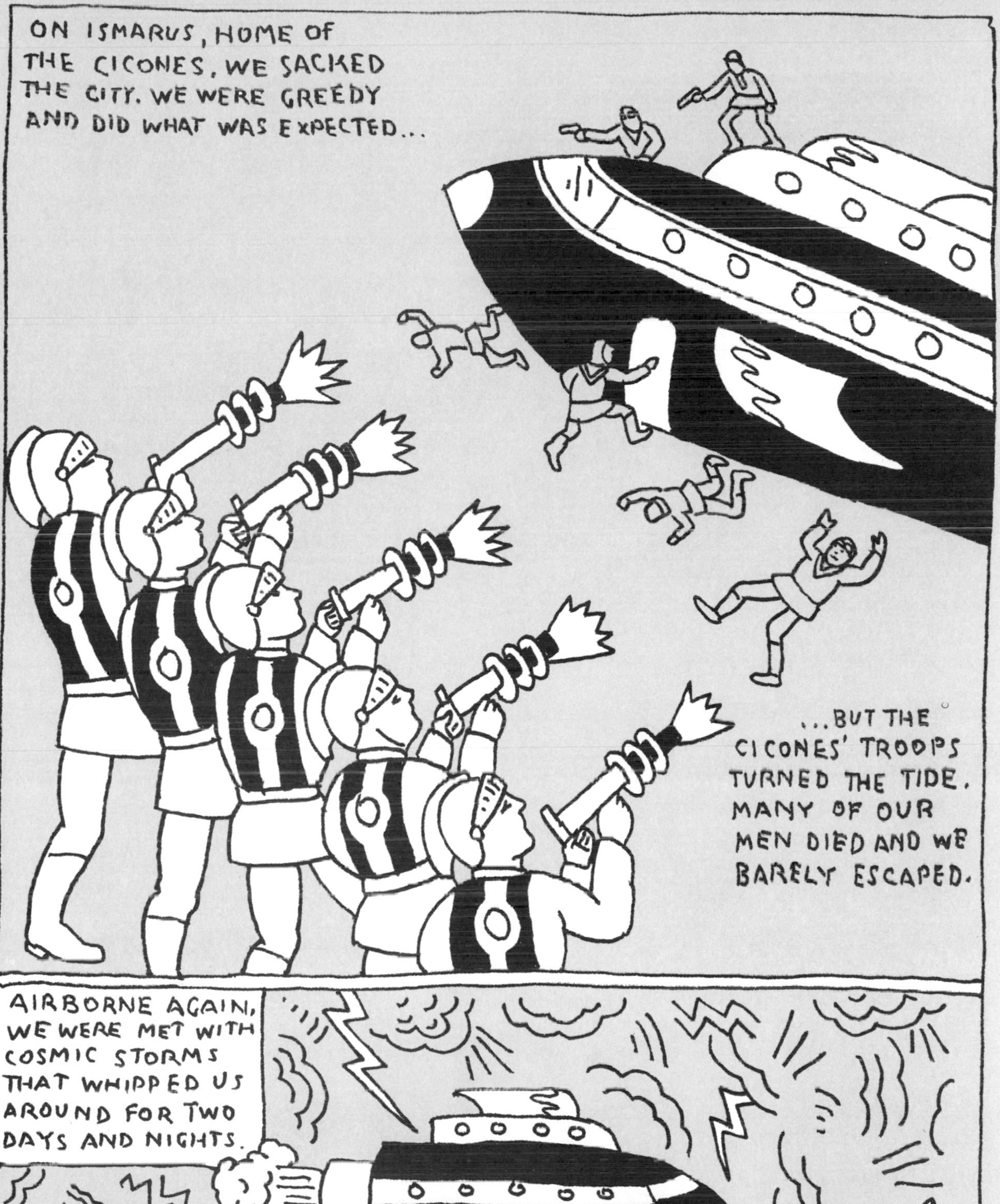
ON ISMARUS, HOME OF THE CICONES, WE SACKED THE CITY. WE WERE GREEDY AND DID WHAT WAS EXPECTED...
...BUT THE CICONES' TROOPS TURNED THE TIDE. MANY OF OUR MEN DIED AND WE BARELY ESCAPED.

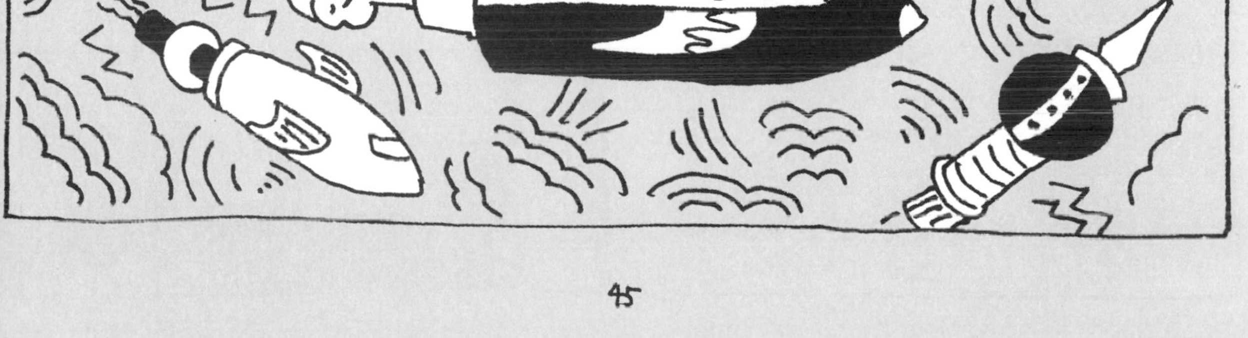
AIRBORNE AGAIN, WE WERE MET WITH COSMIC STORMS THAT WHIPPED US AROUND FOR TWO DAYS AND NIGHTS.

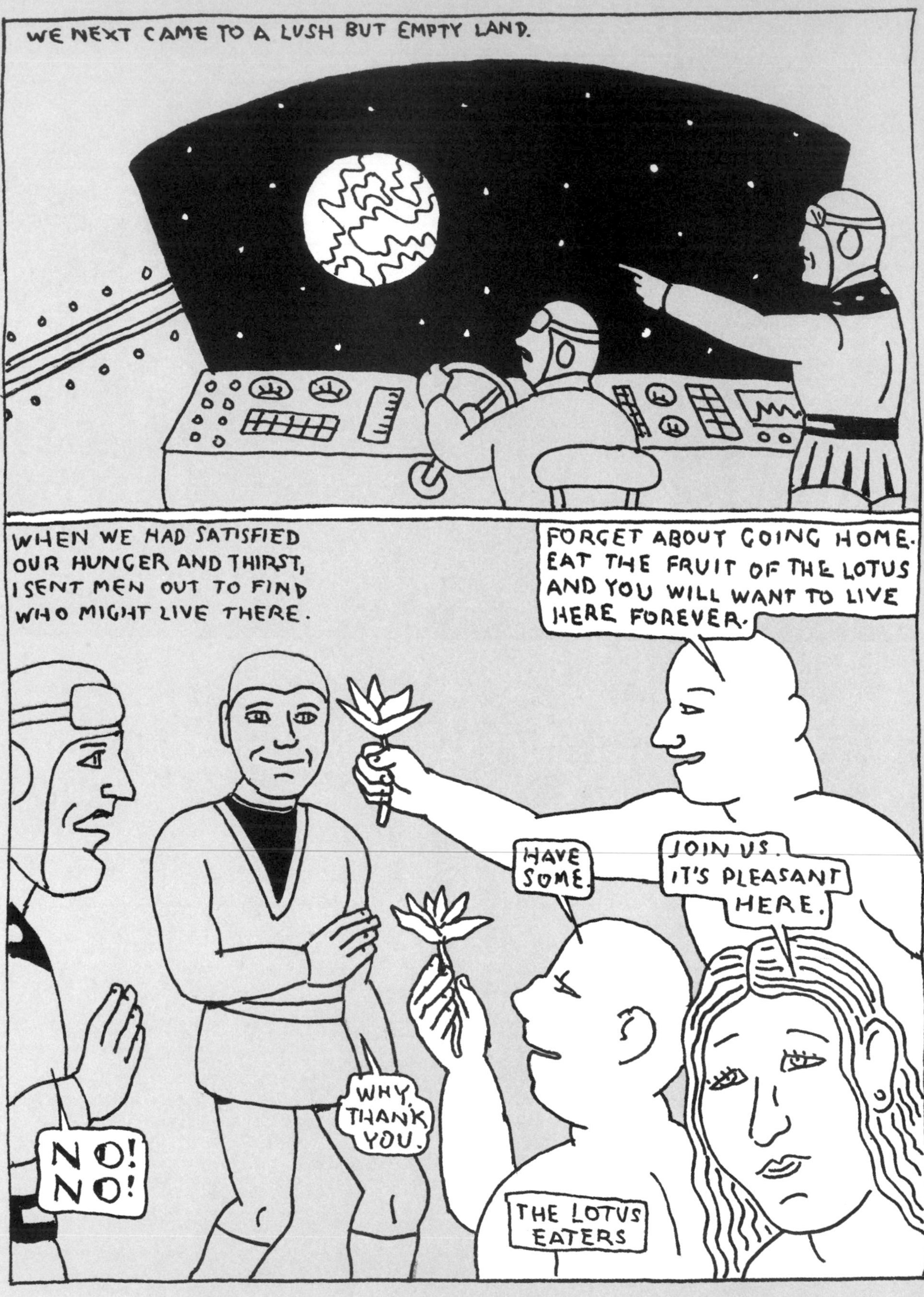
WE NEXT CAME TO A LUSH BUT EMPTY LAND.
WHEN WE HAD SATISFIED OUR HUNGER AND THIRST, I SENT MEN OUT TO FIND WHO MIGHT LIVE THERE.
FORGET ABOUT GOING HOME. EAT THE FRUIT OF THE LOTUS AND YOU WILL WANT TO LIVE HERE FOREVER.
HAVE SOME.
JOIN US. IT'S PLEASANT HERE.
WHY, THANK YOU.
NO! NO!
THE LOTUS EATERS

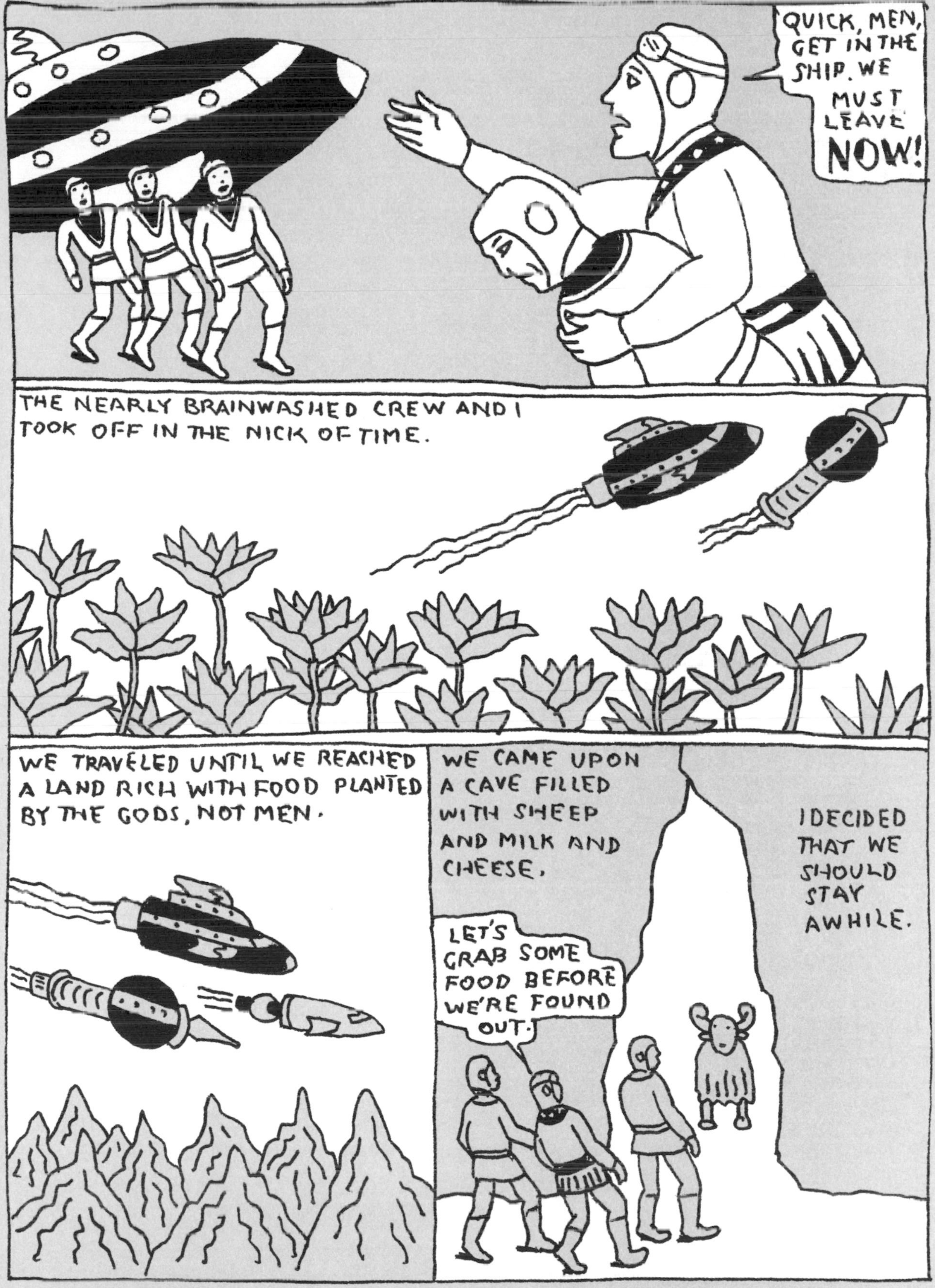
QUICK, MEN, GET IN THE SHIP. WE MUST LEAVE NOW!
THE NEARLY BRAINWASHED CREW AND I TOOK OFF IN THE NICK OF TIME.
WE TRAVELED UNTIL WE REACHED A LAND RICH WITH FOOD PLANTED BY THE GODS, NOT MEN.
WE CAME UPON A CAVE FILLED WITH SHEEP AND MILK AND CHEESE.
I DECIDED THAT WE SHOULD STAY AWHILE.
LET'S GRAB SOME FOOD BEFORE WE'RE FOUND OUT.

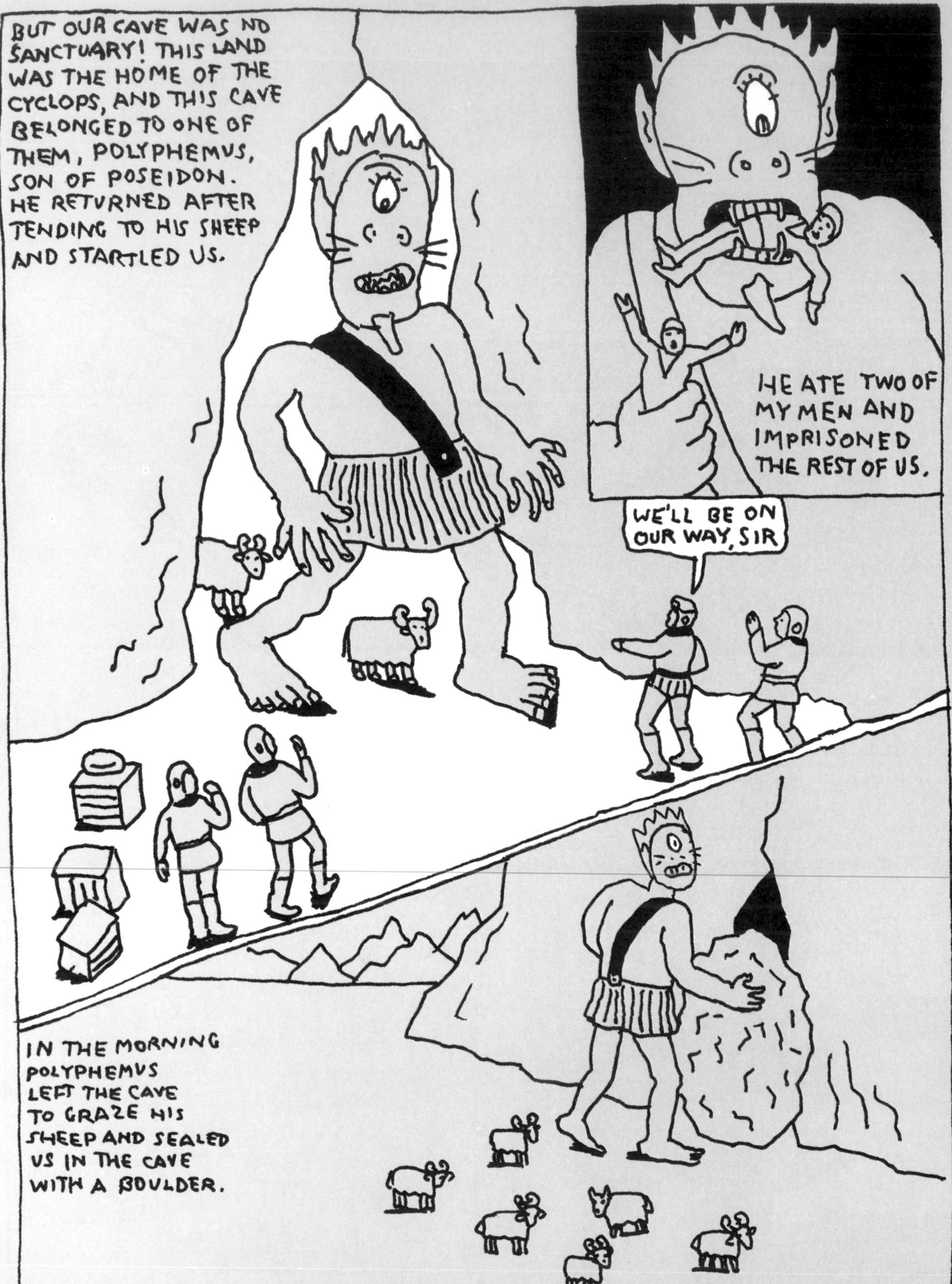
BUT OUR CAVE WAS NO SANCTUARY! THIS LAND WAS THE HOME OF THE CYCLOPS, AND THIS CAVE BELONGED TO ONE OF THEM, POLYPHEMUS, SON OF POSEIDON. HE RETURNED AFTER TENDING TO HIS SHEEP AND STARTLED US.
HE ATE TWO OF MY MEN AND IMPRISONED THE REST OF US.
WE'LL BE ON OUR WAY, SIR
IN THE MORNING POLYPHEMUS LEFT THE CAVE TO GRAZE HIS SHEEP AND SEALED US IN THE CAVE WITH A BOULDER.

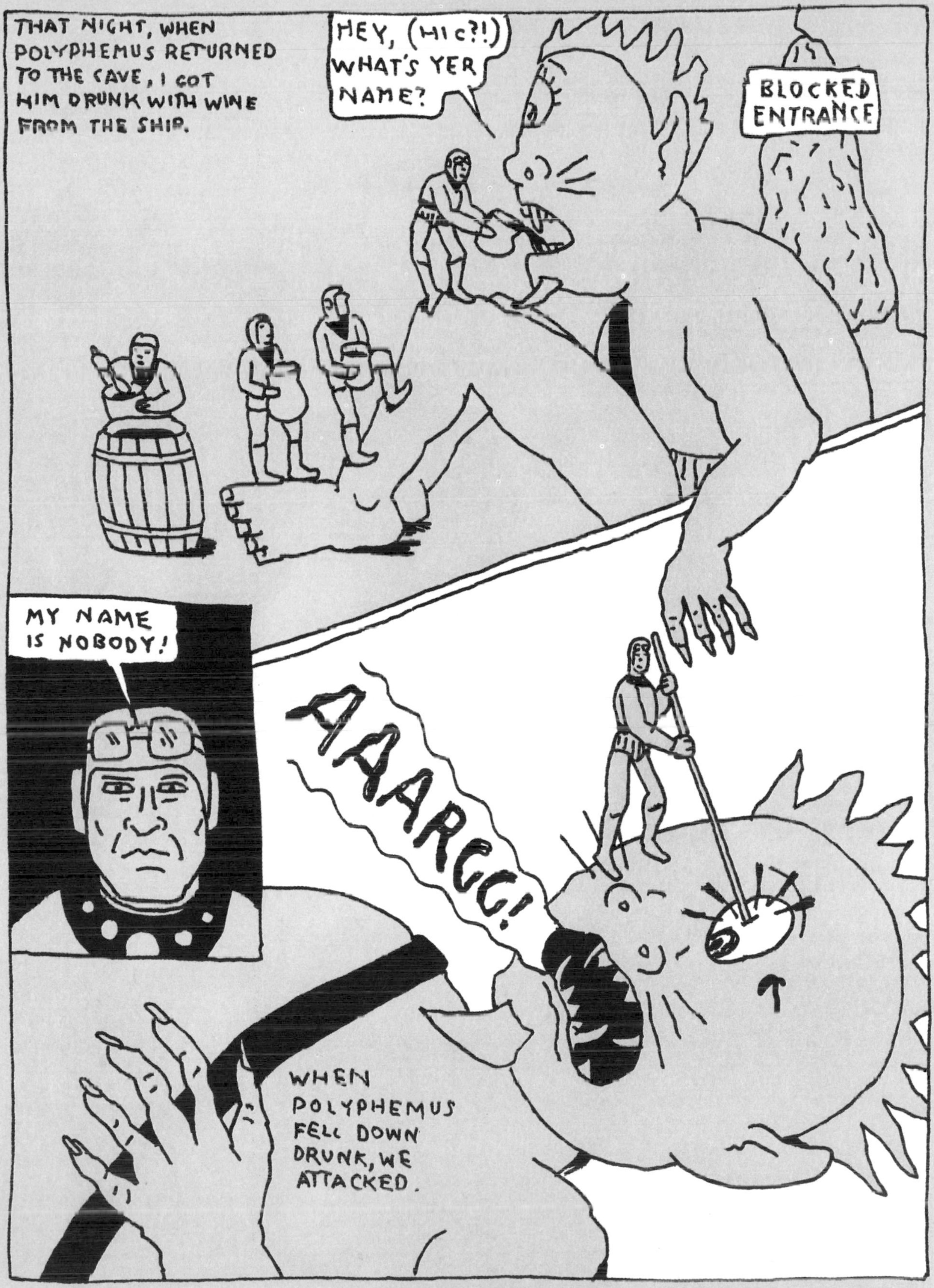

THAT NIGHT, WHEN POLYPHEMUS RETURNED TO THE CAVE, I GOT HIM DRUNK WITH WINE FROM THE SHIP.
HEY, (HIC?!) WHAT'S YER NAME?
BLOCKED ENTRANCE
MY NAME IS NOBODY!
AAAARGG!
WHEN POLYPHEMUS FELL DOWN DRUNK, WE ATTACKED.

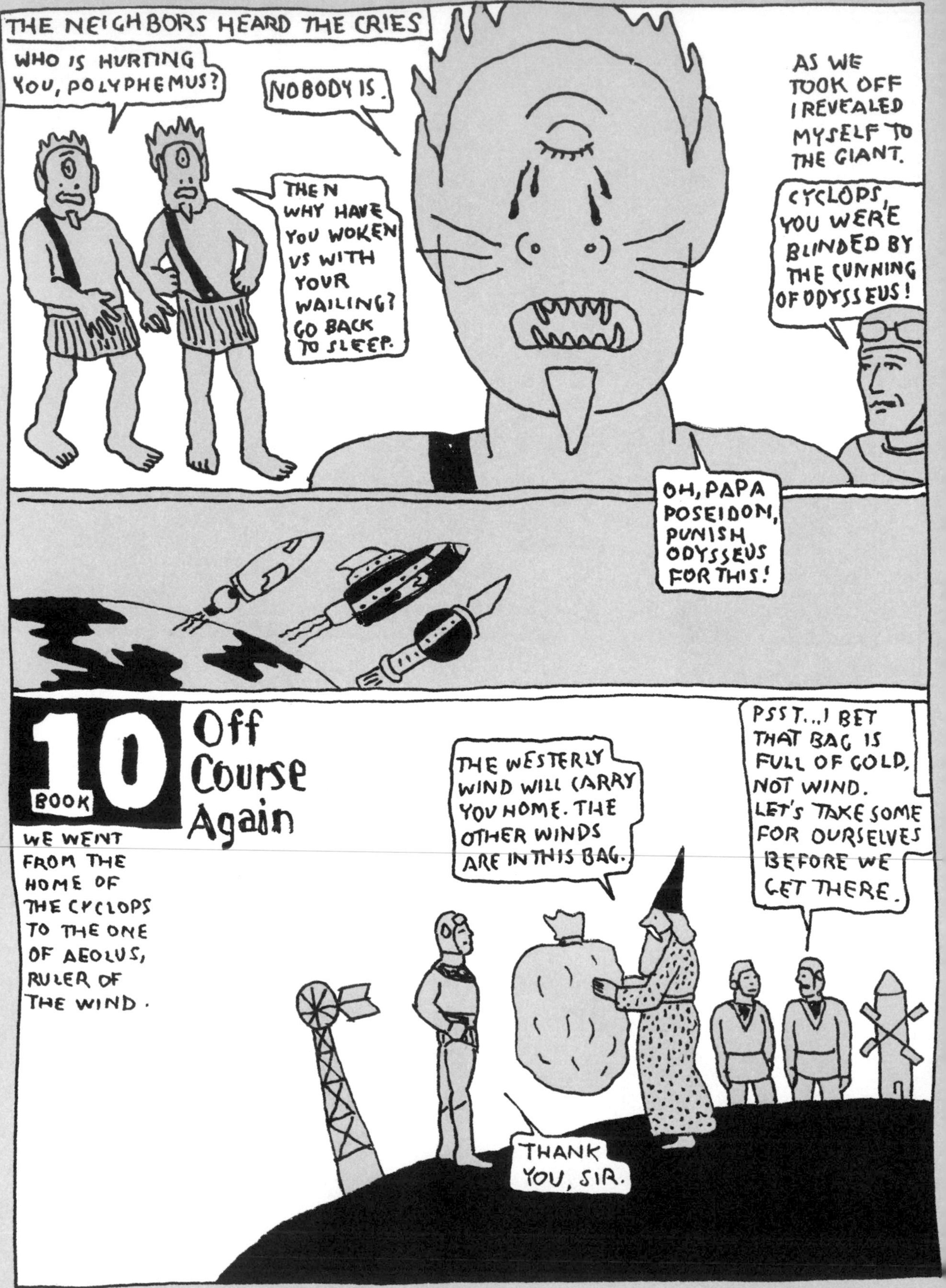
THE NEIGHBORS HEARD THE CRIES
WHO IS HURTING YOU, POLYPHEMUS?
NOBODY IS.
THEN WHY HAVE YOU WOKEN US WITH YOUR WAILING? GO BACK TO SLEEP.
AS WE TOOK OFF I REVEALED MYSELF TO THE GIANT.
CYCLOPS, YOU WERE BLINDED BY THE CUNNING OF ODYSSEUS!
OH, PAPA POSEIDON, PUNISH ODYSSEUS FOR THIS!
BOOK 10 Off Course Again
WE WENT FROM THE HOME OF THE CYCLOPS TO THE ONE OF AEOLUS, RULER OF THE WIND.
THE WESTERLY WIND WILL CARRY YOU HOME. THE OTHER WINDS ARE IN THIS BAG.
THANK YOU, SIR.
PSST... I BET THAT BAG IS FULL OF GOLD, NOT WIND. LET'S TAKE SOME FOR OURSELVES BEFORE WE GET THERE.

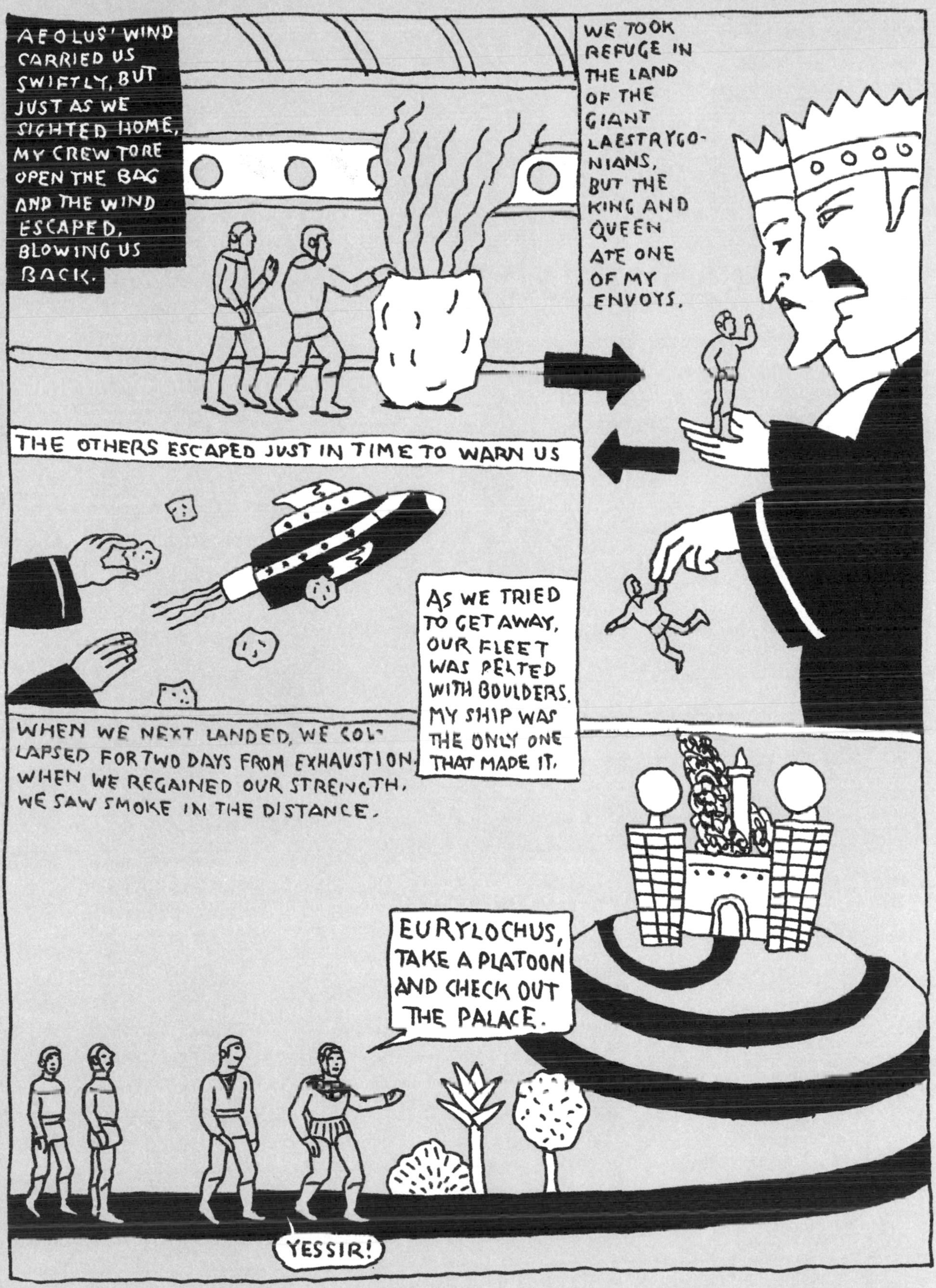
AEOLUS' WIND CARRIED US SWIFTLY, BUT JUST AS WE SIGHTED HOME, MY CREW TORE OPEN THE BAG AND THE WIND ESCAPED, BLOWING US BACK.
WE TOOK REFUGE IN THE LAND OF THE GIANT LAESTRYGONIANS, BUT THE KING AND QUEEN ATE ONE OF MY ENVOYS.
THE OTHERS ESCAPED JUST IN TIME TO WARN US
AS WE TRIED TO GET AWAY, OUR FLEET WAS PELTED WITH BOULDERS. MY SHIP WAS THE ONLY ONE THAT MADE IT.
WHEN WE NEXT LANDED, WE COLLAPSED FOR TWO DAYS FROM EXHAUSTION. WHEN WE REGAINED OUR STRENGTH, WE SAW SMOKE IN THE DISTANCE.
EURYLOCHUS, TAKE A PLATOON AND CHECK OUT THE PALACE.
YESSIR!

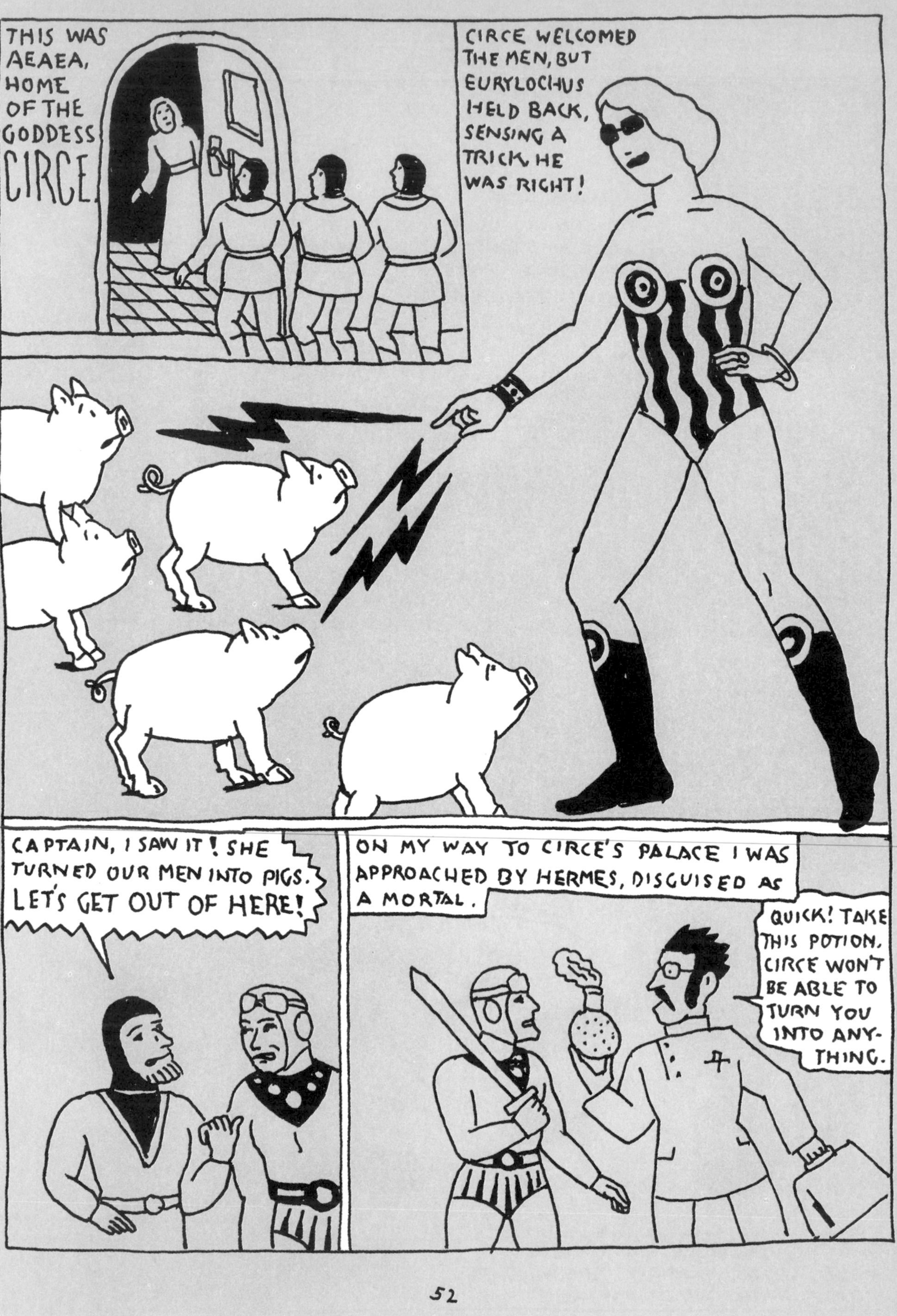
THIS WAS AEAEA, HOME OF THE GODDESS CIRCE.
CIRCE WELCOMED THE MEN, BUT EURYLOCHUS HELD BACK, SENSING A TRICK. HE WAS RIGHT!
CAPTAIN, I SAW IT! SHE TURNED OUR MEN INTO PIGS. LET'S GET OUT OF HERE!
ON MY WAY TO CIRCE'S PALACE I WAS APPROACHED BY HERMES, DISGUISED AS A MORTAL.
QUICK! TAKE THIS POTION. CIRCE WON'T BE ABLE TO TURN YOU INTO ANYTHING.

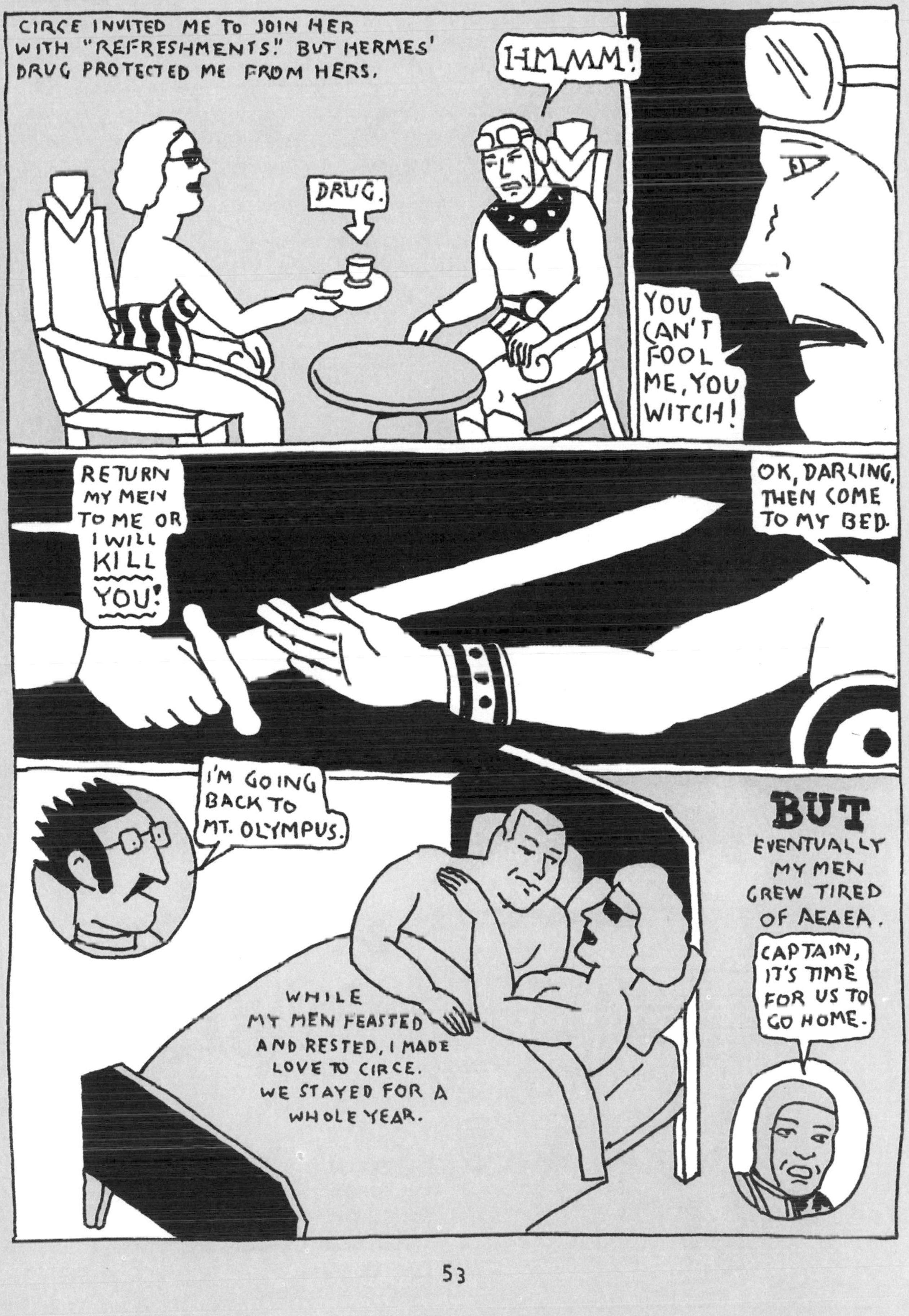
CIRCE INVITED ME TO JOIN HER WITH "REFRESHMENTS." BUT HERMES' DRUG PROTECTED ME FROM HERS.
DRUG.
HMMM!
YOU CAN'T FOOL ME, YOU WITCH!
RETURN MY MEN TO ME OR I WILL KILL YOU!
OK, DARLING, THEN COME TO MY BED.
I'M GOING BACK TO MT. OLYMPUS.
WHILE MY MEN FEASTED AND RESTED, I MADE LOVE TO CIRCE. WE STAYED FOR A WHOLE YEAR.
BUT EVENTUALLY MY MEN GREW TIRED OF AEAEA.
CAPTAIN, IT'S TIME FOR US TO GO HOME.

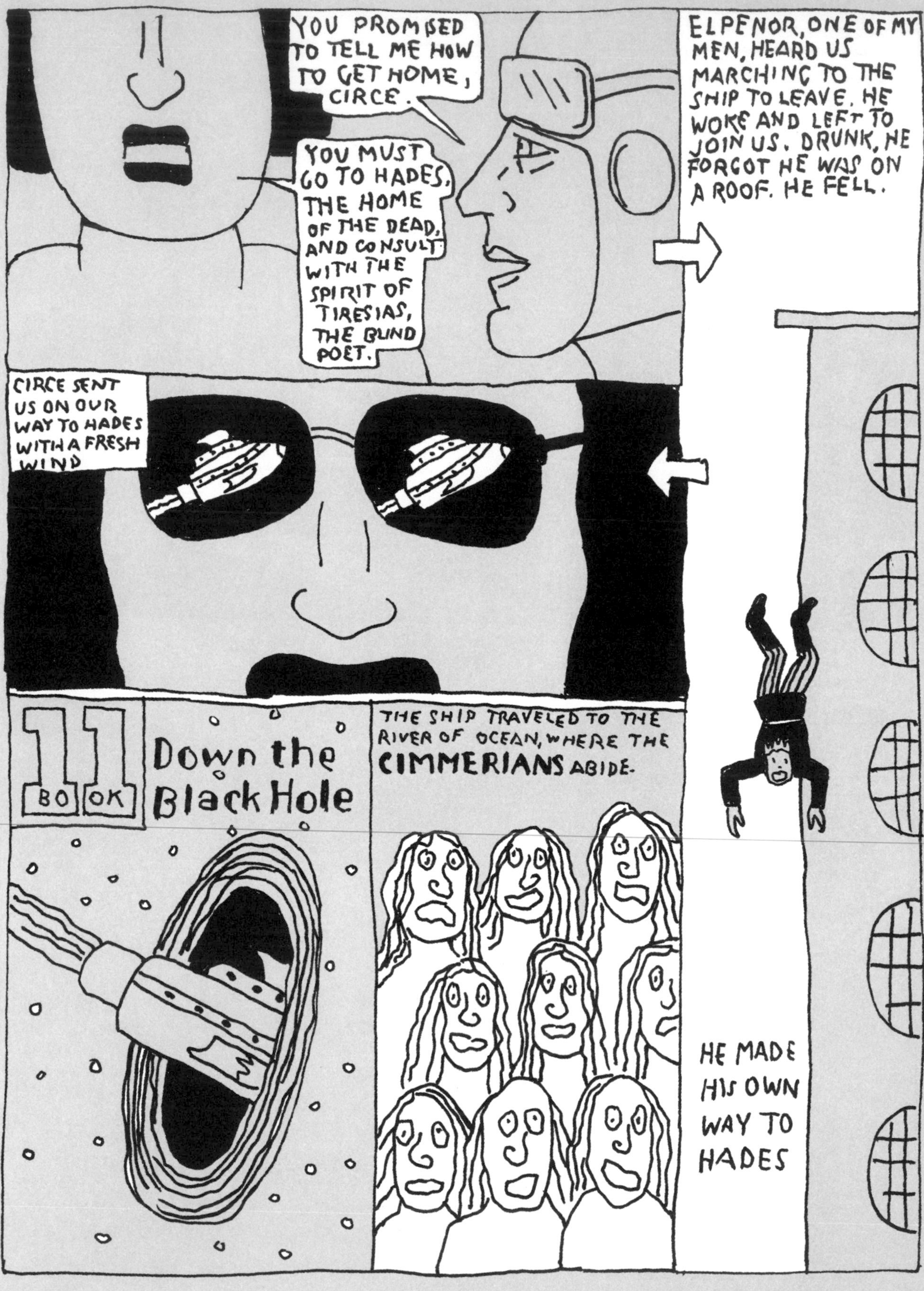

YOU PROMISED TO TELL ME HOW TO GET HOME, CIRCE.
YOU MUST GO TO HADES, THE HOME OF THE DEAD, AND CONSULT WITH THE SPIRIT OF TIRESIAS, THE BLIND POET.
ELPENOR, ONE OF MY MEN, HEARD US MARCHING TO THE SHIP TO LEAVE. HE WOKE AND LEFT TO JOIN US. DRUNK, HE FORGOT HE WAS ON A ROOF. HE FELL.
CIRCE SENT US ON OUR WAY TO HADES WITH A FRESH WIND
BOOK 11
Down the Black Hole
THE SHIP TRAVELED TO THE RIVER OF OCEAN, WHERE THE CIMMERIANS ABIDE.
HE MADE HIS OWN WAY TO HADES

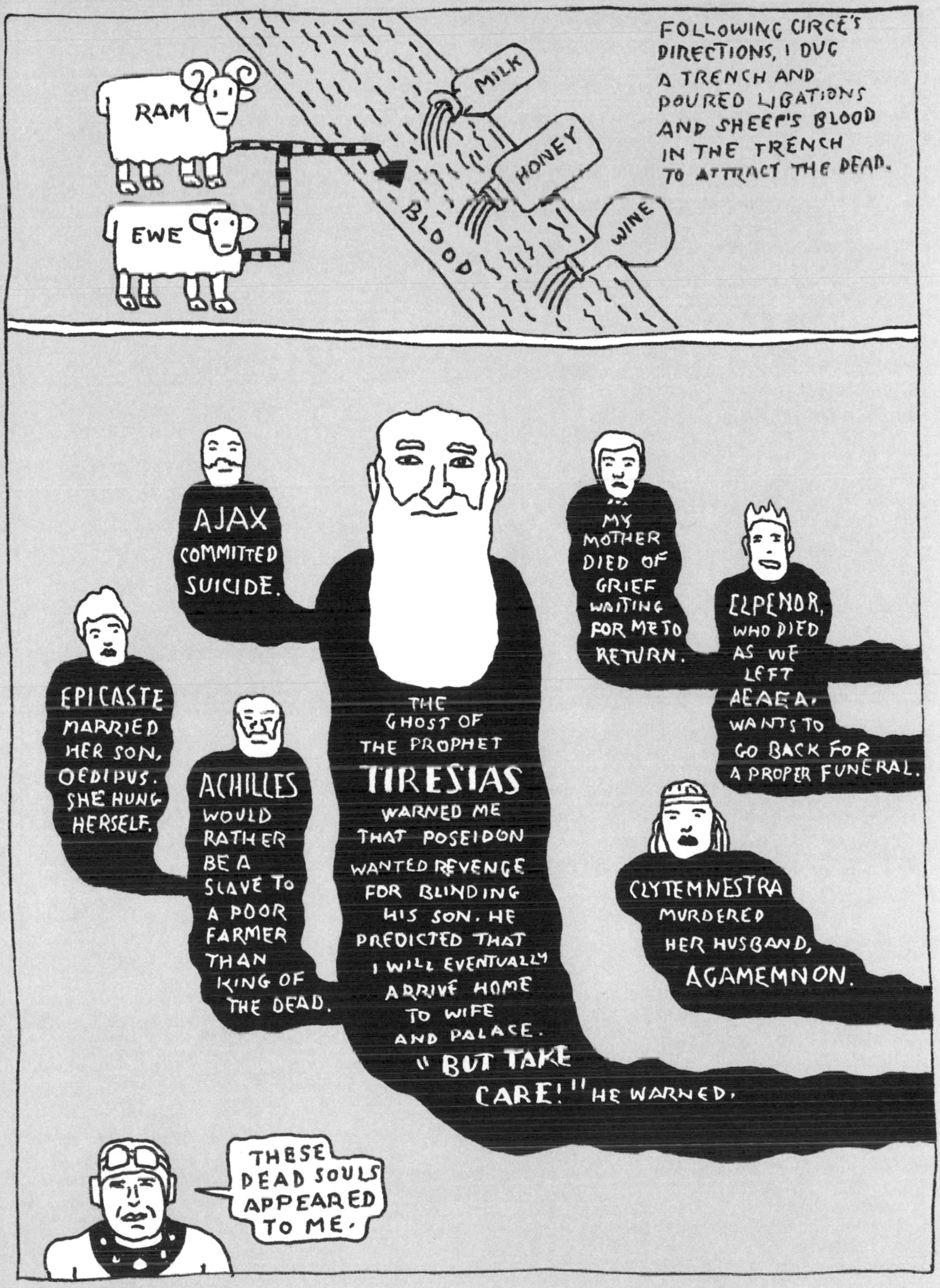
FOLLOWING CIRCE'S DIRECTIONS, I DUG A TRENCH AND POURED LIBATIONS AND SHEEP'S BLOOD IN THE TRENCH TO ATTRACT THE DEAD.
RAM
EWE
BLOOD
MILK
HONEY
WINE
AJAX COMMITTED SUICIDE.
EPICASTE MARRIED HER SON, OEDIPUS. SHE HUNG HERSELF.
ACHILLES WOULD RATHER BE A SLAVE TO A POOR FARMER THAN KING OF THE DEAD.
THE GHOST OF THE PROPHET TIRESIAS WARNED ME THAT POSEIDON WANTED REVENGE FOR BLINDING HIS SON. HE PREDICTED THAT I WILL EVENTUALLY ARRIVE HOME TO WIFE AND PALACE.
"BUT TAKE CARE!" HE WARNED.
MY MOTHER DIED OF GRIEF WAITING FOR ME TO RETURN.
ELPENOR, WHO DIED AS WE LEFT AEAEA, WANTS TO GO BACK FOR A PROPER FUNERAL.
CLYTEMNESTRA MURDERED HER HUSBAND, AGAMEMNON.
THESE DEAD SOULS APPEARED TO ME.

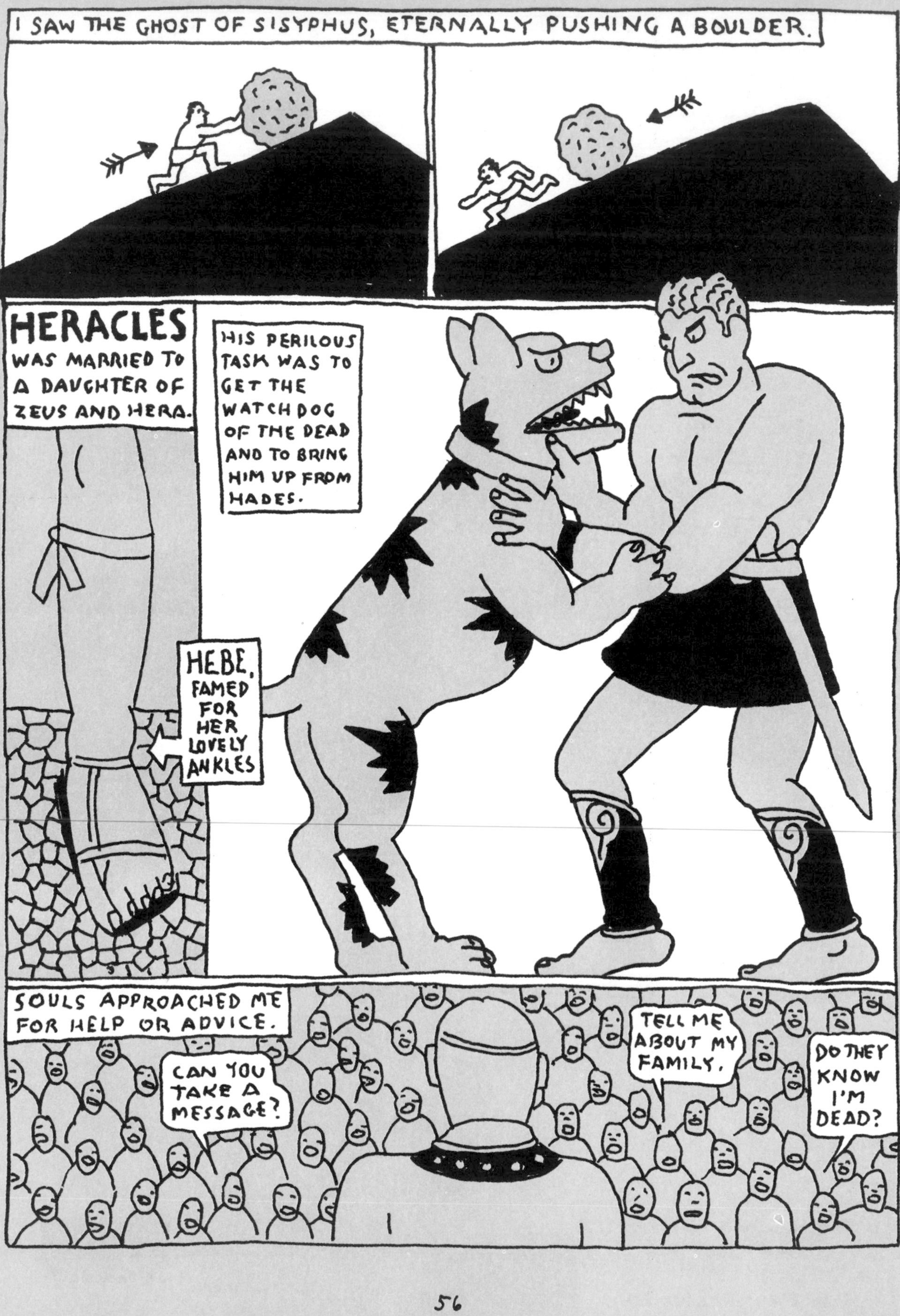
I SAW THE GHOST OF SISYPHUS, ETERNALLY PUSHING A BOULDER.
HERACLES WAS MARRIED TO A DAUGHTER OF ZEUS AND HERA.
HIS PERILOUS TASK WAS TO GET THE WATCHDOG OF THE DEAD AND TO BRING HIM UP FROM HADES.
HEBE, FAMED FOR HER LOVELY ANKLES
SOULS APPROACHED ME FOR HELP OR ADVICE.
CAN YOU TAKE A MESSAGE?
TELL ME ABOUT MY FAMILY.
DO THEY KNOW I'M DEAD?

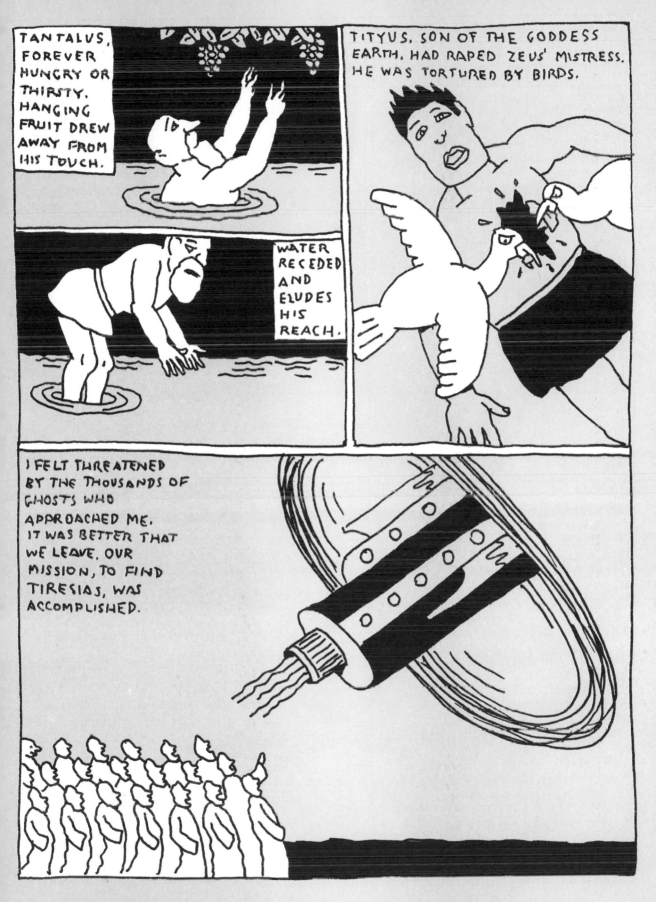

TANTALUS, FOREVER HUNGRY OR THIRSTY. HANGING FRUIT DREW AWAY FROM HIS TOUCH.

TITYUS, SON OF THE GODDESS EARTH, HAD RAPED ZEUS' MISTRESS. HE WAS TORTURED BY BIRDS.

WATER RECEDED AND ELUDES HIS REACH.

I FELT THREATENED BY THE THOUSANDS OF GHOSTS WHO APPROACHED ME. IT WAS BETTER THAT WE LEAVE. OUR MISSION, TO FIND TIRESIAS, WAS ACCOMPLISHED.

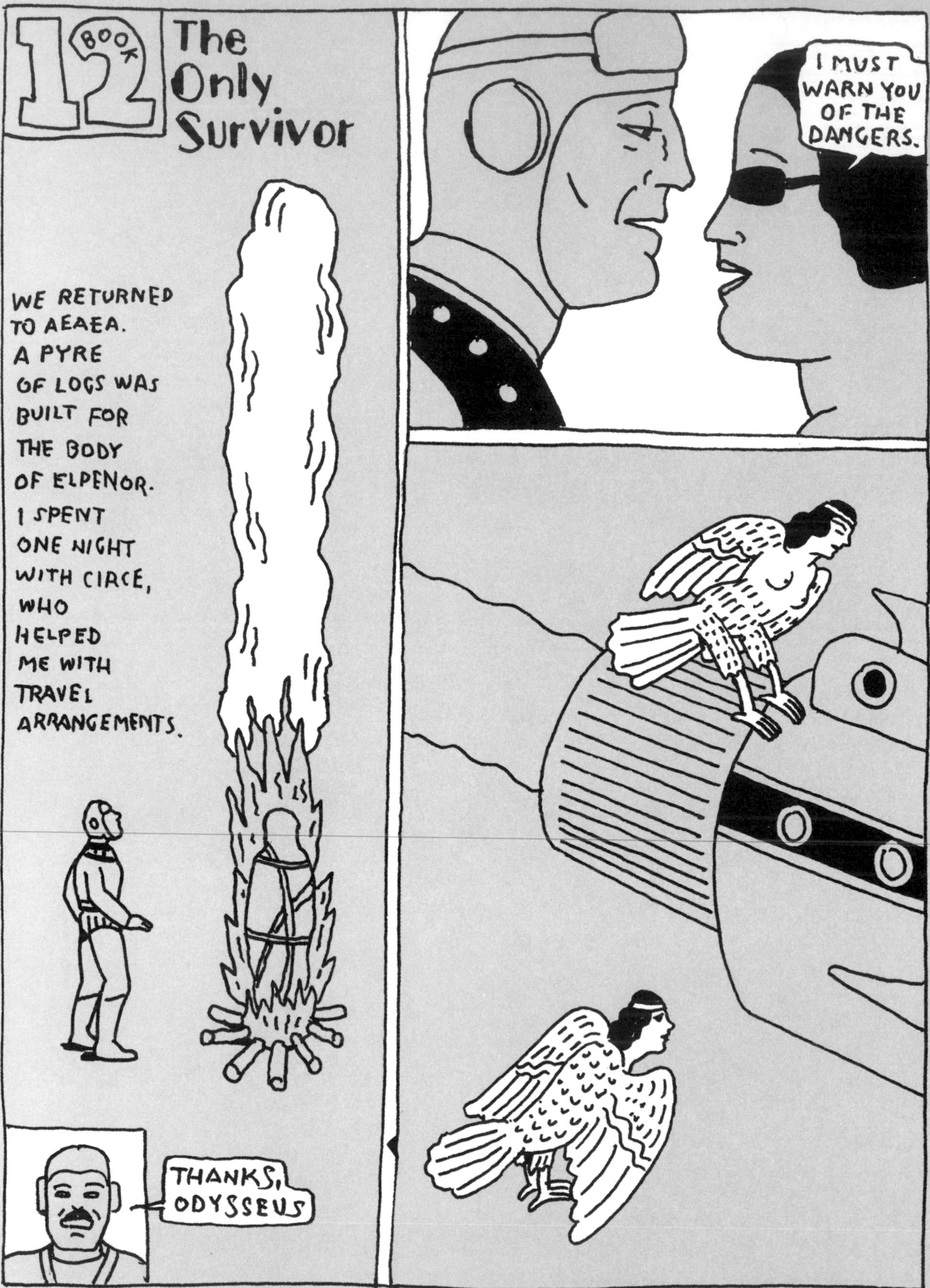
BOOK 12
The Only Survivor
WE RETURNED TO AEAEA. A PYRE OF LOGS WAS BUILT FOR THE BODY OF ELPENOR. I SPENT ONE NIGHT WITH CIRCE, WHO HELPED ME WITH TRAVEL ARRANGEMENTS.
THANKS, ODYSSEUS
I MUST WARN YOU OF THE DANGERS.

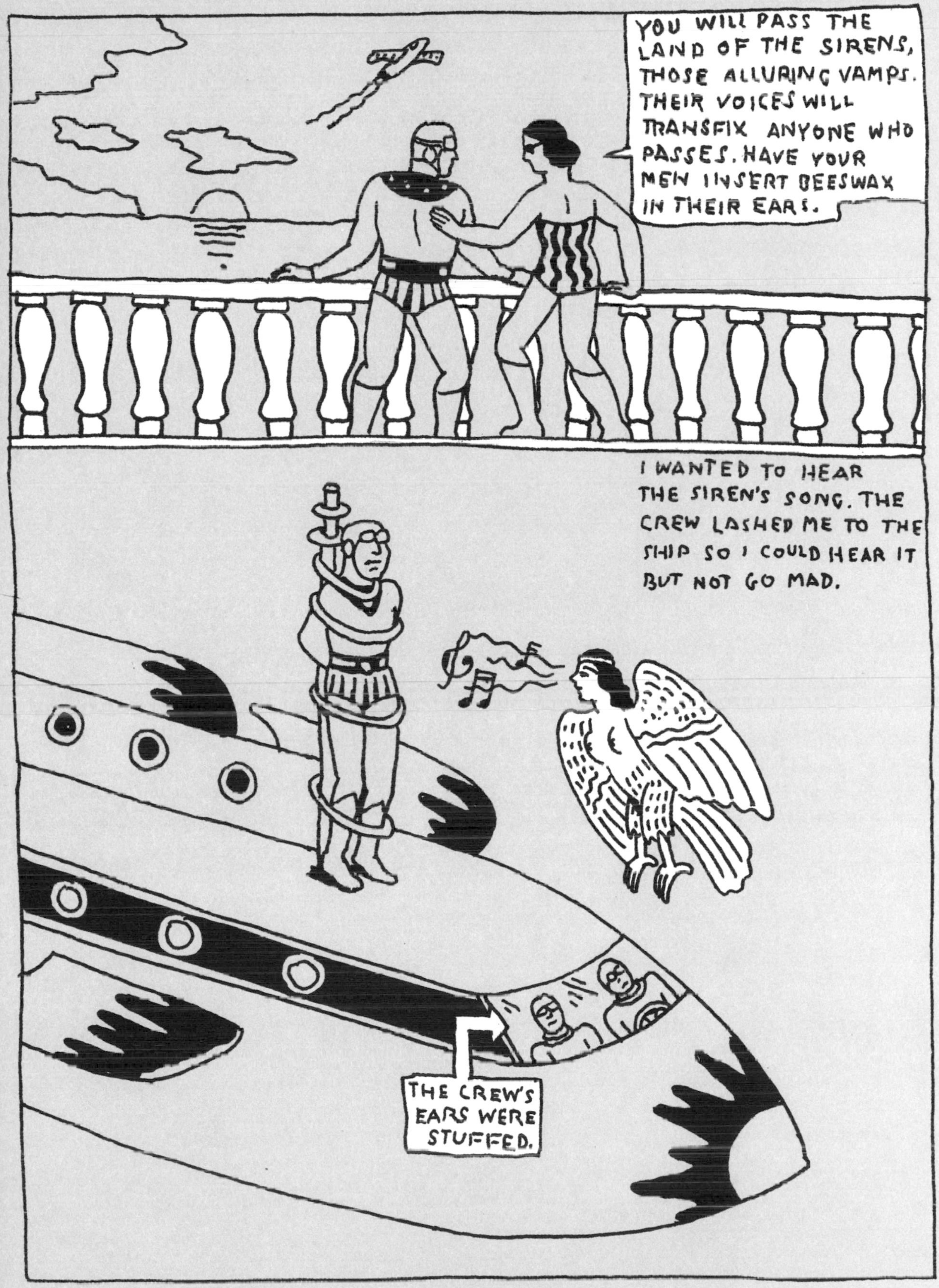
YOU WILL PASS THE LAND OF THE SIRENS, THOSE ALLURING VAMPS. THEIR VOICES WILL TRANSFIX ANYONE WHO PASSES. HAVE YOUR MEN INSERT BEESWAX IN THEIR EARS.
I WANTED TO HEAR THE SIREN'S SONG. THE CREW LASHED ME TO THE SHIP SO I COULD HEAR IT BUT NOT GO MAD.
THE CREW'S EARS WERE STUFFED.

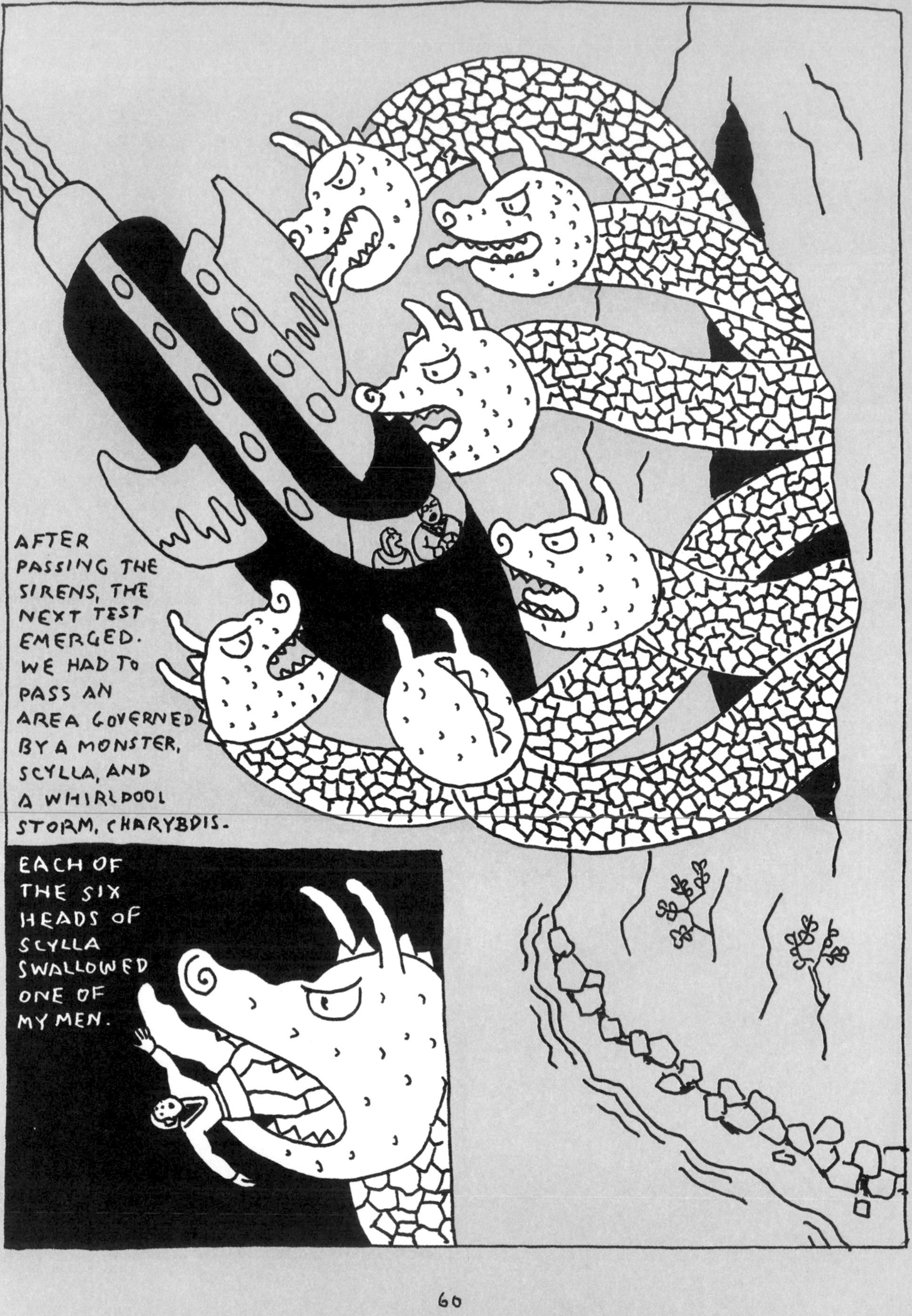
AFTER PASSING THE SIRENS, THE NEXT TEST EMERGED. WE HAD TO PASS AN AREA GOVERNED BY A MONSTER, SCYLLA, AND A WHIRLPOOL STORM, CHARYBDIS.
EACH OF THE SIX HEADS OF SCYLLA SWALLOWED ONE OF MY MEN.

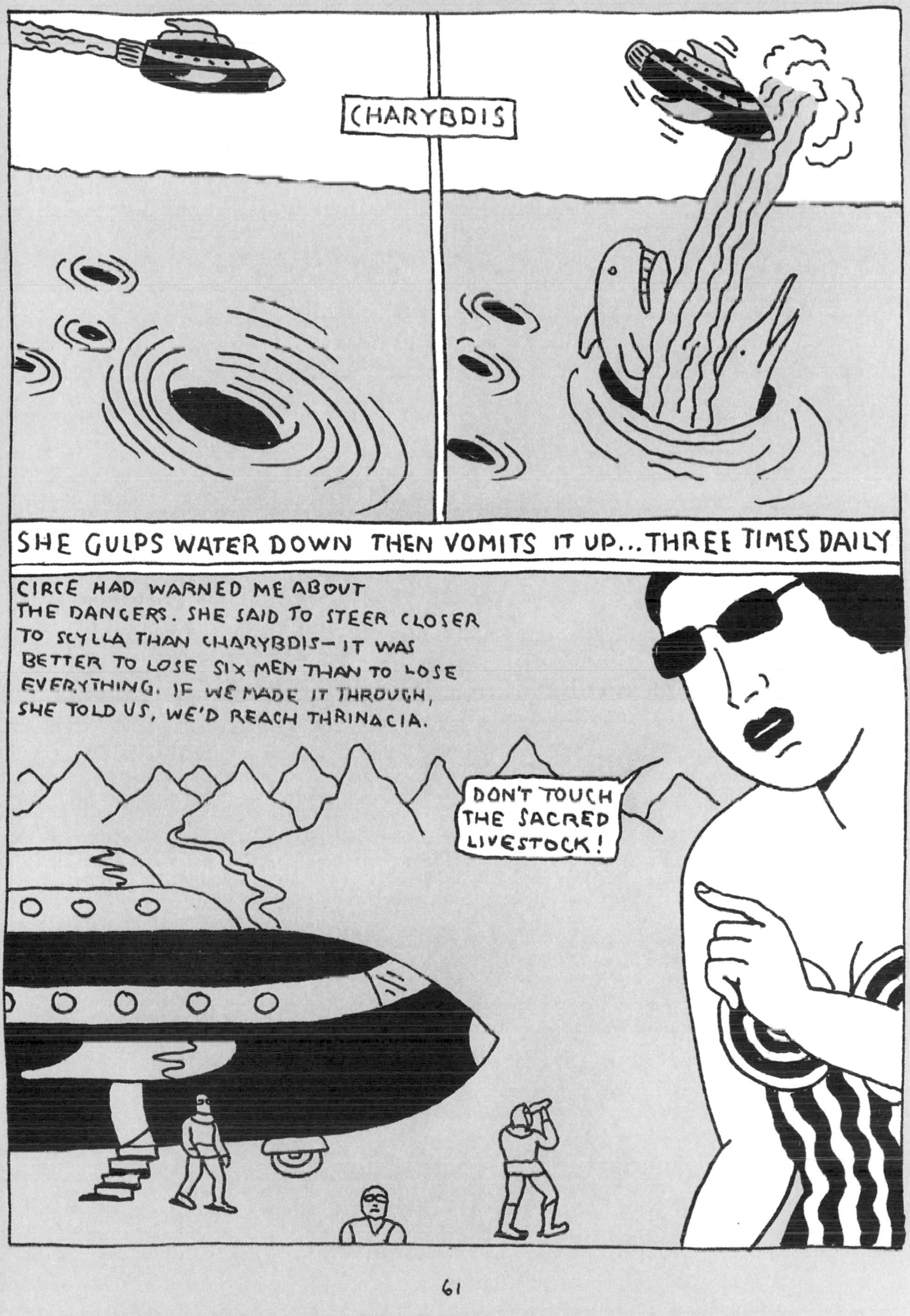
CHARYBDIS
SHE GULPS WATER DOWN THEN VOMITS IT UP... THREE TIMES DAILY
CIRCE HAD WARNED ME ABOUT THE DANGERS. SHE SAID TO STEER CLOSER TO SCYLLA THAN CHARYBDIS— IT WAS BETTER TO LOSE SIX MEN THAN TO LOSE EVERYTHING. IF WE MADE IT THROUGH, SHE TOLD US, WE'D REACH THRINACIA.
DON'T TOUCH THE SACRED LIVESTOCK!

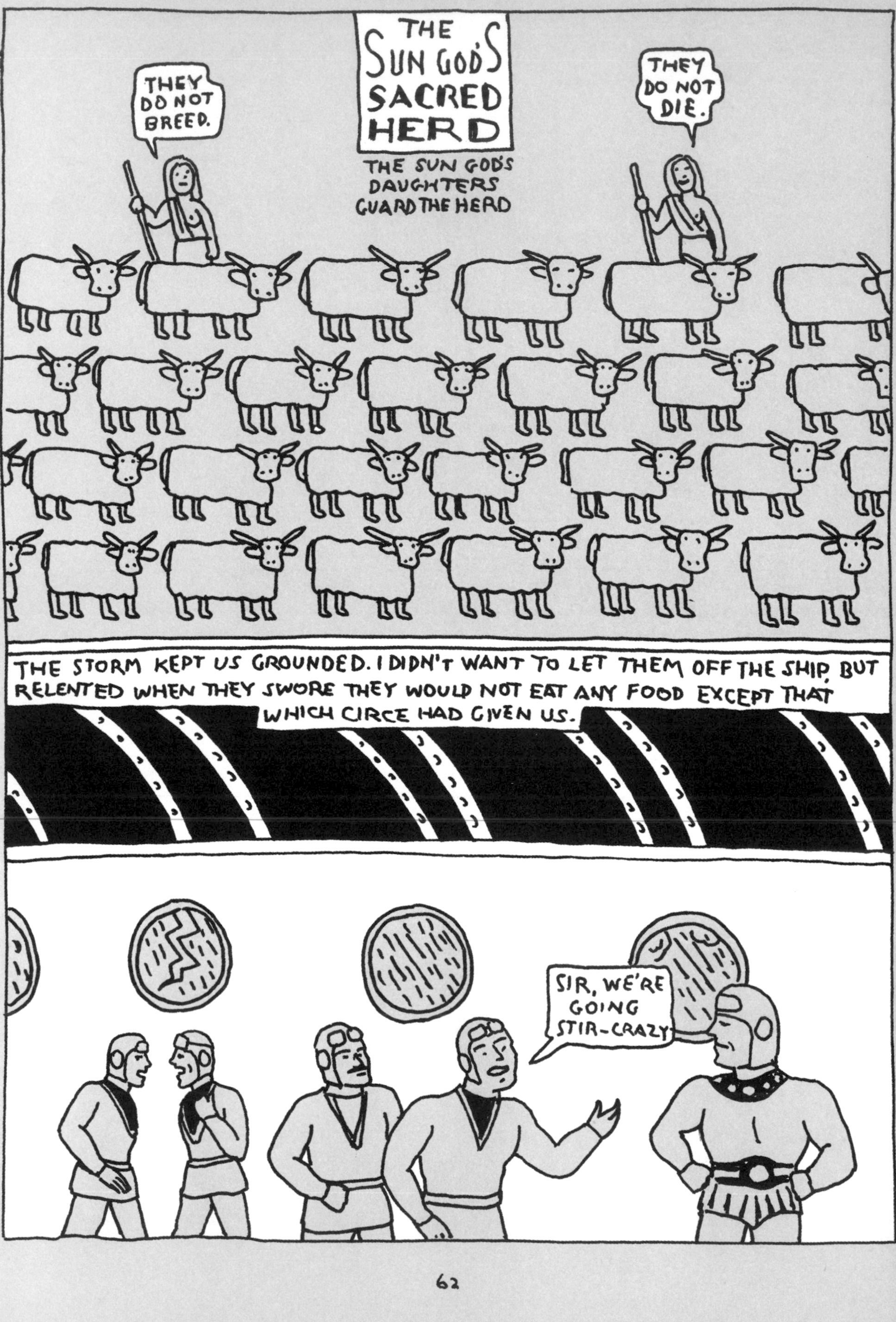
THE SUN GOD'S SACRED HERD
THEY DO NOT BREED.
THEY DO NOT DIE.
THE SUN GOD'S DAUGHTERS GUARD THE HERD
THE STORM KEPT US GROUNDED. I DIDN'T WANT TO LET THEM OFF THE SHIP, BUT RELENTED WHEN THEY SWORE THEY WOULD NOT EAT ANY FOOD EXCEPT THAT WHICH CIRCE HAD GIVEN US.
SIR, WE'RE GOING STIR-CRAZY

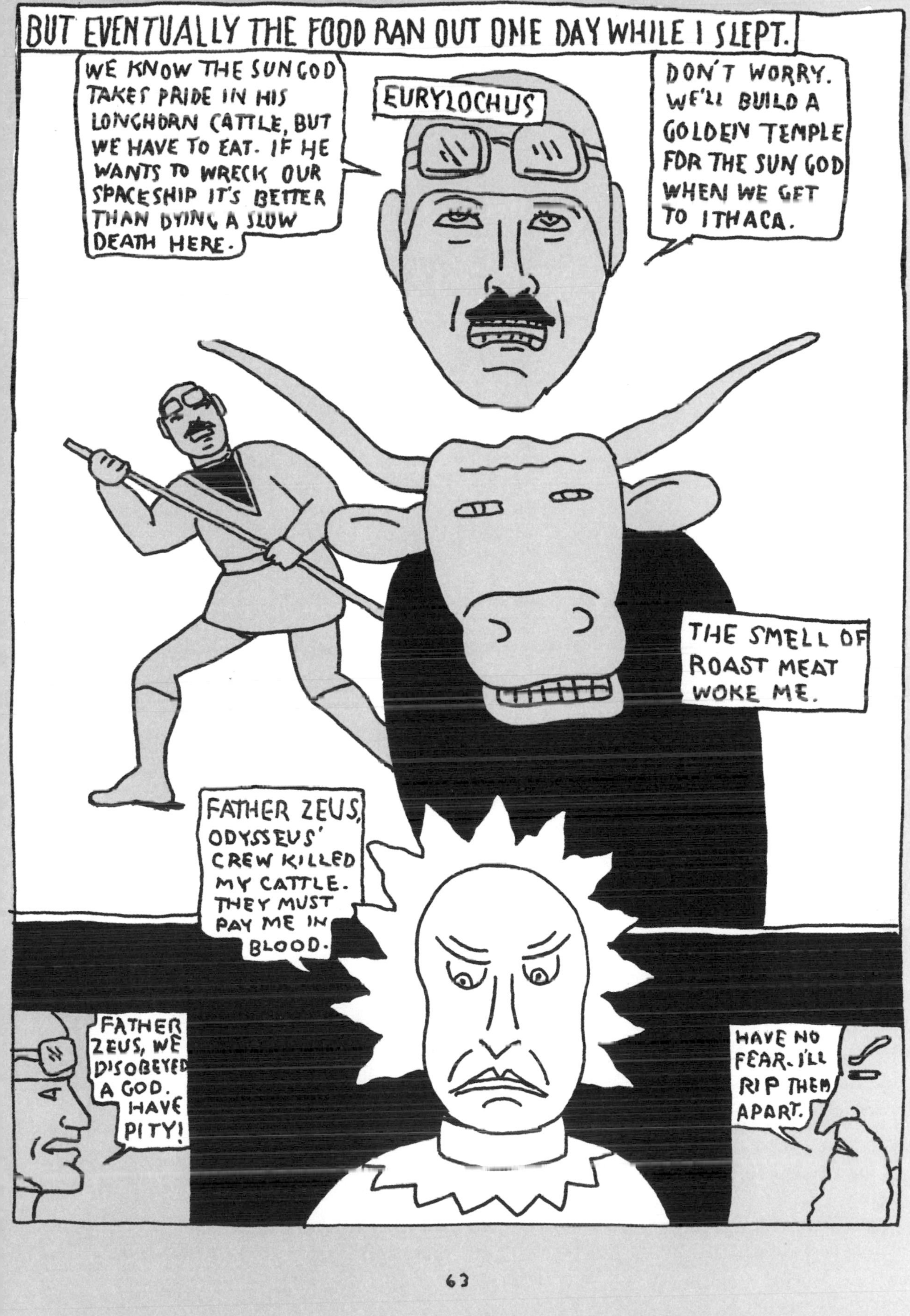
BUT EVENTUALLY THE FOOD RAN OUT ONE DAY WHILE I SLEPT.
WE KNOW THE SUN GOD TAKES PRIDE IN HIS LONGHORN CATTLE, BUT WE HAVE TO EAT. IF HE WANTS TO WRECK OUR SPACESHIP IT'S BETTER THAN DYING A SLOW DEATH HERE.
EURYLOCHUS
DON'T WORRY. WE'LL BUILD A GOLDEN TEMPLE FOR THE SUN GOD WHEN WE GET TO ITHACA.
THE SMELL OF ROAST MEAT WOKE ME.
FATHER ZEUS, ODYSSEUS' CREW KILLED MY CATTLE. THEY MUST PAY ME IN BLOOD.
FATHER ZEUS, WE DISOBEYED A GOD. HAVE PITY!
HAVE NO FEAR. I'LL RIP THEM APART.

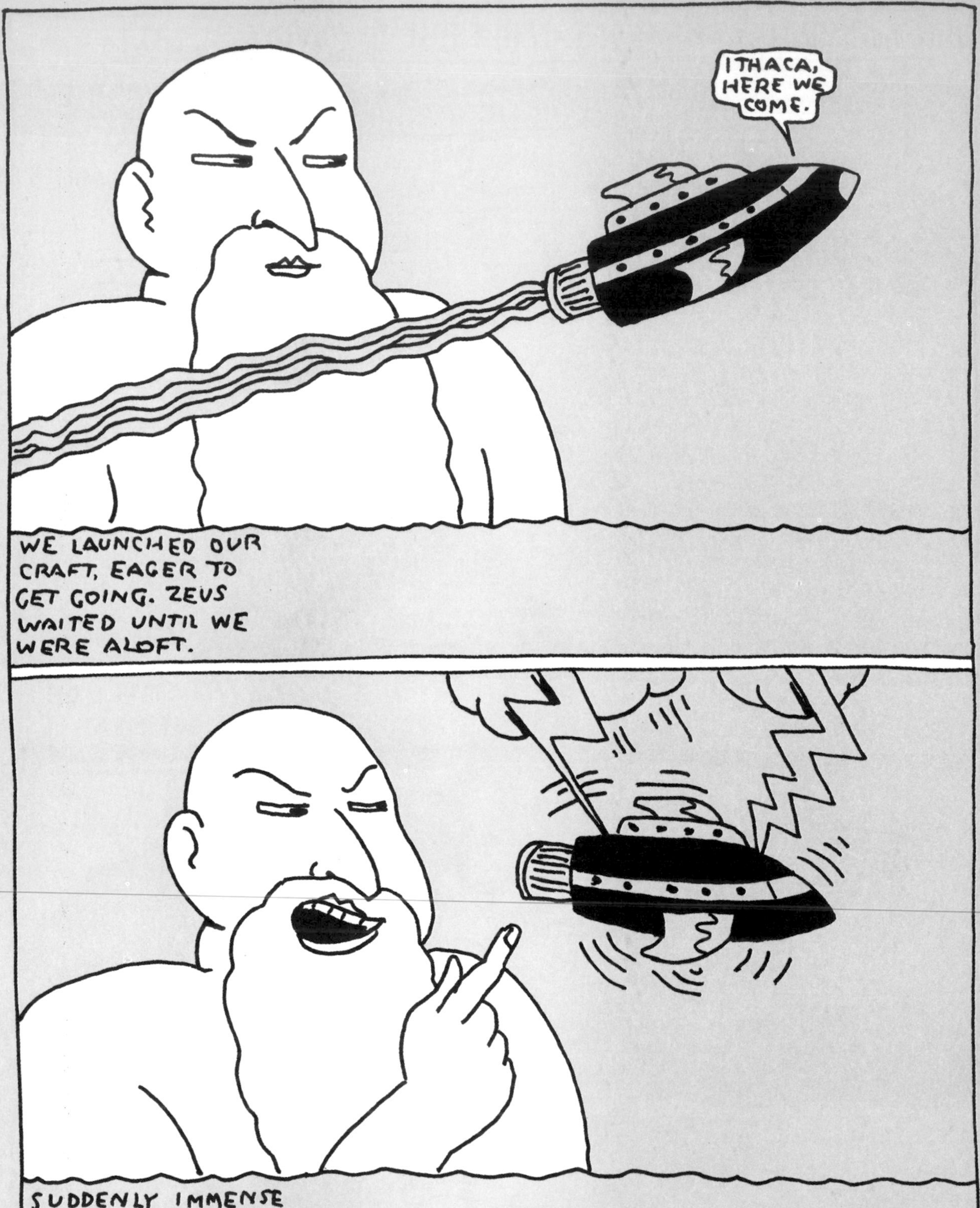
ITHACA, HERE WE COME.
WE LAUNCHED OUR CRAFT, EAGER TO GET GOING. ZEUS WAITED UNTIL WE WERE ALOFT.
SUDDENLY IMMENSE SQUALLS ATTACKED. LIGHTNING HIT US AND RIPPED THROUGH OUR SHIP.

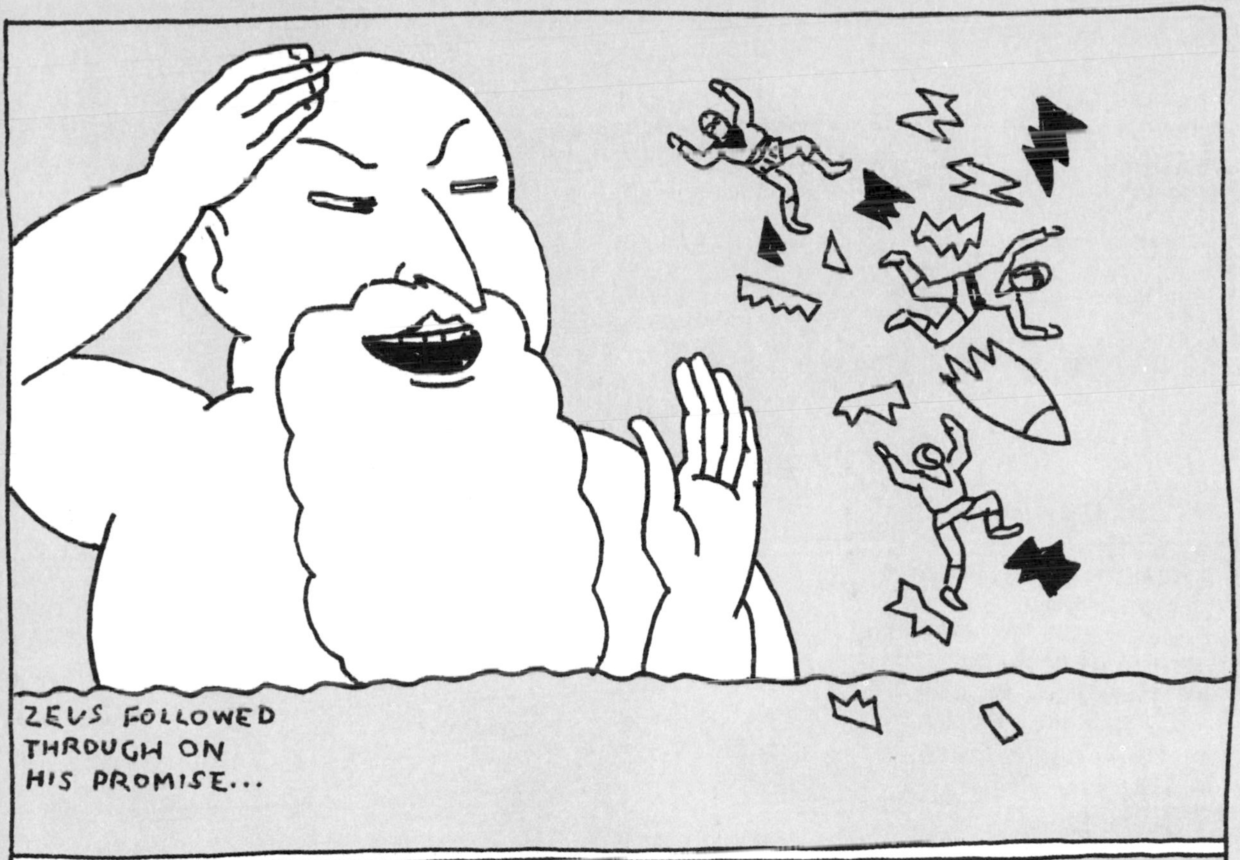
ZEUS FOLLOWED THROUGH ON HIS PROMISE...

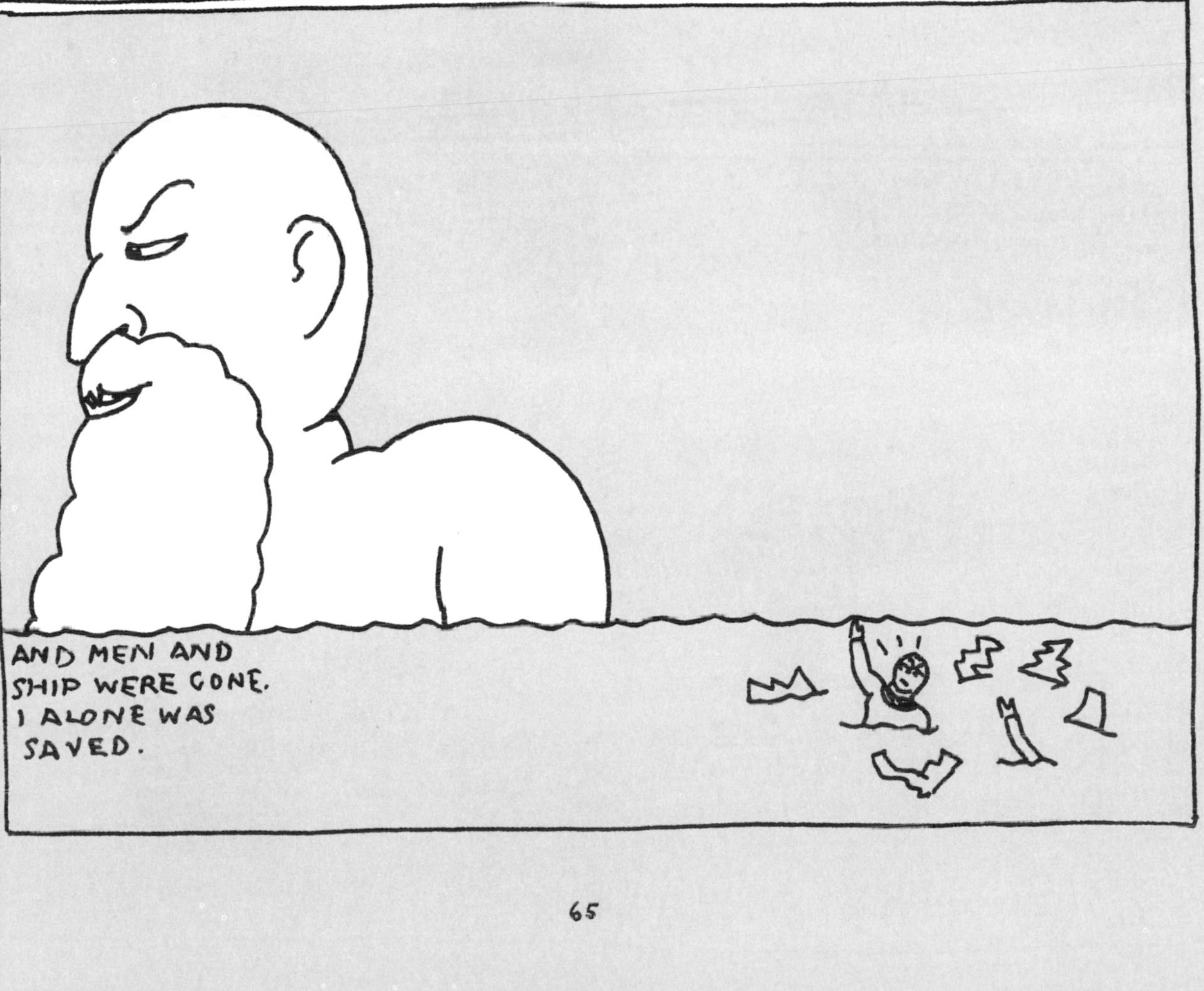
AND MEN AND SHIP WERE GONE. I ALONE WAS SAVED.

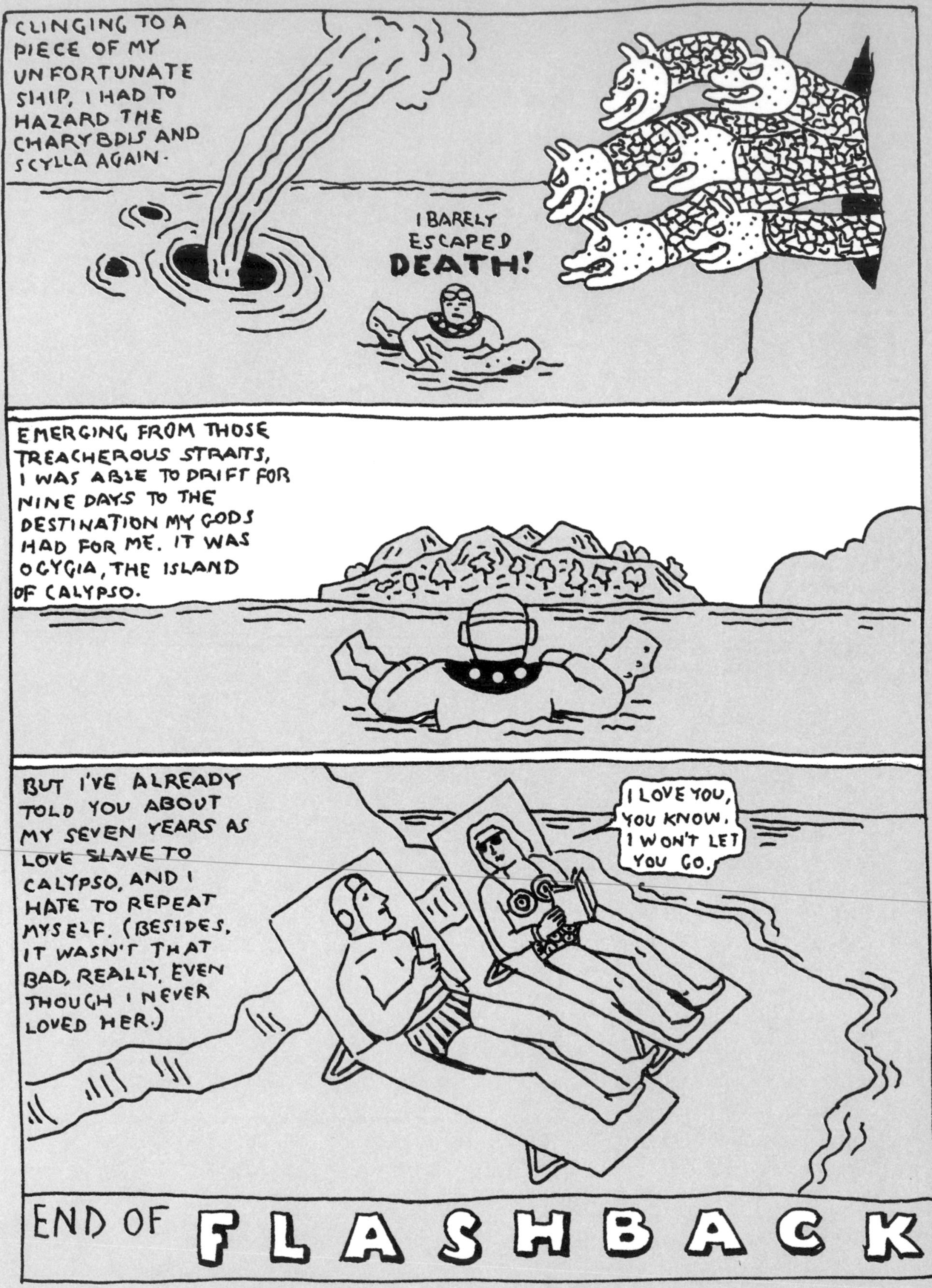
CLINGING TO A PIECE OF MY UNFORTUNATE SHIP, I HAD TO HAZARD THE CHARYBDIS AND SCYLLA AGAIN.
I BARELY ESCAPED DEATH!
EMERGING FROM THOSE TREACHEROUS STRAITS, I WAS ABLE TO DRIFT FOR NINE DAYS TO THE DESTINATION MY GODS HAD FOR ME. IT WAS OGYGIA, THE ISLAND OF CALYPSO.
BUT I'VE ALREADY TOLD YOU ABOUT MY SEVEN YEARS AS LOVE SLAVE TO CALYPSO, AND I HATE TO REPEAT MYSELF. (BESIDES, IT WASN'T THAT BAD, REALLY, EVEN THOUGH I NEVER LOVED HER.)
I LOVE YOU, YOU KNOW. I WON'T LET YOU GO.
END OF FLASHBACK

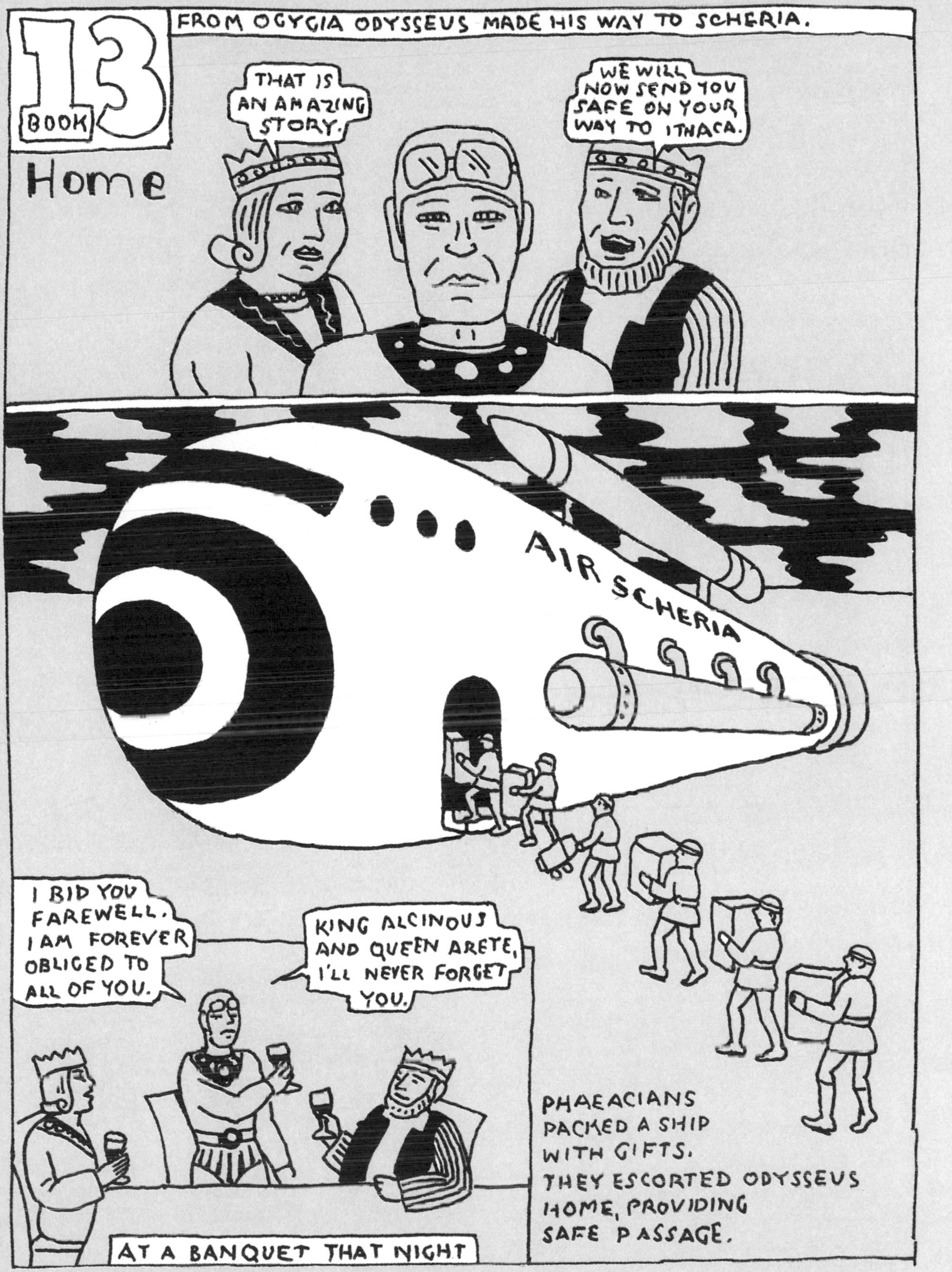

BOOK 13
Home
FROM OGYGIA ODYSSEUS MADE HIS WAY TO SCHERIA.
THAT IS AN AMAZING STORY.
WE WILL NOW SEND YOU SAFE ON YOUR WAY TO ITHACA.
AIR SCHERIA
AT A BANQUET THAT NIGHT
I BID YOU FAREWELL. I AM FOREVER OBLIGED TO ALL OF YOU.
KING ALCINOUS AND QUEEN ARETE, I'LL NEVER FORGET YOU.
PHAEACIANS PACKED A SHIP WITH GIFTS. THEY ESCORTED ODYSSEUS HOME, PROVIDING SAFE PASSAGE.

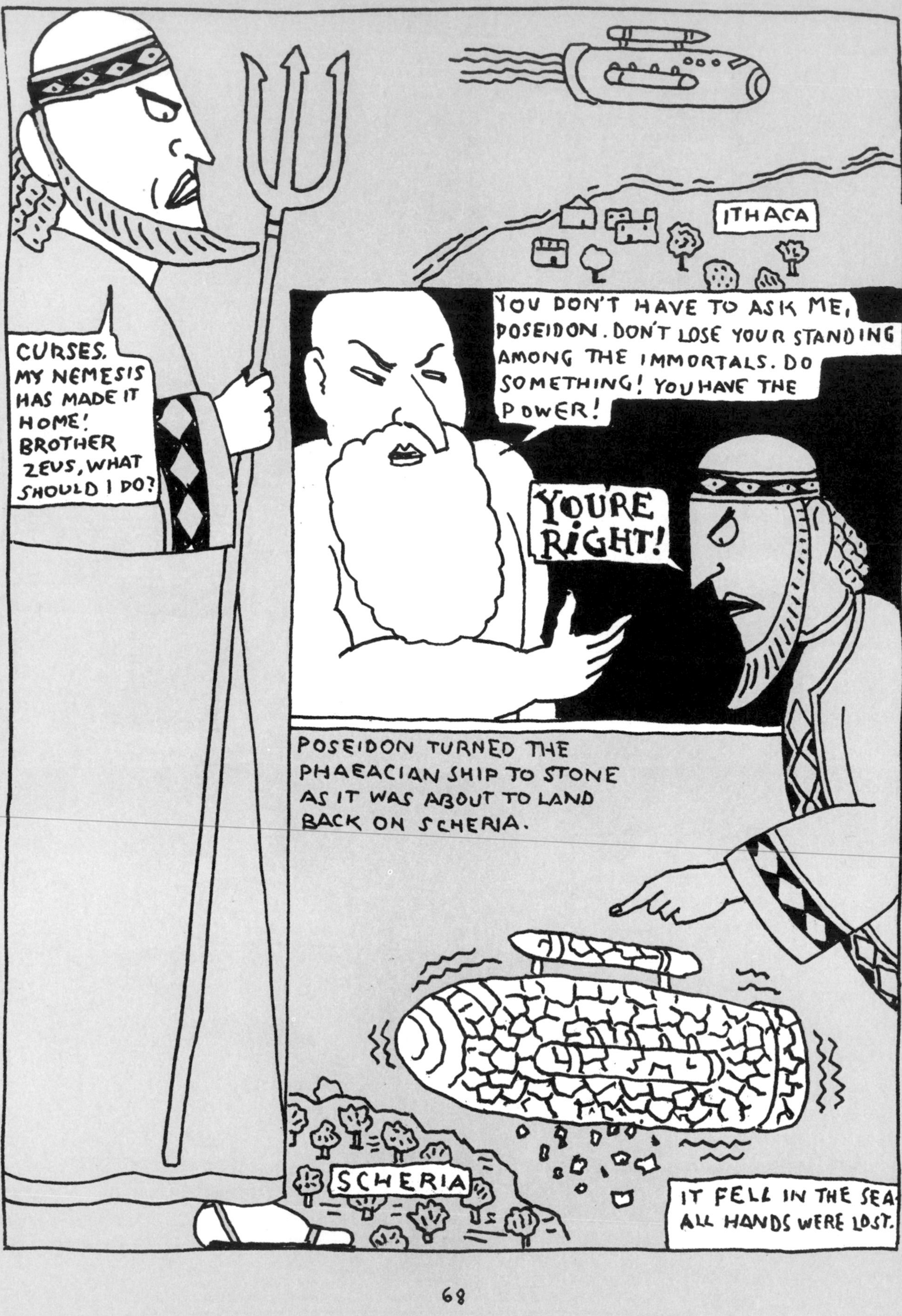
ITHACA
CURSES. MY NEMESIS HAS MADE IT HOME! BROTHER ZEUS, WHAT SHOULD I DO?
YOU DON'T HAVE TO ASK ME, POSEIDON. DON'T LOSE YOUR STANDING AMONG THE IMMORTALS. DO SOMETHING! YOU HAVE THE POWER!
YOU'RE RIGHT!
POSEIDON TURNED THE PHAEACIAN SHIP TO STONE AS IT WAS ABOUT TO LAND BACK ON SCHERIA.
SCHERIA
IT FELL IN THE SEA. ALL HANDS WERE LOST.

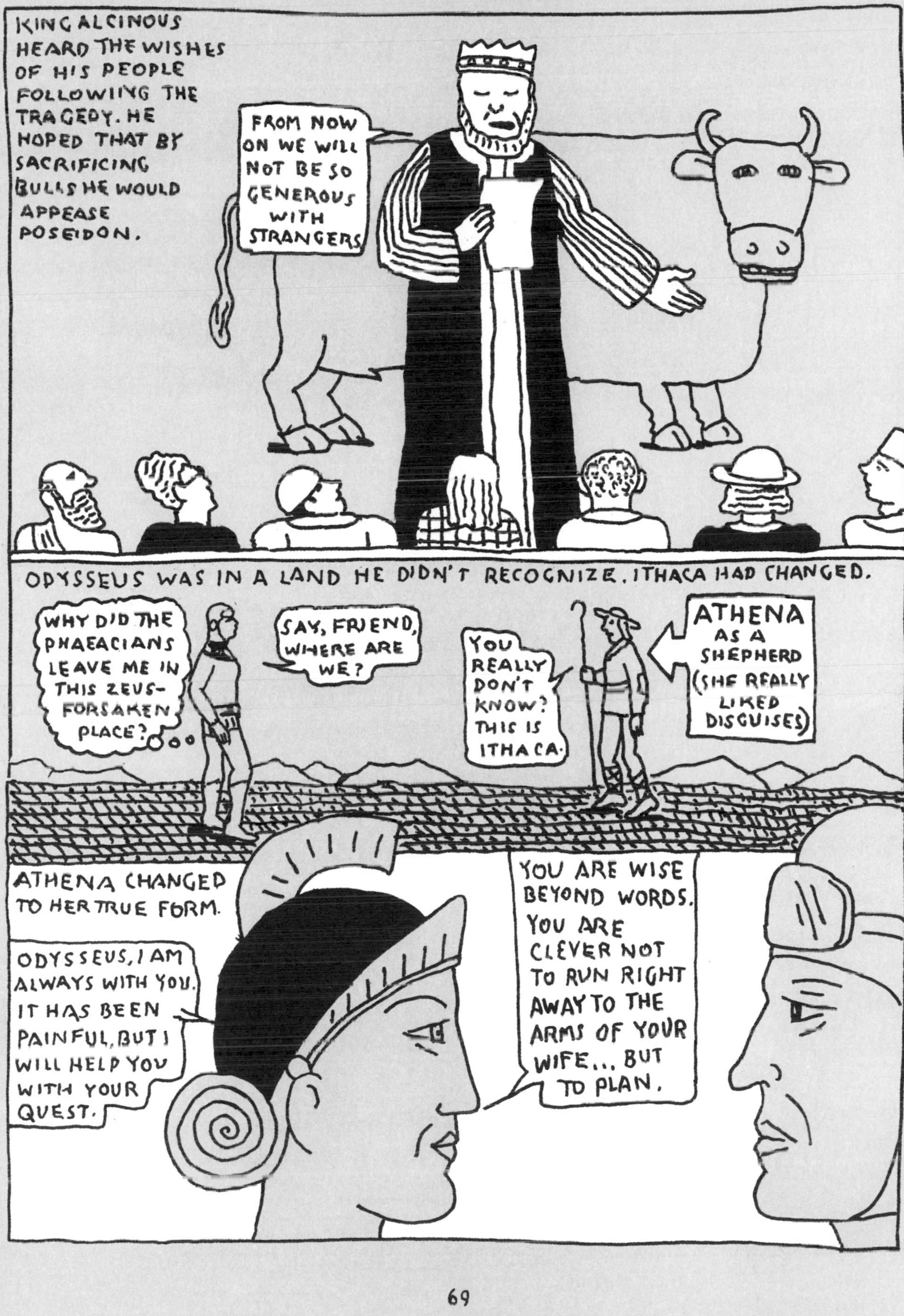
KING ALCINOUS HEARD THE WISHES OF HIS PEOPLE FOLLOWING THE TRAGEDY. HE HOPED THAT BY SACRIFICING BULLS HE WOULD APPEASE POSEIDON.
FROM NOW ON WE WILL NOT BE SO GENEROUS WITH STRANGERS
ODYSSEUS WAS IN A LAND HE DIDN'T RECOGNIZE. ITHACA HAD CHANGED.
WHY DID THE PHAEACIANS LEAVE ME IN THIS ZEUS-FORSAKEN PLACE?
SAY, FRIEND, WHERE ARE WE?
YOU REALLY DON'T KNOW? THIS IS ITHACA.
ATHENA AS A SHEPHERD (SHE REALLY LIKED DISGUISES)
ATHENA CHANGED TO HER TRUE FORM.
ODYSSEUS, I AM ALWAYS WITH YOU. IT HAS BEEN PAINFUL, BUT I WILL HELP YOU WITH YOUR QUEST.
YOU ARE WISE BEYOND WORDS. YOU ARE CLEVER NOT TO RUN RIGHT AWAY TO THE ARMS OF YOUR WIFE... BUT TO PLAN.

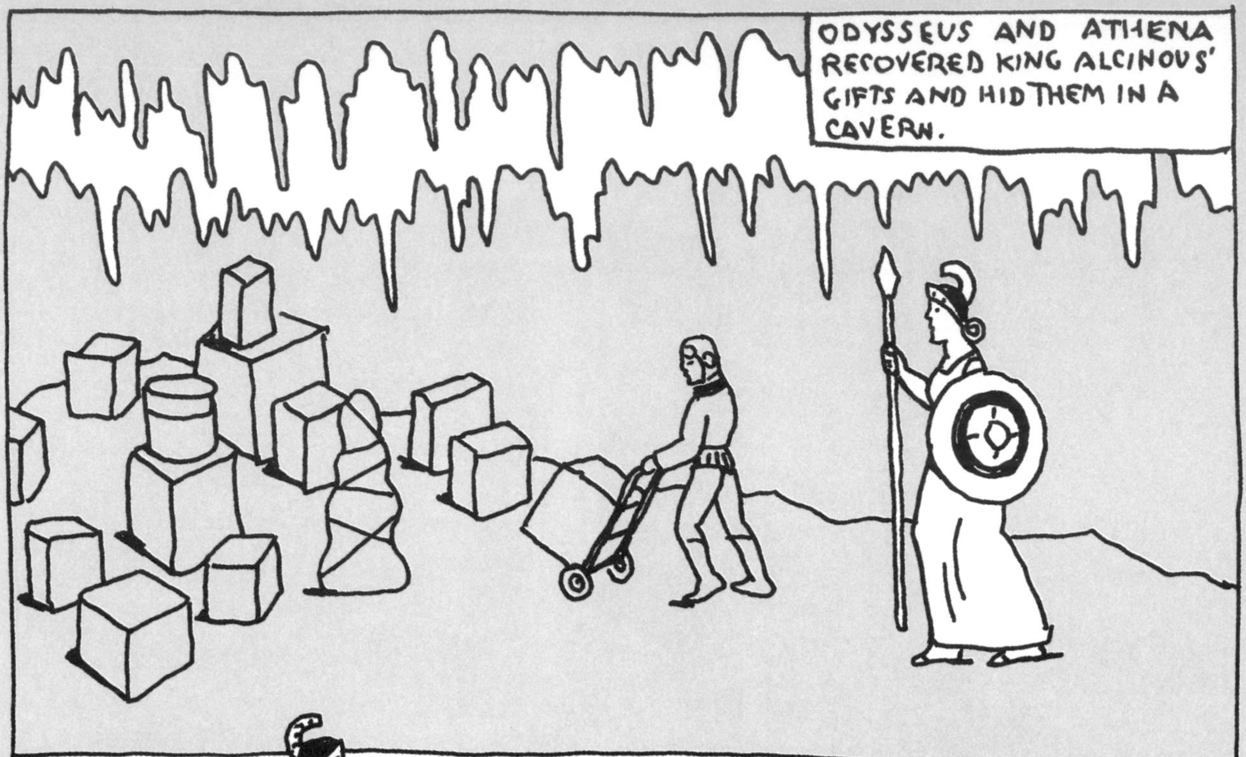
ODYSSEUS AND ATHENA RECOVERED KING ALCINOUS' GIFTS AND HID THEM IN A CAVERN.

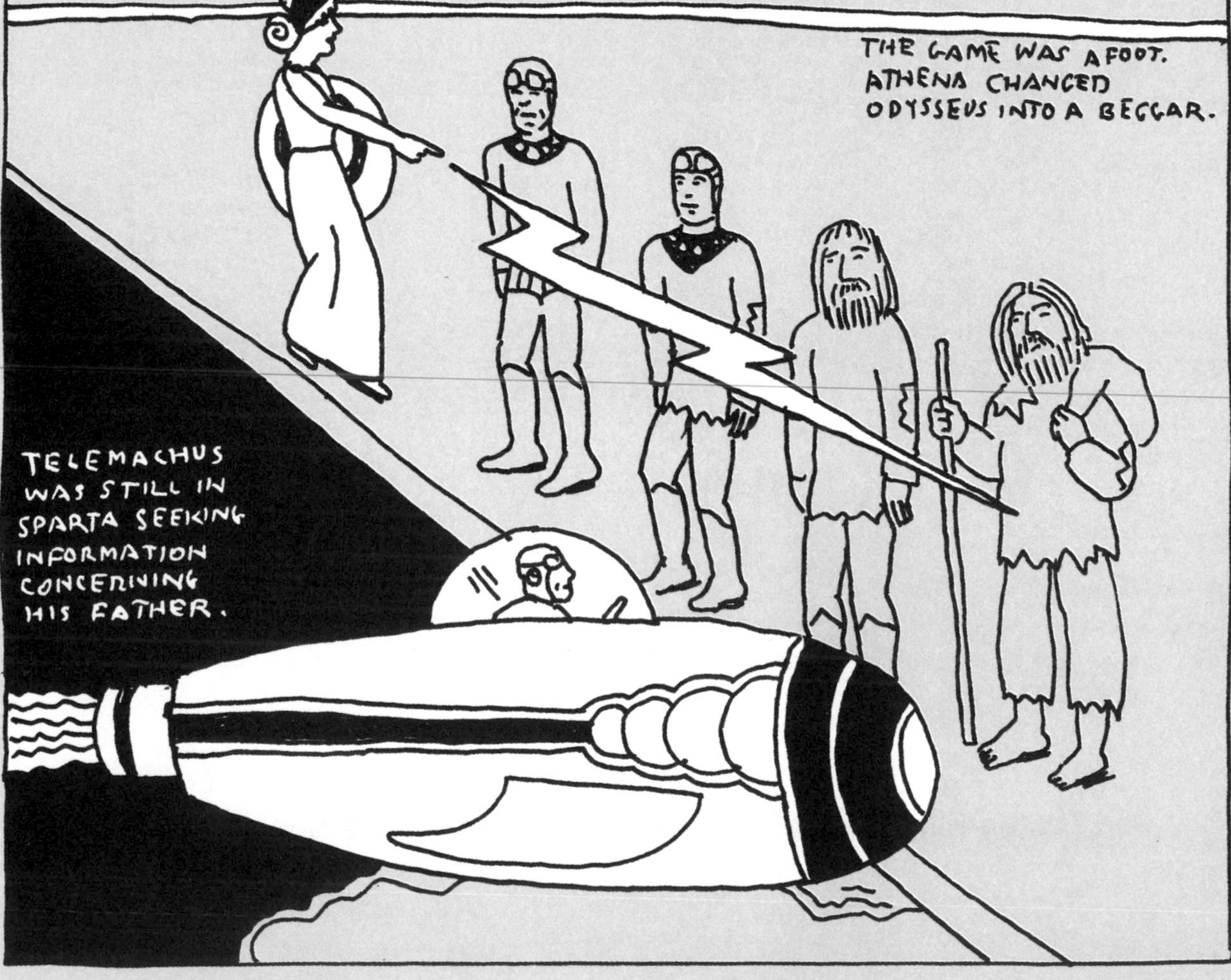
THE GAME WAS AFOOT. ATHENA CHANGED ODYSSEUS INTO A BEGGAR.
TELEMACHUS WAS STILL IN SPARTA SEEKING INFORMATION CONCERNING HIS FATHER.

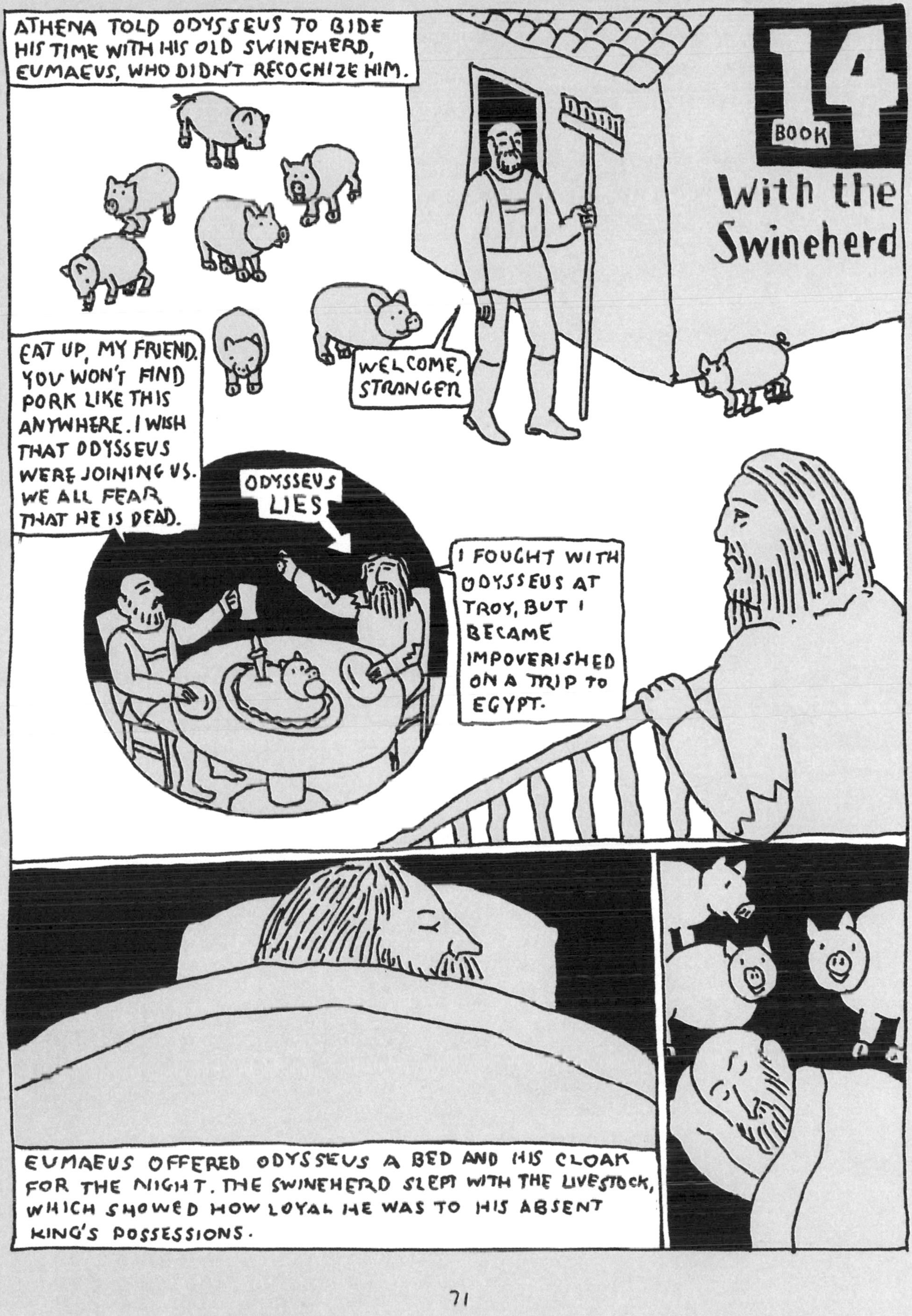
ATHENA TOLD ODYSSEUS TO BIDE HIS TIME WITH HIS OLD SWINEHERD, EUMAEUS, WHO DIDN'T RECOGNIZE HIM.
BOOK 14
With the Swineherd
WELCOME, STRANGER.
EAT UP, MY FRIEND. YOU WON'T FIND PORK LIKE THIS ANYWHERE. I WISH THAT ODYSSEUS WERE JOINING US. WE ALL FEAR THAT HE IS DEAD.
ODYSSEUS LIES
I FOUGHT WITH ODYSSEUS AT TROY, BUT I BECAME IMPOVERISHED ON A TRIP TO EGYPT.
EUMAEUS OFFERED ODYSSEUS A BED AND HIS CLOAK FOR THE NIGHT. THE SWINEHERD SLEPT WITH THE LIVESTOCK, WHICH SHOWED HOW LOYAL HE WAS TO HIS ABSENT KING'S POSSESSIONS.

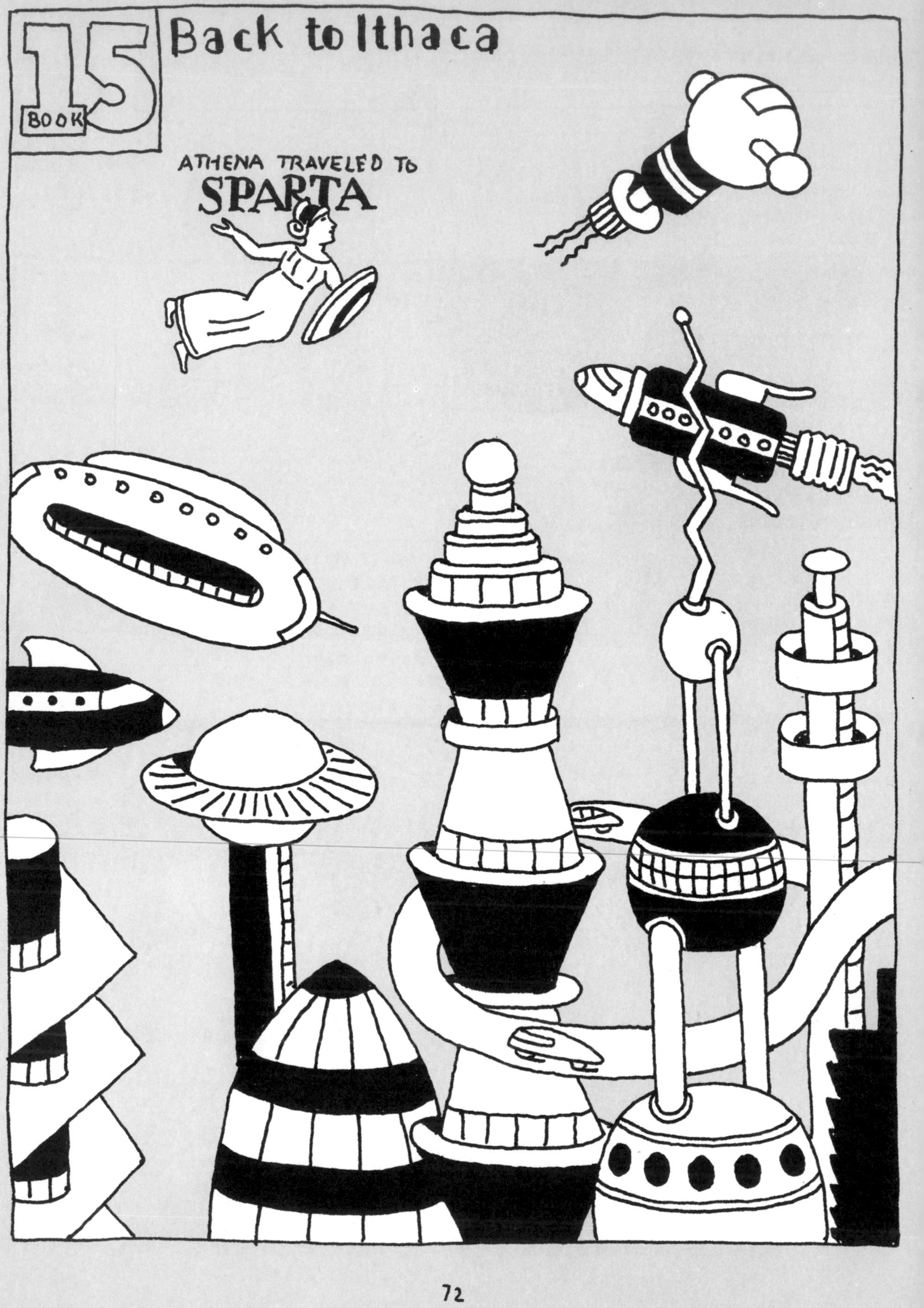
BOOK 15
Back to Ithaca
ATHENA TRAVELED TO
SPARTA

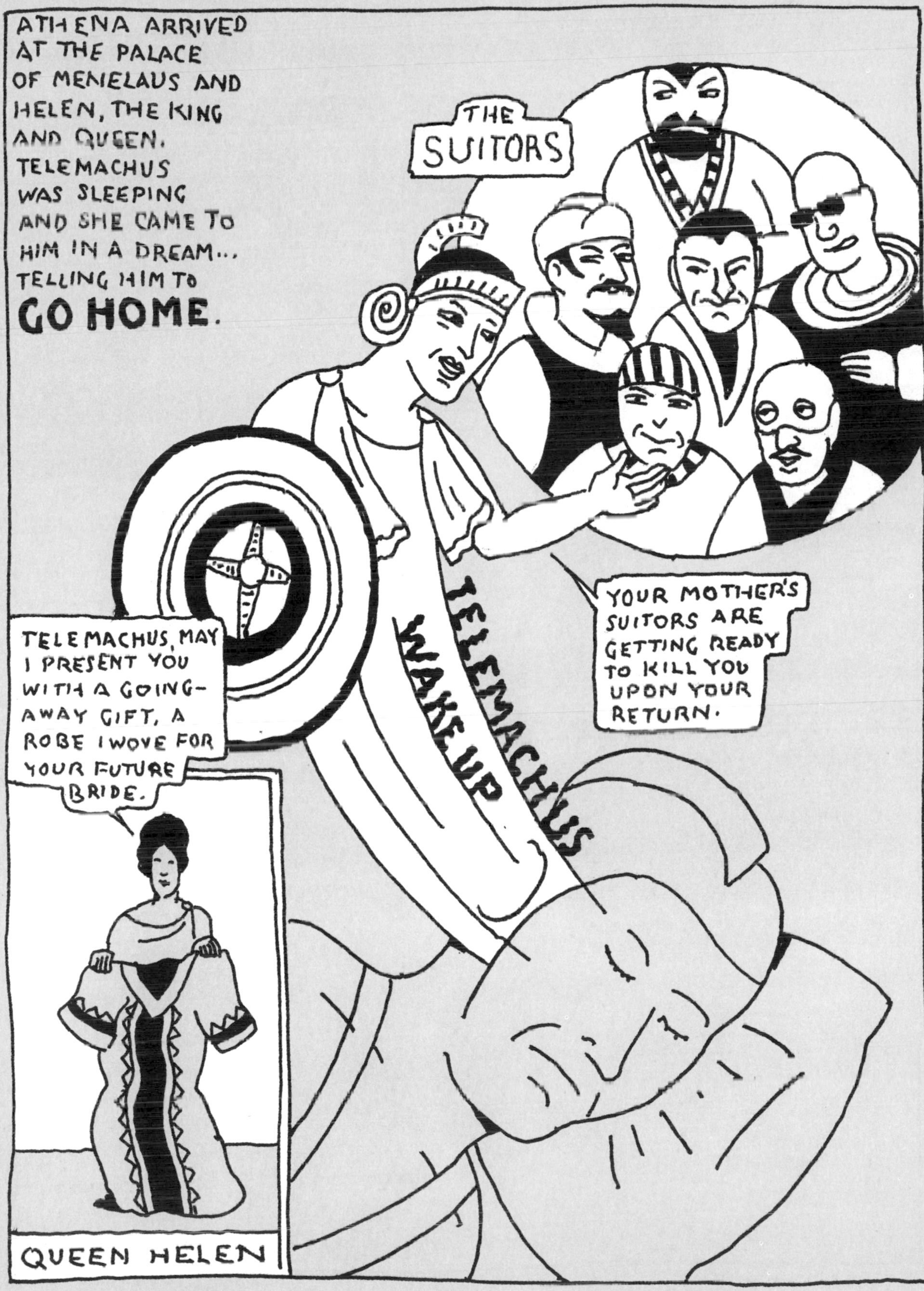
ATHENA ARRIVED AT THE PALACE OF MENELAUS AND HELEN, THE KING AND QUEEN. TELEMACHUS WAS SLEEPING AND SHE CAME TO HIM IN A DREAM... TELLING HIM TO GO HOME.
THE SUITORS
TELEMACHUS
WAKE UP
YOUR MOTHER'S SUITORS ARE GETTING READY TO KILL YOU UPON YOUR RETURN.
TELEMACHUS, MAY I PRESENT YOU WITH A GOING-AWAY GIFT, A ROBE I WOVE FOR YOUR FUTURE BRIDE.
QUEEN HELEN

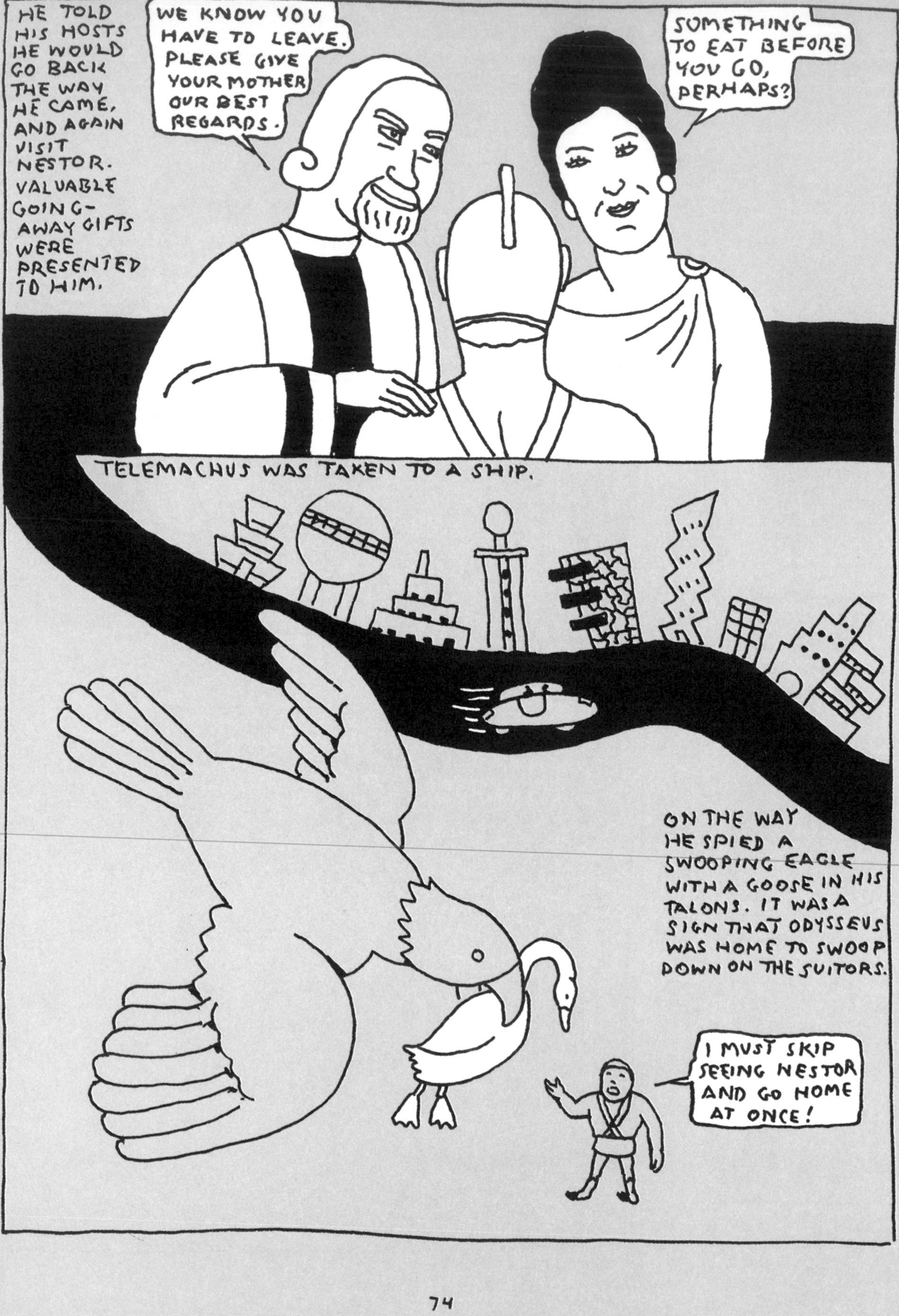
HE TOLD HIS HOSTS HE WOULD GO BACK THE WAY HE CAME, AND AGAIN VISIT NESTOR. VALUABLE GOING-AWAY GIFTS WERE PRESENTED TO HIM.
WE KNOW YOU HAVE TO LEAVE. PLEASE GIVE YOUR MOTHER OUR BEST REGARDS.
SOMETHING TO EAT BEFORE YOU GO, PERHAPS?
TELEMACHUS WAS TAKEN TO A SHIP.
ON THE WAY HE SPIED A SWOOPING EAGLE WITH A GOOSE IN HIS TALONS. IT WAS A SIGN THAT ODYSSEUS WAS HOME TO SWOOP DOWN ON THE SUITORS.
I MUST SKIP SEEING NESTOR AND GO HOME AT ONCE!

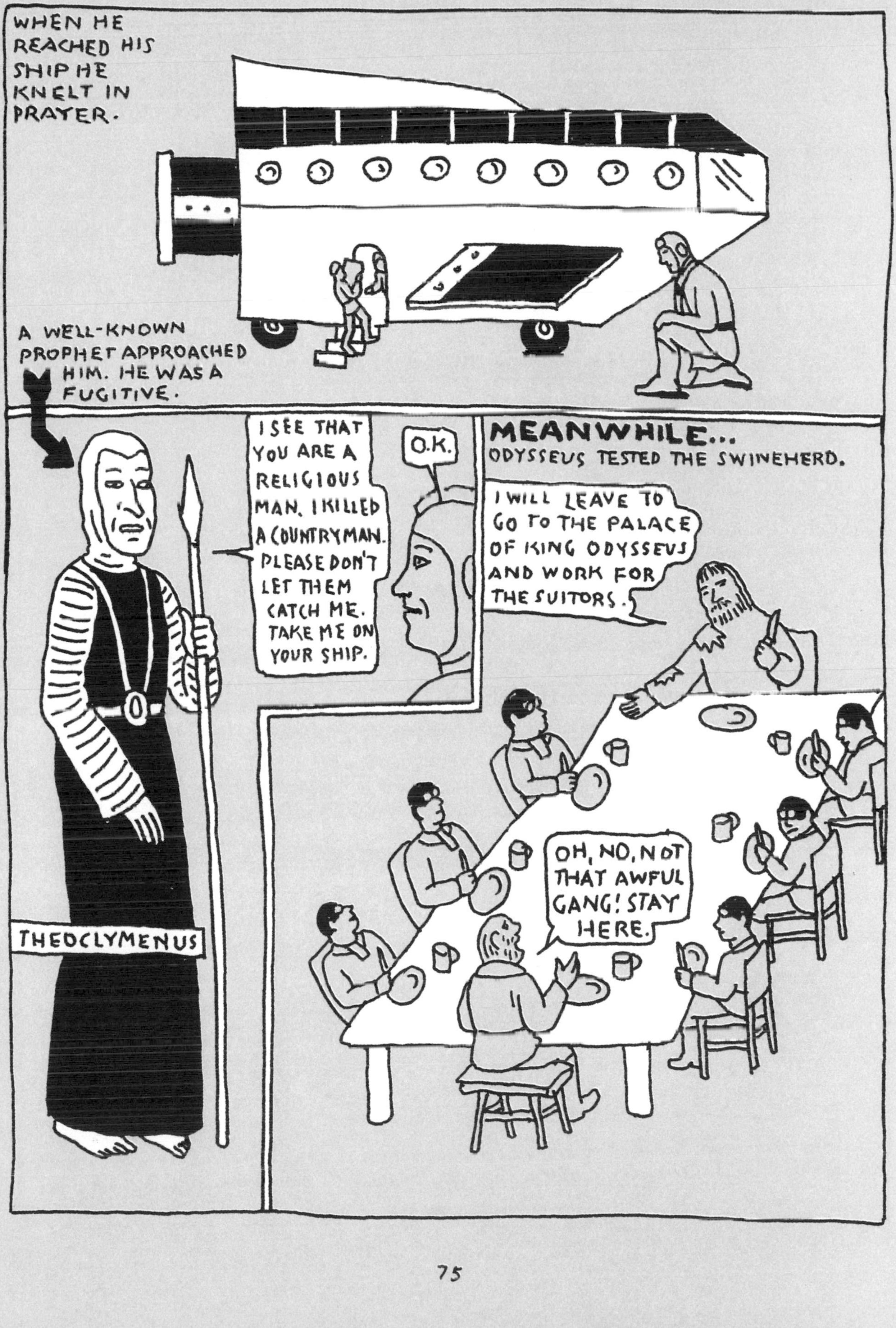
WHEN HE REACHED HIS SHIP HE KNELT IN PRAYER.
A WELL-KNOWN PROPHET APPROACHED HIM. HE WAS A FUGITIVE.
THEOCLYMENUS
I SEE THAT YOU ARE A RELIGIOUS MAN. I KILLED A COUNTRYMAN. PLEASE DON'T LET THEM CATCH ME. TAKE ME ON YOUR SHIP.
O.K.
MEANWHILE...
ODYSSEUS TESTED THE SWINEHERD.
I WILL LEAVE TO GO TO THE PALACE OF KING ODYSSEUS AND WORK FOR THE SUITORS.
OH, NO, NOT THAT AWFUL GANG! STAY HERE.

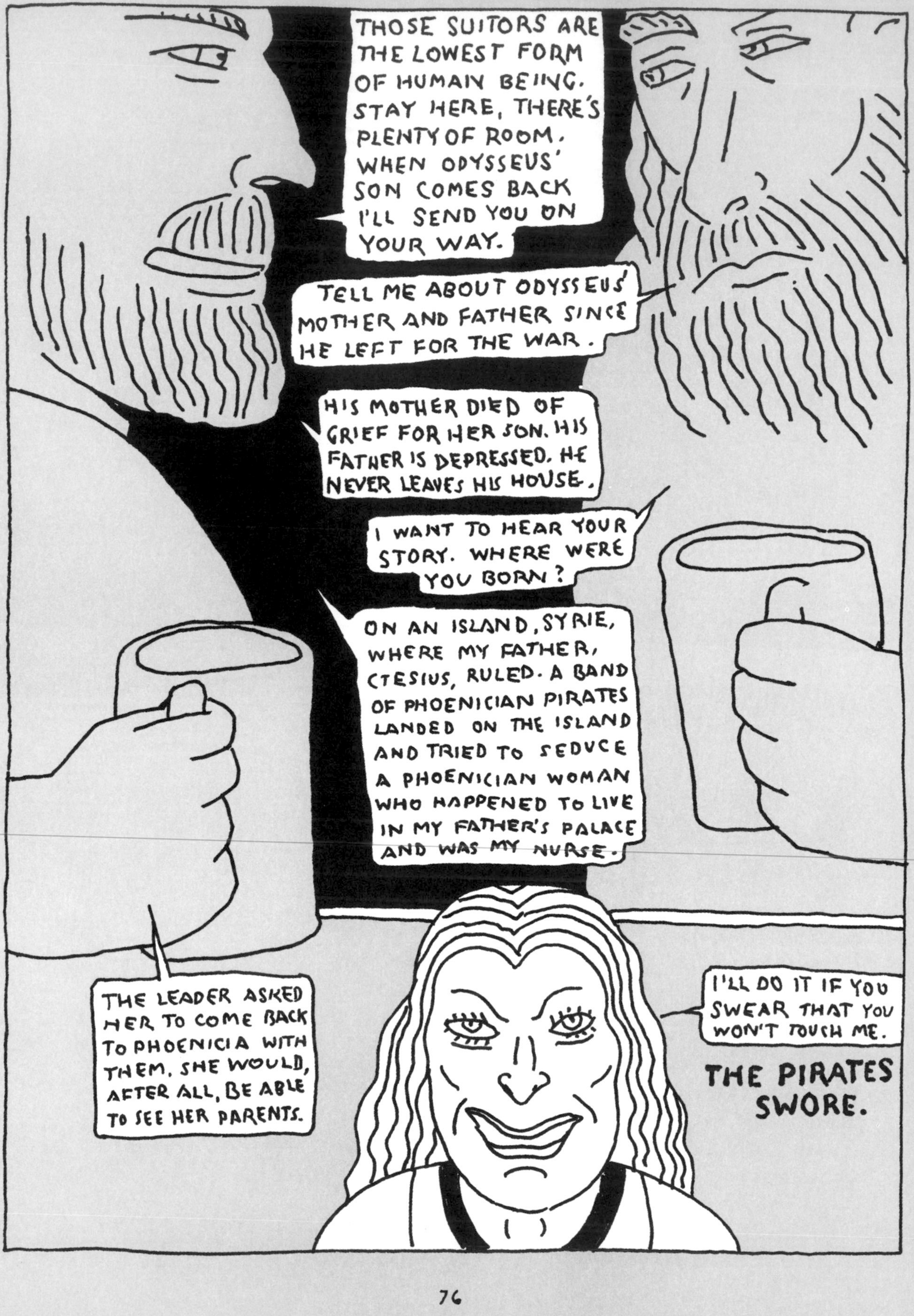
THOSE SUITORS ARE THE LOWEST FORM OF HUMAN BEING. STAY HERE, THERE'S PLENTY OF ROOM. WHEN ODYSSEUS' SON COMES BACK I'LL SEND YOU ON YOUR WAY.
TELL ME ABOUT ODYSSEUS' MOTHER AND FATHER SINCE HE LEFT FOR THE WAR.
HIS MOTHER DIED OF GRIEF FOR HER SON. HIS FATHER IS DEPRESSED. HE NEVER LEAVES HIS HOUSE.
I WANT TO HEAR YOUR STORY. WHERE WERE YOU BORN?
ON AN ISLAND, SYRIE, WHERE MY FATHER, CTESIUS, RULED. A BAND OF PHOENICIAN PIRATES LANDED ON THE ISLAND AND TRIED TO SEDUCE A PHOENICIAN WOMAN WHO HAPPENED TO LIVE IN MY FATHER'S PALACE AND WAS MY NURSE.
THE LEADER ASKED HER TO COME BACK TO PHOENICIA WITH THEM. SHE WOULD, AFTER ALL, BE ABLE TO SEE HER PARENTS.
I'LL DO IT IF YOU SWEAR THAT YOU WON'T TOUCH ME.
THE PIRATES SWORE.

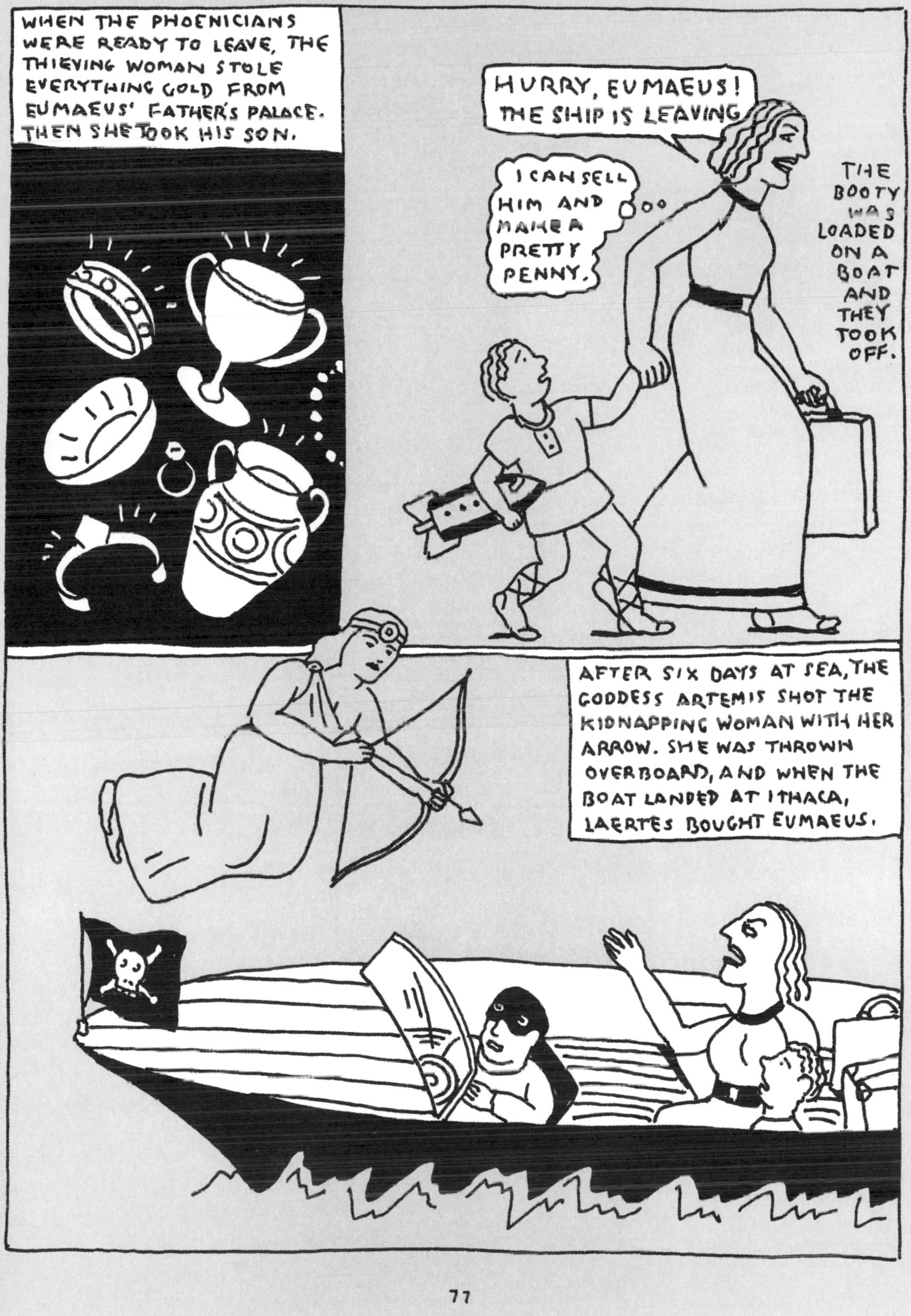

WHEN THE PHOENICIANS WERE READY TO LEAVE, THE THIEVING WOMAN STOLE EVERYTHING GOLD FROM EUMAEUS' FATHER'S PALACE. THEN SHE TOOK HIS SON.
HURRY, EUMAEUS! THE SHIP IS LEAVING.
I CAN SELL HIM AND MAKE A PRETTY PENNY.
THE BOOTY WAS LOADED ON A BOAT AND THEY TOOK OFF.
AFTER SIX DAYS AT SEA, THE GODDESS ARTEMIS SHOT THE KIDNAPPING WOMAN WITH HER ARROW. SHE WAS THROWN OVERBOARD, AND WHEN THE BOAT LANDED AT ITHACA, LAERTES BOUGHT EUMAEUS.

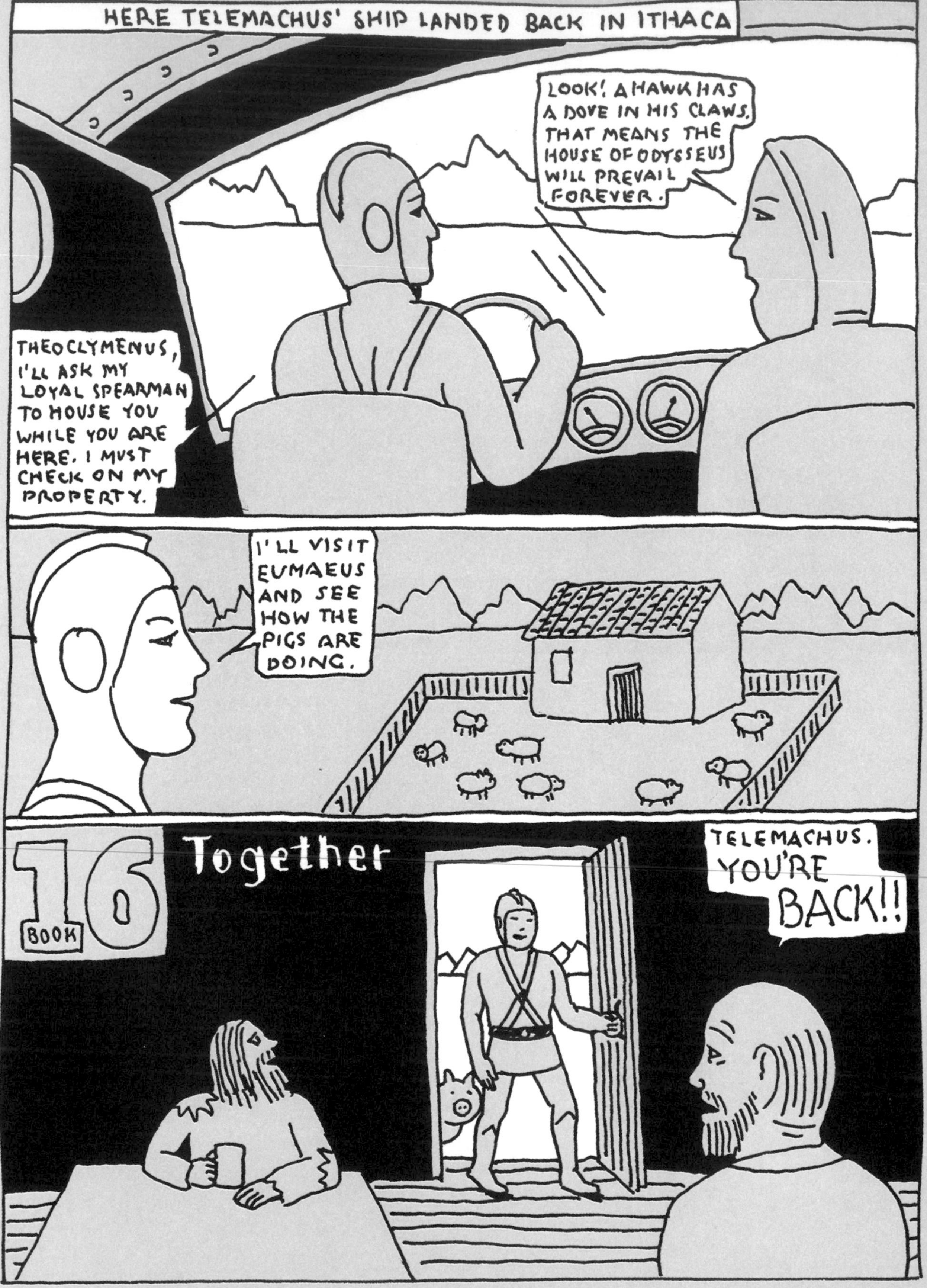
HERE TELEMACHUS' SHIP LANDED BACK IN ITHACA
LOOK! A HAWK HAS A DOVE IN HIS CLAWS. THAT MEANS THE HOUSE OF ODYSSEUS WILL PREVAIL FOREVER.
THEOCLYMENUS, I'LL ASK MY LOYAL SPEARMAN TO HOUSE YOU WHILE YOU ARE HERE. I MUST CHECK ON MY PROPERTY.
I'LL VISIT EUMAEUS AND SEE HOW THE PIGS ARE DOING.
BOOK 16
Together
TELEMACHUS. YOU'RE BACK!!

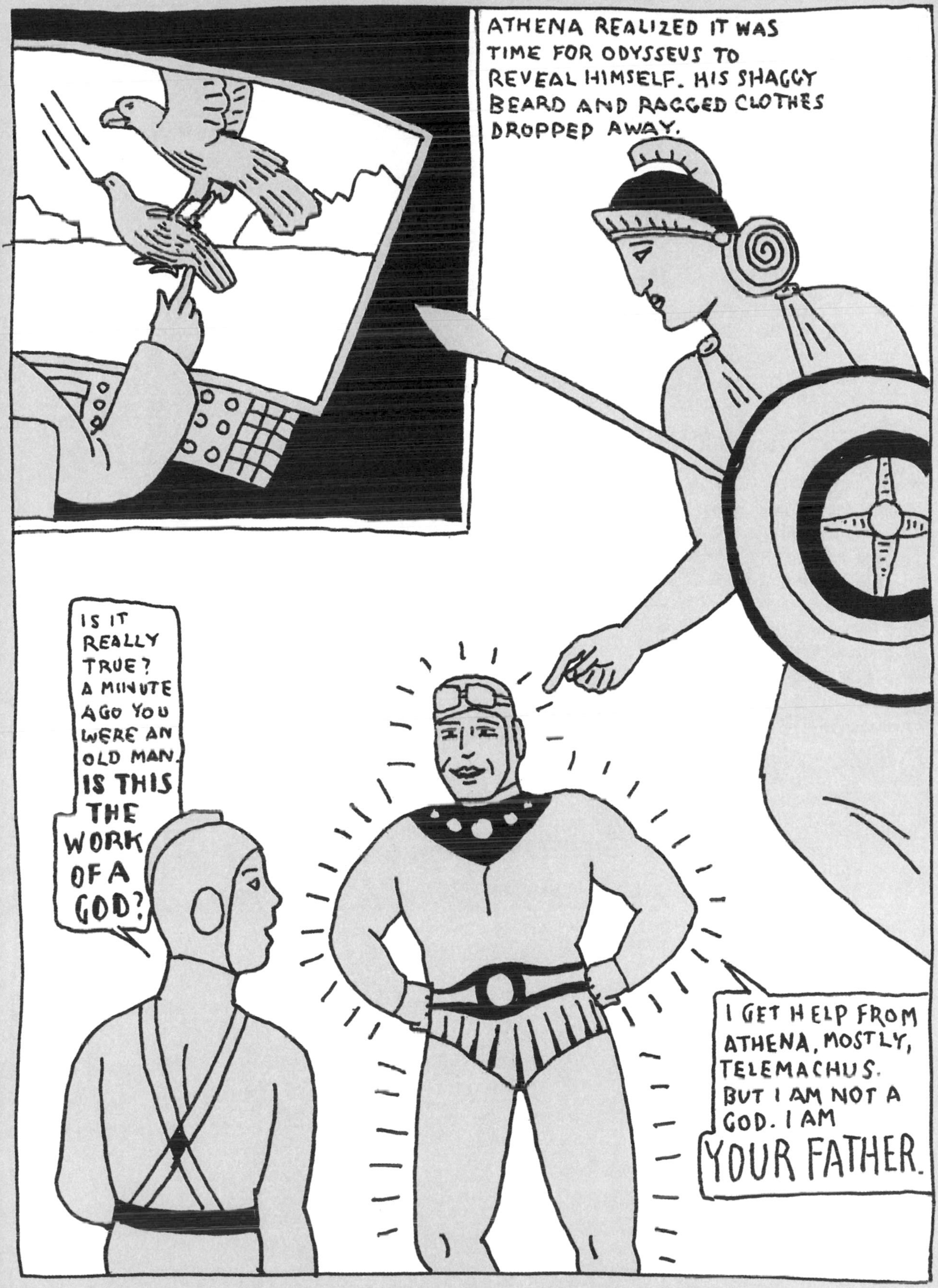

ATHENA REALIZED IT WAS TIME FOR ODYSSEUS TO REVEAL HIMSELF. HIS SHAGGY BEARD AND RAGGED CLOTHES DROPPED AWAY.
IS IT REALLY TRUE? A MINUTE AGO YOU WERE AN OLD MAN. IS THIS THE WORK OF A GOD?
I GET HELP FROM ATHENA, MOSTLY, TELEMACHUS. BUT I AM NOT A GOD. I AM YOUR FATHER.

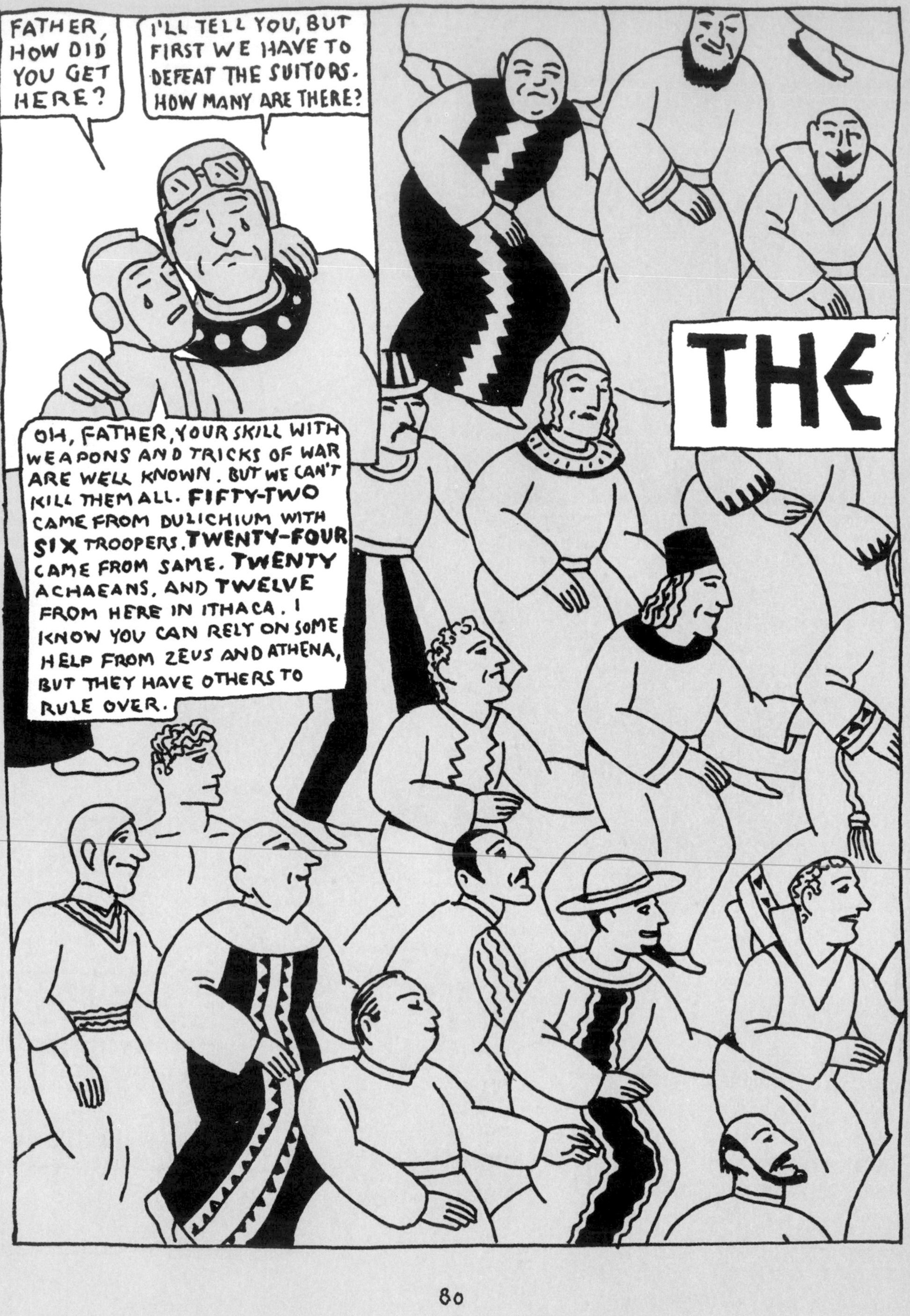
FATHER, HOW DID YOU GET HERE?
I'LL TELL YOU, BUT FIRST WE HAVE TO DEFEAT THE SUITORS. HOW MANY ARE THERE?
OH, FATHER, YOUR SKILL WITH WEAPONS AND TRICKS OF WAR ARE WELL KNOWN. BUT WE CAN'T KILL THEM ALL. FIFTY-TWO CAME FROM DULICHIUM WITH SIX TROOPERS. TWENTY-FOUR CAME FROM SAME. TWENTY ACHAEANS, AND TWELVE FROM HERE IN ITHACA. I KNOW YOU CAN RELY ON SOME HELP FROM ZEUS AND ATHENA, BUT THEY HAVE OTHERS TO RULE OVER.
THE

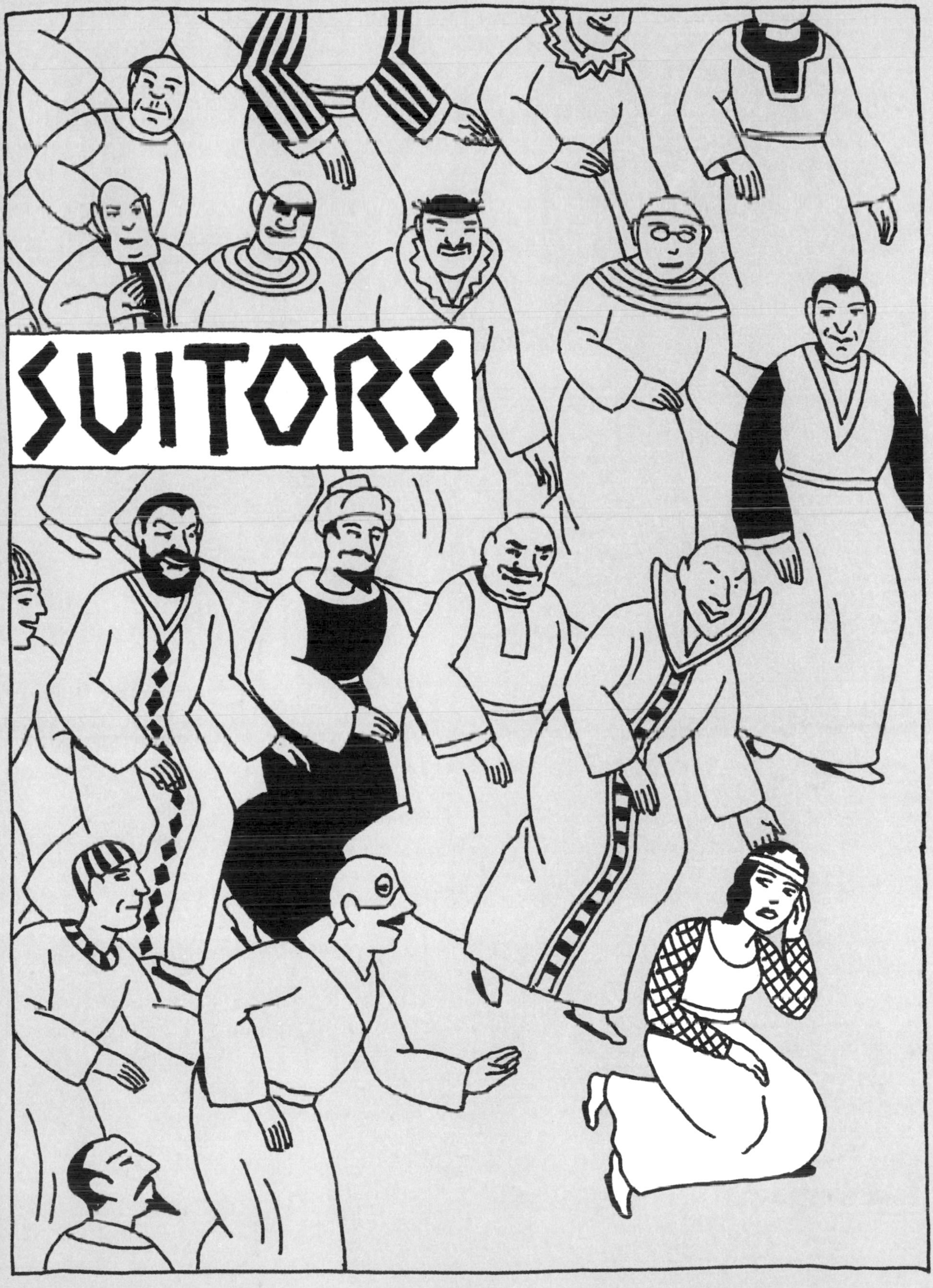
SUITORS

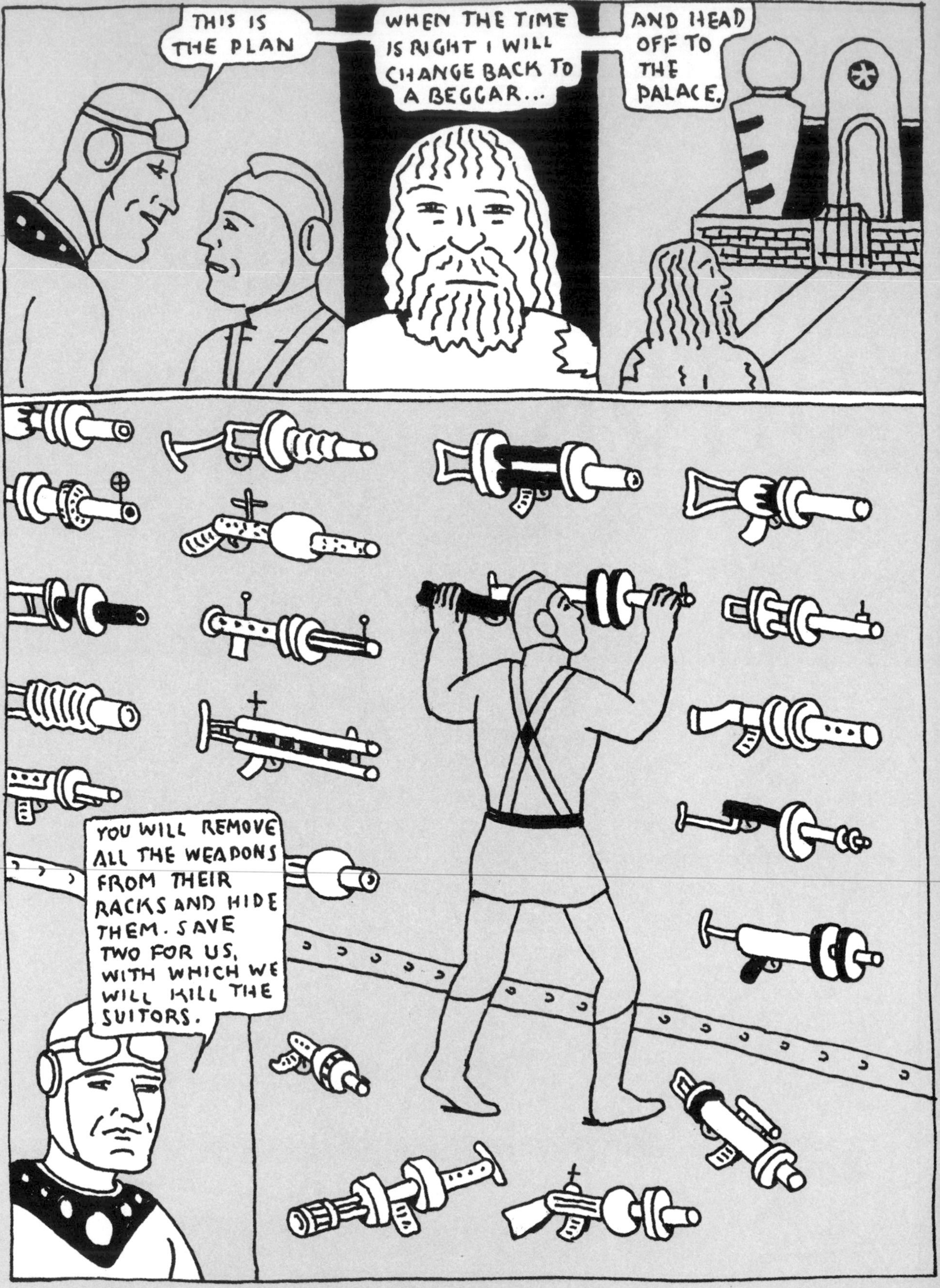
THIS IS THE PLAN
WHEN THE TIME IS RIGHT I WILL CHANGE BACK TO A BEGGAR...
AND HEAD OFF TO THE PALACE.
YOU WILL REMOVE ALL THE WEAPONS FROM THEIR RACKS AND HIDE THEM. SAVE TWO FOR US, WITH WHICH WE WILL KILL THE SUITORS.

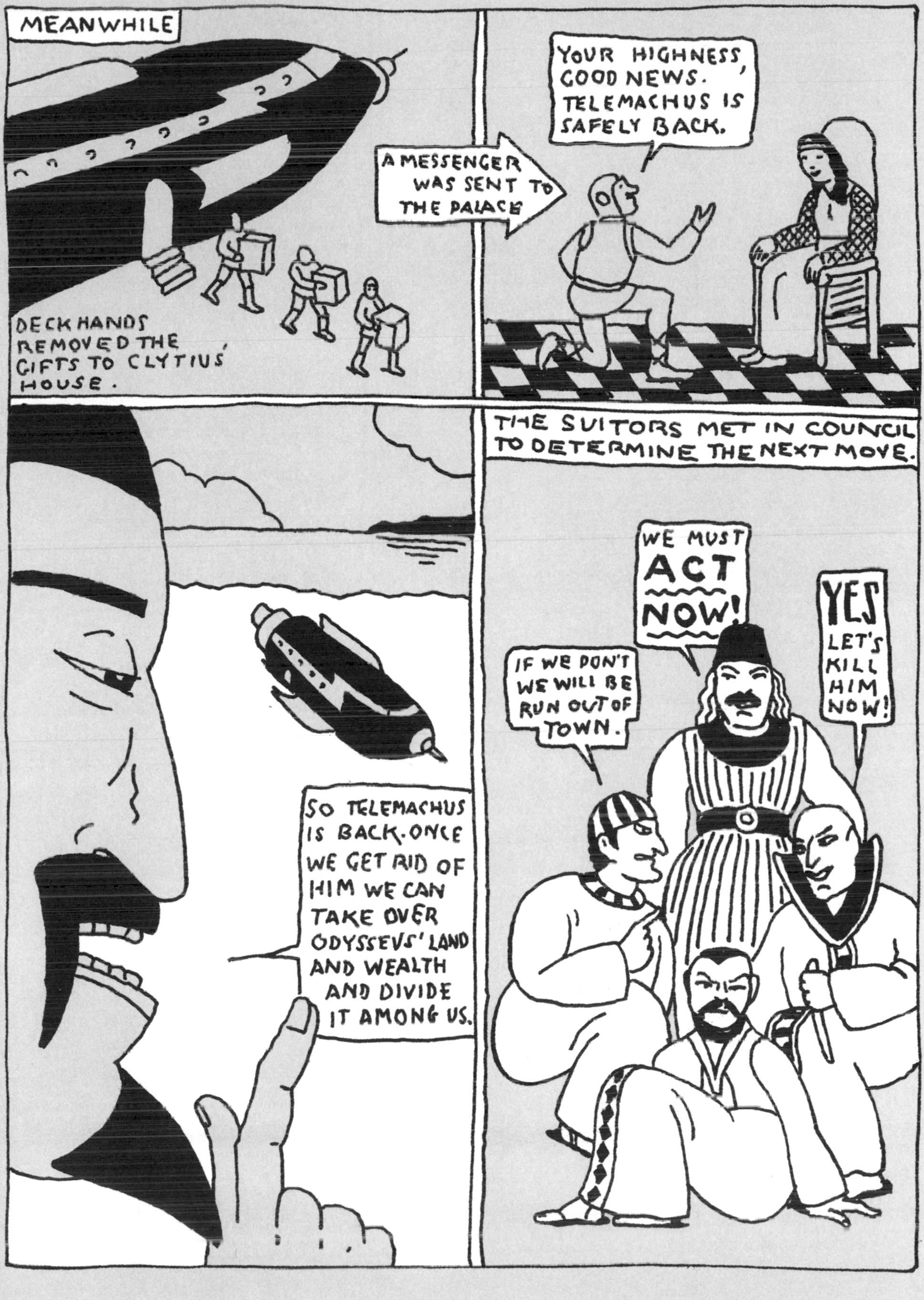
MEANWHILE
DECK HANDS REMOVED THE GIFTS TO CLYTIUS' HOUSE.
A MESSENGER WAS SENT TO THE PALACE
YOUR HIGHNESS, GOOD NEWS. TELEMACHUS IS SAFELY BACK.
SO TELEMACHUS IS BACK. ONCE WE GET RID OF HIM WE CAN TAKE OVER ODYSSEUS' LAND AND WEALTH AND DIVIDE IT AMONG US.
THE SUITORS MET IN COUNCIL TO DETERMINE THE NEXT MOVE.
WE MUST ACT NOW!
YES LET'S KILL HIM NOW!
IF WE DON'T WE WILL BE RUN OUT OF TOWN.

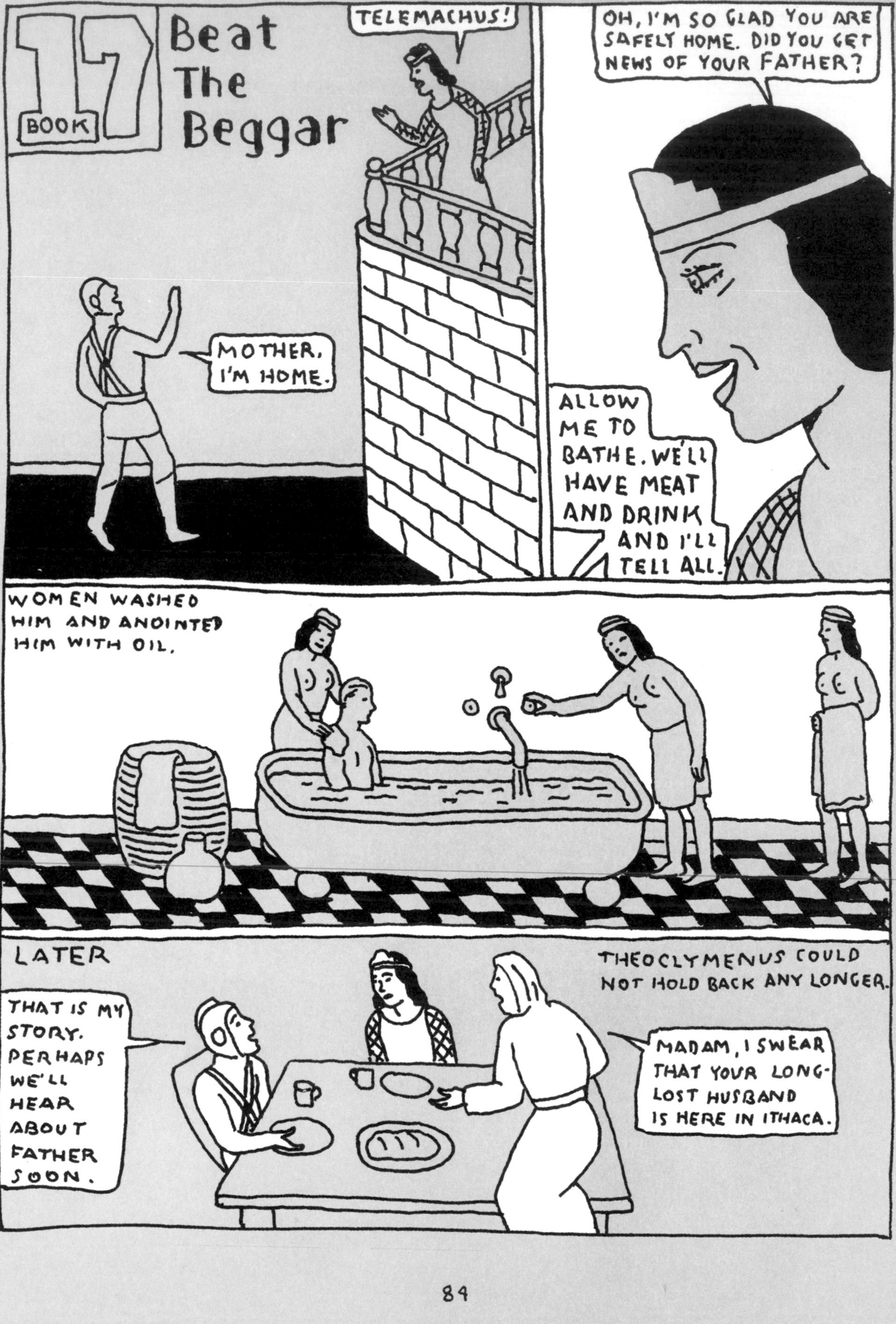
BOOK 17 Beat The Beggar
TELEMACHUS!
MOTHER, I'M HOME.
OH, I'M SO GLAD YOU ARE SAFELY HOME. DID YOU GET NEWS OF YOUR FATHER?
ALLOW ME TO BATHE. WE'LL HAVE MEAT AND DRINK AND I'LL TELL ALL.
WOMEN WASHED HIM AND ANOINTED HIM WITH OIL.
LATER
THAT IS MY STORY. PERHAPS WE'LL HEAR ABOUT FATHER SOON.
THEOCLYMENUS COULD NOT HOLD BACK ANY LONGER.
MADAM, I SWEAR THAT YOUR LONG-LOST HUSBAND IS HERE IN ITHACA.

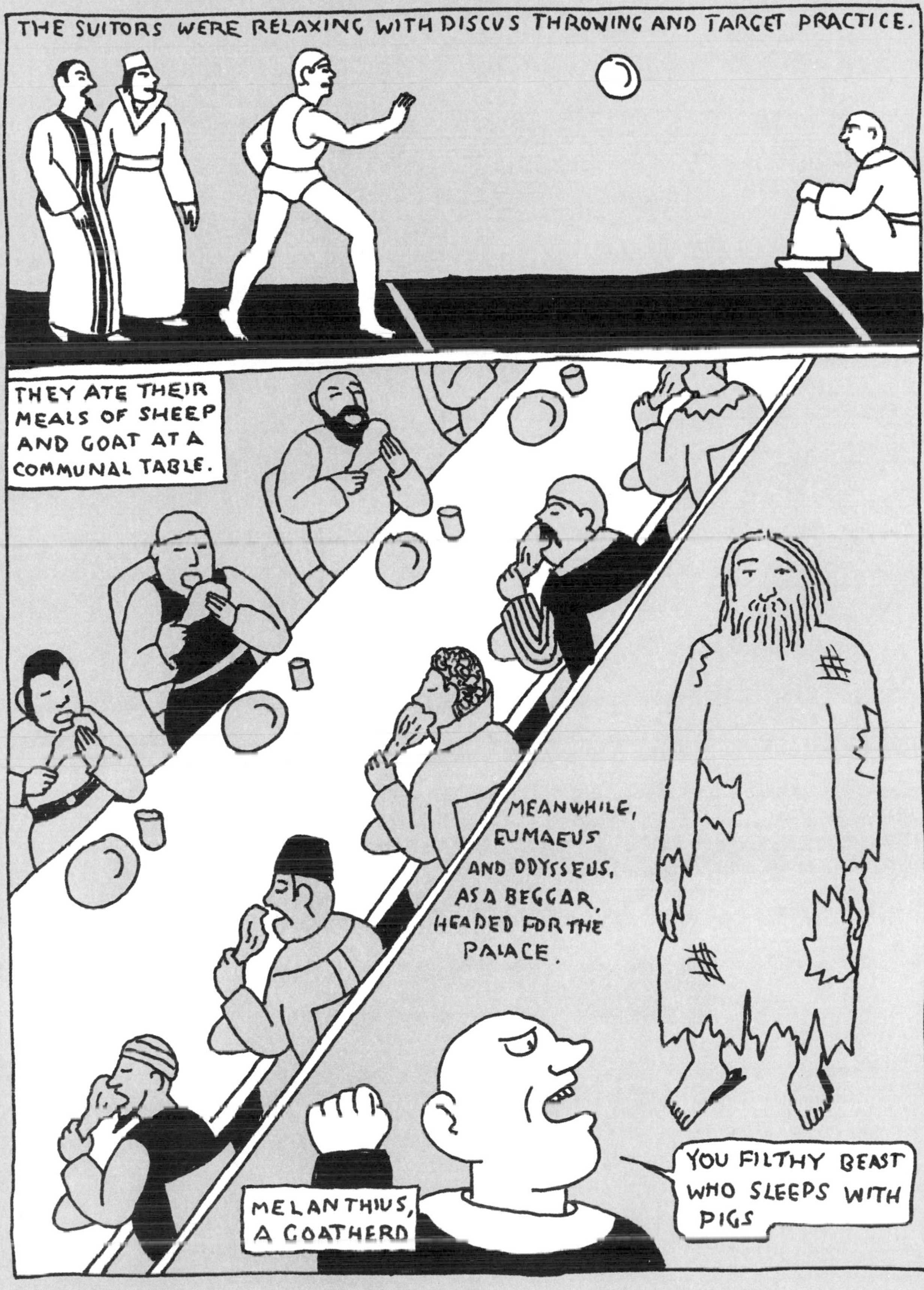
THE SUITORS WERE RELAXING WITH DISCUS THROWING AND TARGET PRACTICE.
THEY ATE THEIR MEALS OF SHEEP AND GOAT AT A COMMUNAL TABLE.
MEANWHILE, EUMAEUS AND ODYSSEUS, AS A BEGGAR, HEADED FOR THE PALACE.
MELANTHIUS, A GOATHERD
YOU FILTHY BEAST WHO SLEEPS WITH PIGS

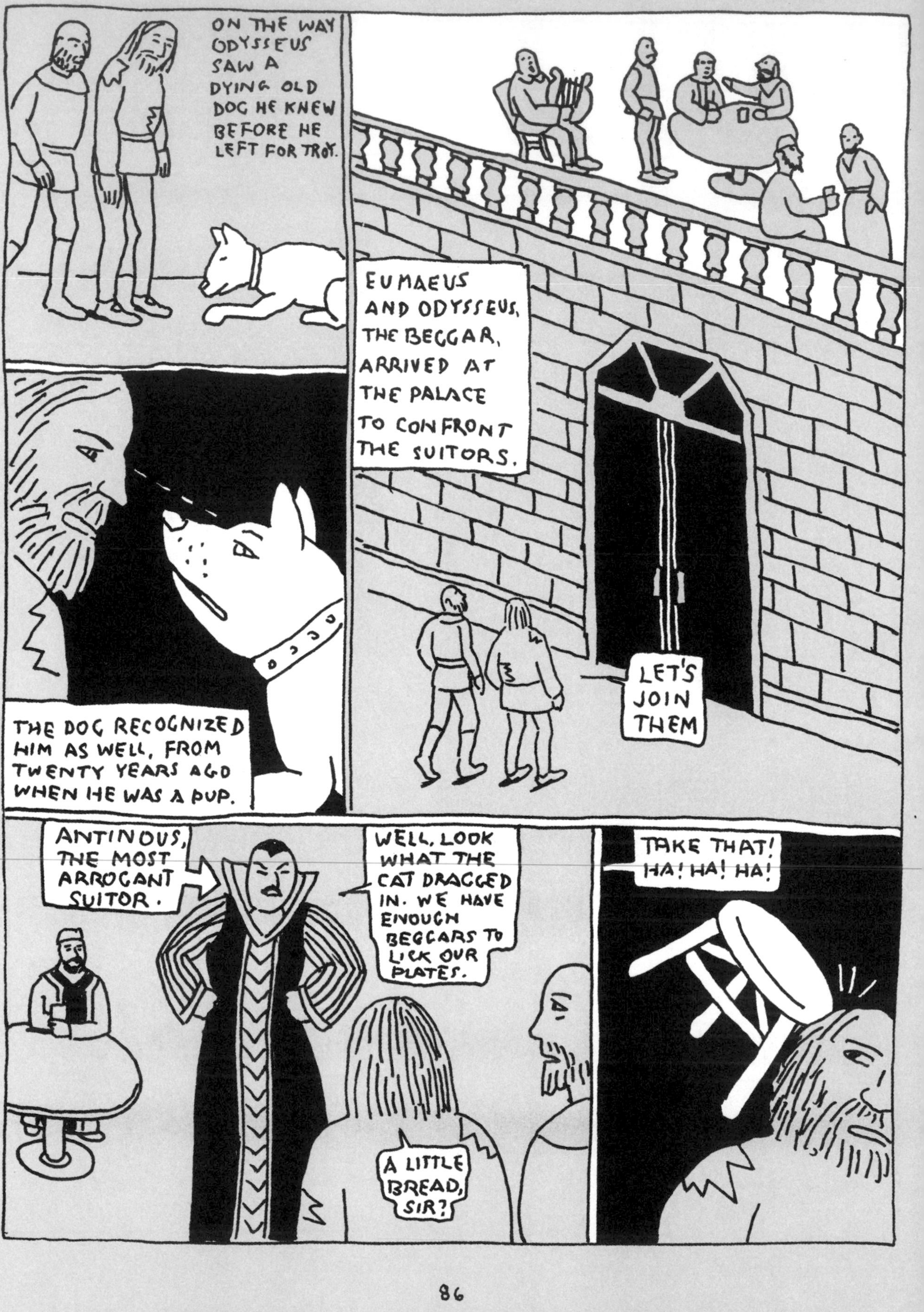
ON THE WAY ODYSSEUS SAW A DYING OLD DOG HE KNEW BEFORE HE LEFT FOR TROY.
THE DOG RECOGNIZED HIM AS WELL, FROM TWENTY YEARS AGO WHEN HE WAS A PUP.
EUMAEUS AND ODYSSEUS, THE BEGGAR, ARRIVED AT THE PALACE TO CONFRONT THE SUITORS.
LET'S JOIN THEM
ANTINOUS, THE MOST ARROGANT SUITOR.
WELL, LOOK WHAT THE CAT DRAGGED IN. WE HAVE ENOUGH BEGGARS TO LICK OUR PLATES.
A LITTLE BREAD, SIR?
TAKE THAT! HA! HA! HA!

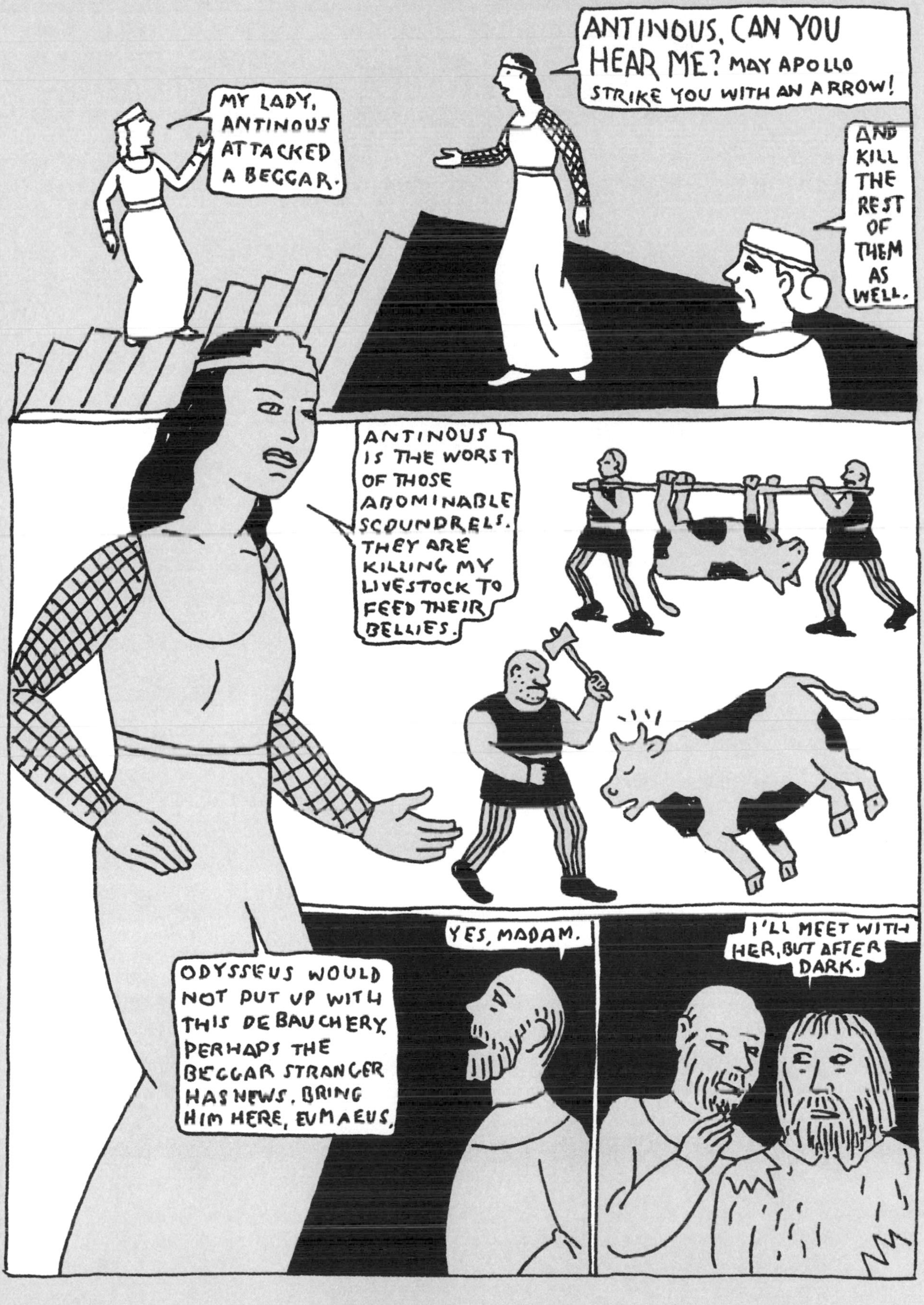
MY LADY, ANTINOUS ATTACKED A BEGGAR.
ANTINOUS, CAN YOU HEAR ME? MAY APOLLO STRIKE YOU WITH AN ARROW!
AND KILL THE REST OF THEM AS WELL.
ANTINOUS IS THE WORST OF THOSE ABOMINABLE SCOUNDRELS. THEY ARE KILLING MY LIVESTOCK TO FEED THEIR BELLIES.
ODYSSEUS WOULD NOT PUT UP WITH THIS DEBAUCHERY. PERHAPS THE BEGGAR STRANGER HAS NEWS. BRING HIM HERE, EUMAEUS.
YES, MADAM.
I'LL MEET WITH HER, BUT AFTER DARK.

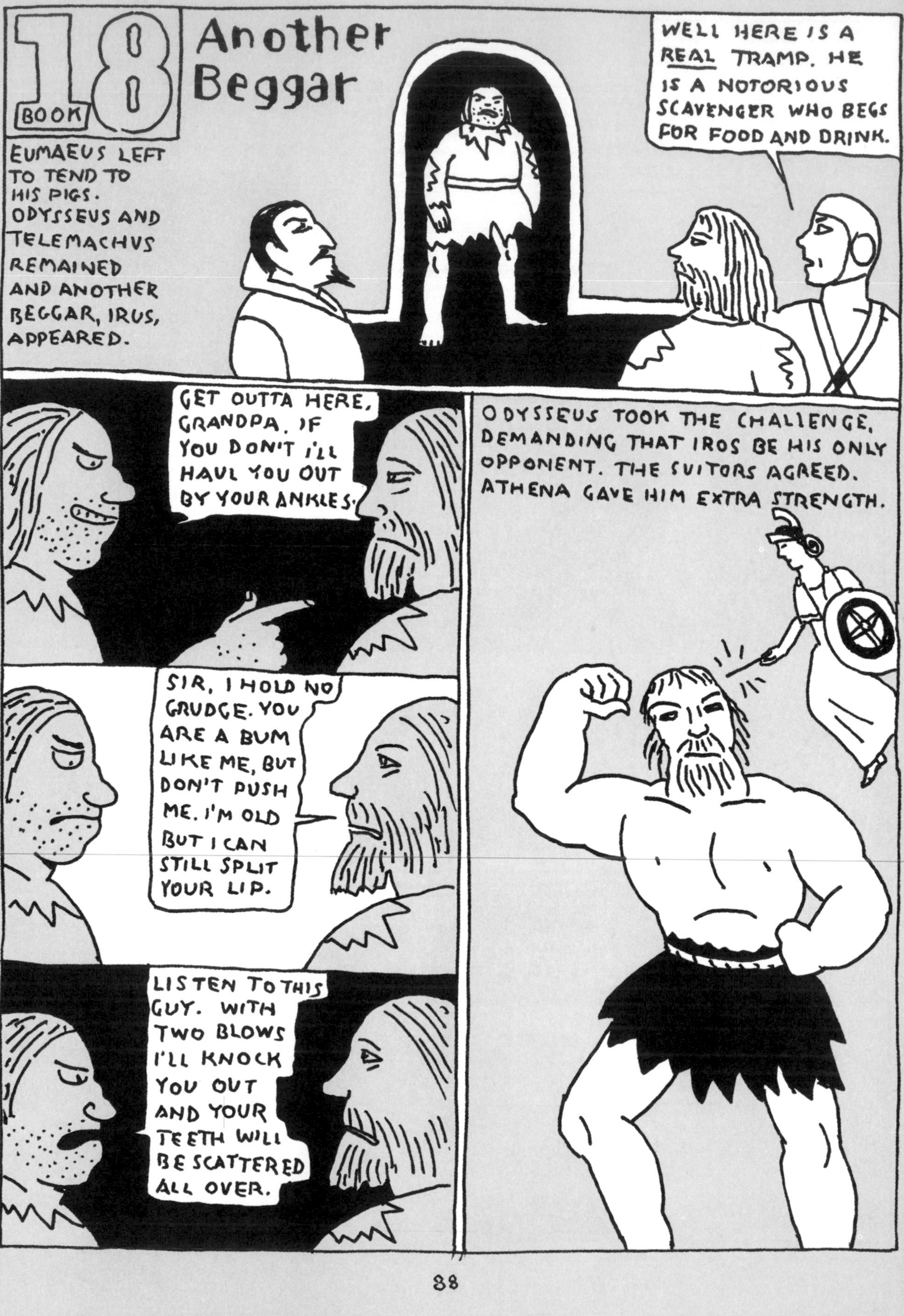
BOOK 18 Another Beggar
EUMAEUS LEFT TO TEND TO HIS PIGS. ODYSSEUS AND TELEMACHUS REMAINED AND ANOTHER BEGGAR, IRUS, APPEARED.
WELL HERE IS A REAL TRAMP. HE IS A NOTORIOUS SCAVENGER WHO BEGS FOR FOOD AND DRINK.
GET OUTTA HERE, GRANDPA. IF YOU DON'T I'LL HAUL YOU OUT BY YOUR ANKLES.
SIR, I HOLD NO GRUDGE. YOU ARE A BUM LIKE ME, BUT DON'T PUSH ME. I'M OLD BUT I CAN STILL SPLIT YOUR LIP.
LISTEN TO THIS GUY. WITH TWO BLOWS I'LL KNOCK YOU OUT AND YOUR TEETH WILL BE SCATTERED ALL OVER.
ODYSSEUS TOOK THE CHALLENGE, DEMANDING THAT IROS BE HIS ONLY OPPONENT. THE SUITORS AGREED. ATHENA GAVE HIM EXTRA STRENGTH.

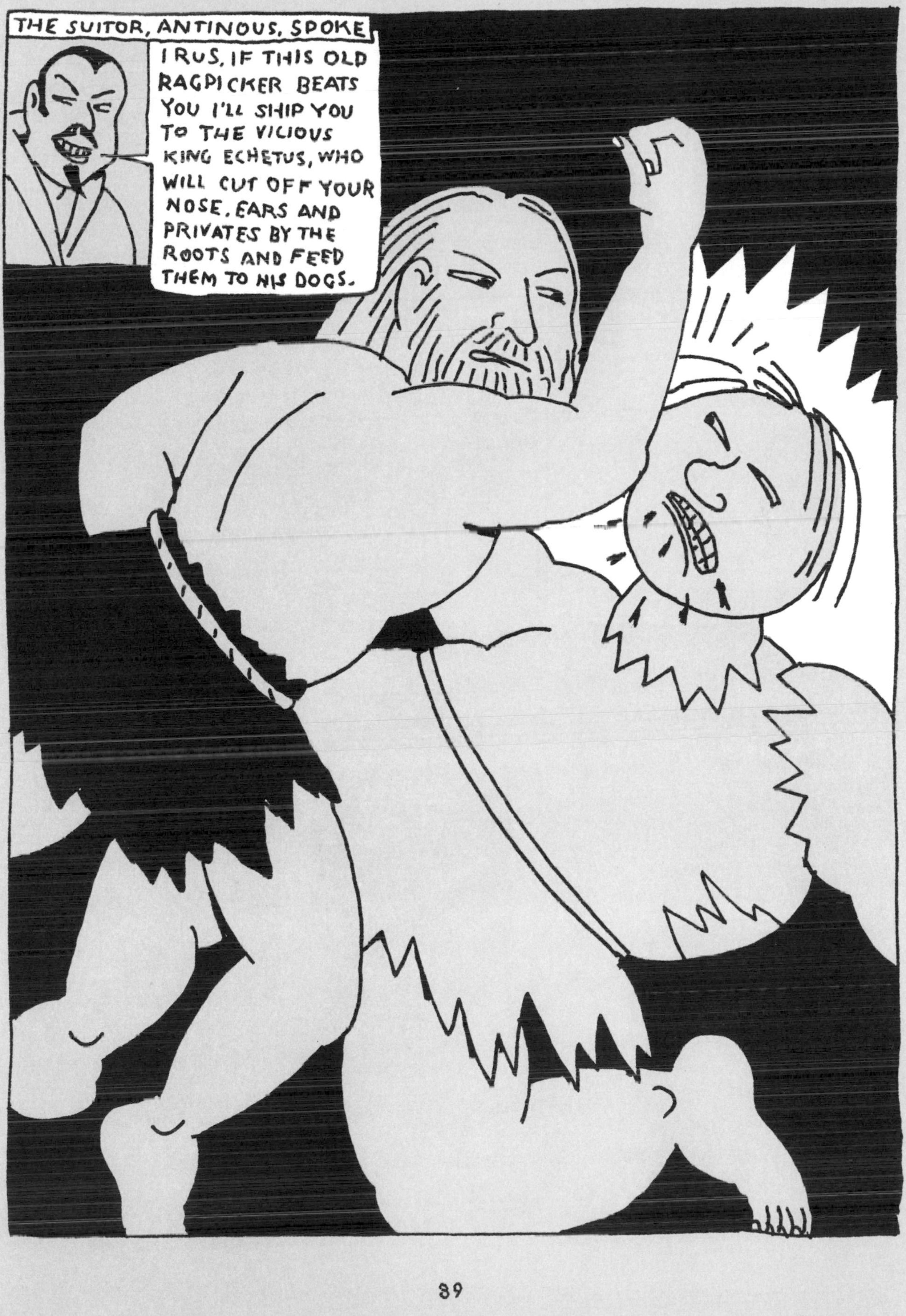
THE SUITOR, ANTINOUS, SPOKE
IRUS, IF THIS OLD RAGPICKER BEATS YOU I'LL SHIP YOU TO THE VICIOUS KING ECHETUS, WHO WILL CUT OFF YOUR NOSE, EARS AND PRIVATES BY THE ROOTS AND FEED THEM TO HIS DOGS.

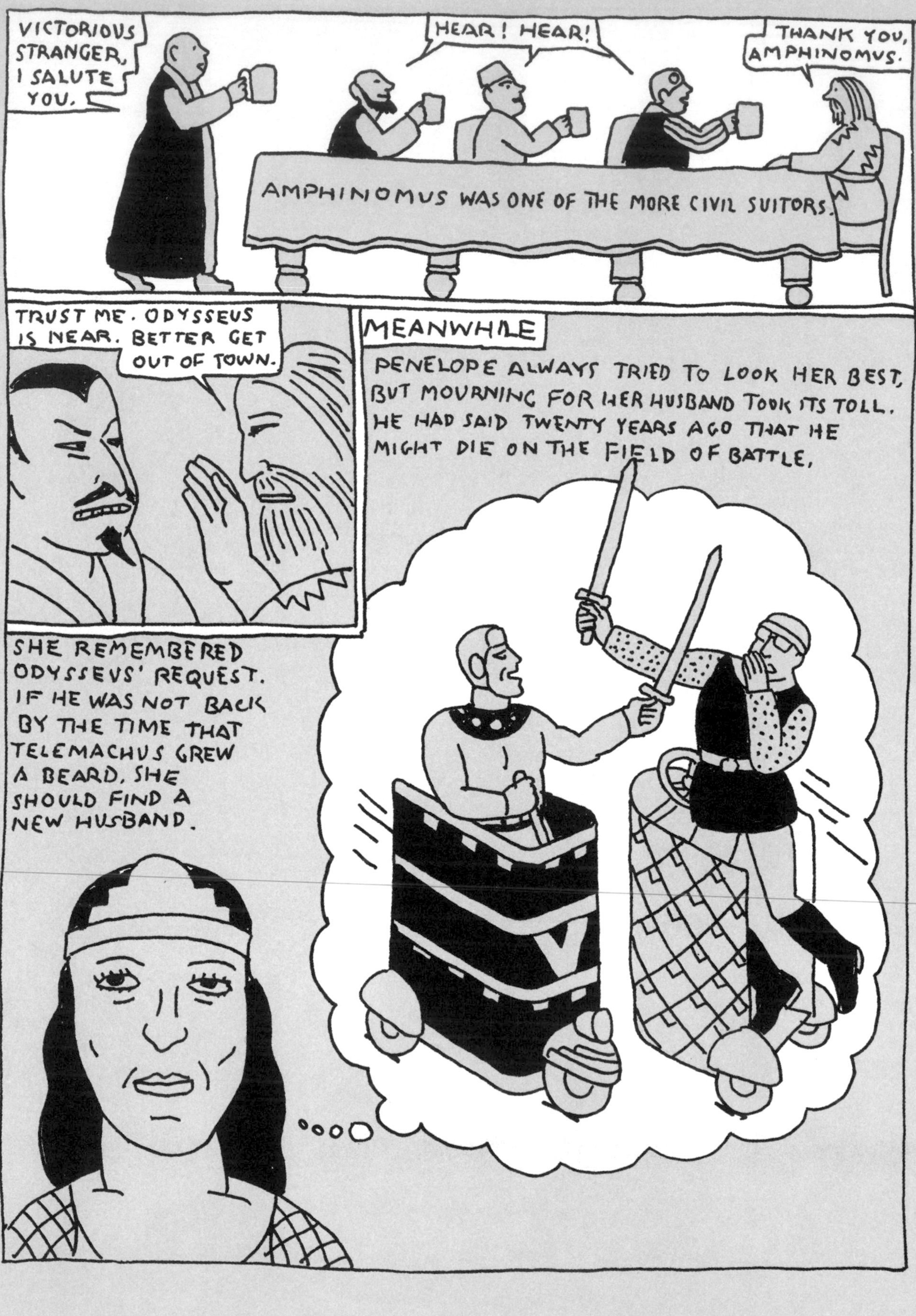
VICTORIOUS STRANGER, I SALUTE YOU.
HEAR! HEAR!
THANK YOU, AMPHINOMUS.
AMPHINOMUS WAS ONE OF THE MORE CIVIL SUITORS.
TRUST ME. ODYSSEUS IS NEAR. BETTER GET OUT OF TOWN.
MEANWHILE
PENELOPE ALWAYS TRIED TO LOOK HER BEST, BUT MOURNING FOR HER HUSBAND TOOK ITS TOLL. HE HAD SAID TWENTY YEARS AGO THAT HE MIGHT DIE ON THE FIELD OF BATTLE.
V
SHE REMEMBERED ODYSSEUS' REQUEST. IF HE WAS NOT BACK BY THE TIME THAT TELEMACHUS GREW A BEARD, SHE SHOULD FIND A NEW HUSBAND.

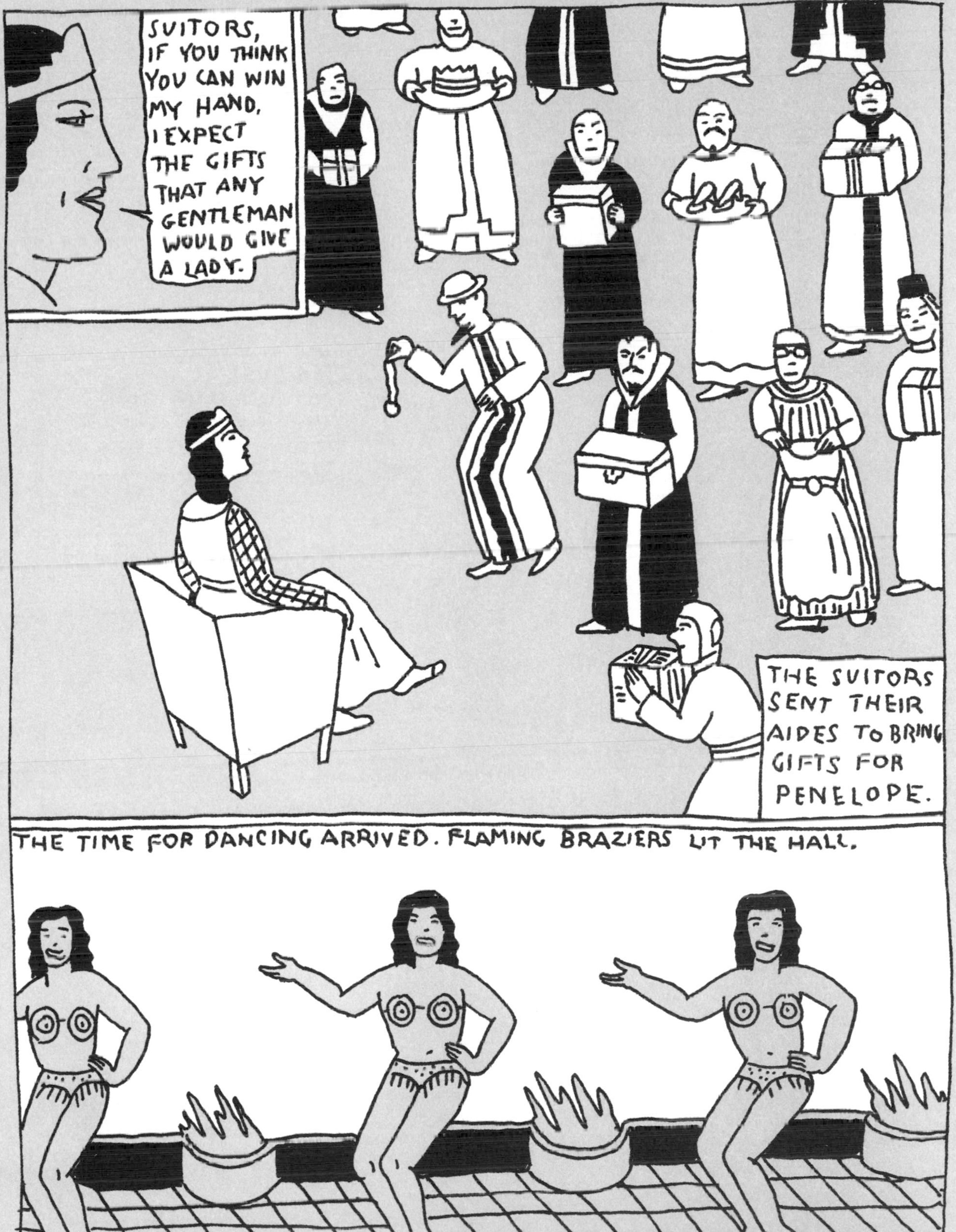
SUITORS, IF YOU THINK YOU CAN WIN MY HAND, I EXPECT THE GIFTS THAT ANY GENTLEMAN WOULD GIVE A LADY.
THE SUITORS SENT THEIR AIDES TO BRING GIFTS FOR PENELOPE.
THE TIME FOR DANCING ARRIVED. FLAMING BRAZIERS LIT THE HALL.

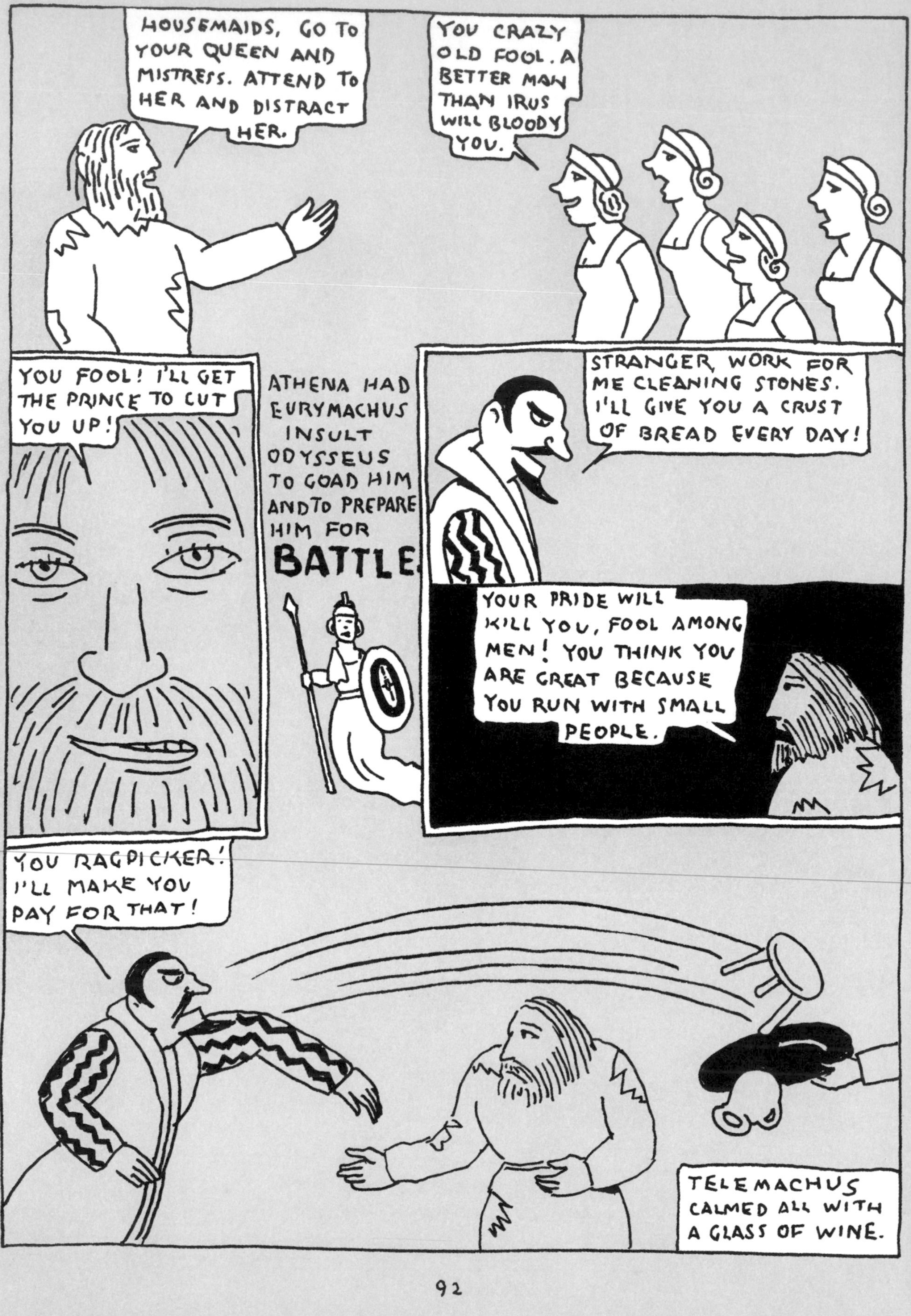

HOUSEMAIDS, GO TO YOUR QUEEN AND MISTRESS. ATTEND TO HER AND DISTRACT HER.
YOU CRAZY OLD FOOL. A BETTER MAN THAN IRUS WILL BLOODY YOU.
YOU FOOL! I'LL GET THE PRINCE TO CUT YOU UP!
ATHENA HAD EURYMACHUS INSULT ODYSSEUS TO GOAD HIM AND TO PREPARE HIM FOR BATTLE.
STRANGER, WORK FOR ME CLEANING STONES. I'LL GIVE YOU A CRUST OF BREAD EVERY DAY!
YOUR PRIDE WILL KILL YOU, FOOL AMONG MEN! YOU THINK YOU ARE GREAT BECAUSE YOU RUN WITH SMALL PEOPLE.
YOU RAGPICKER! I'LL MAKE YOU PAY FOR THAT!
TELEMACHUS CALMED ALL WITH A GLASS OF WINE.

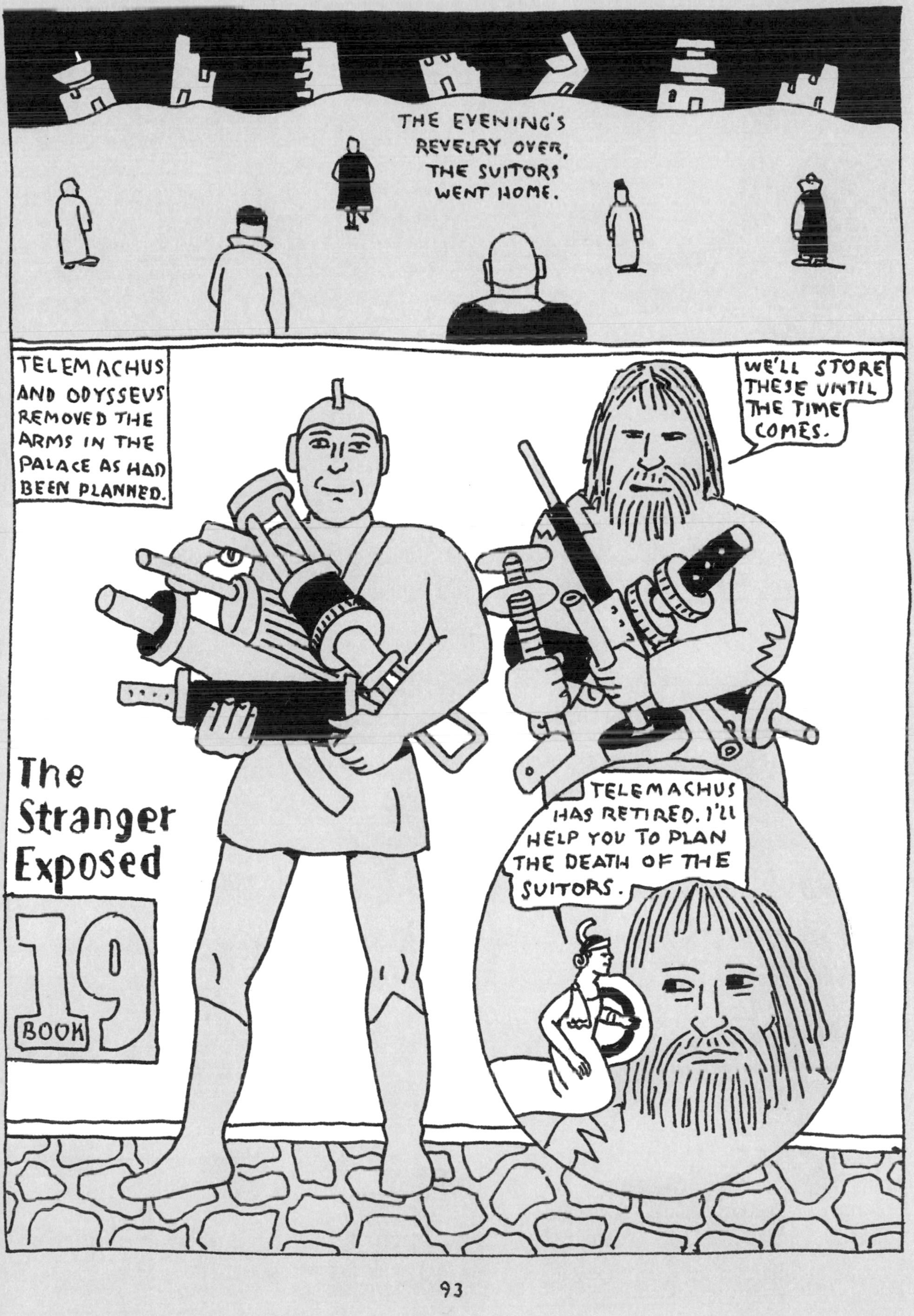
THE EVENING'S REVELRY OVER, THE SUITORS WENT HOME.
TELEMACHUS AND ODYSSEUS REMOVED THE ARMS IN THE PALACE AS HAD BEEN PLANNED.
WE'LL STORE THESE UNTIL THE TIME COMES.
The Stranger Exposed
BOOK 19
TELEMACHUS HAS RETIRED. I'LL HELP YOU TO PLAN THE DEATH OF THE SUITORS.

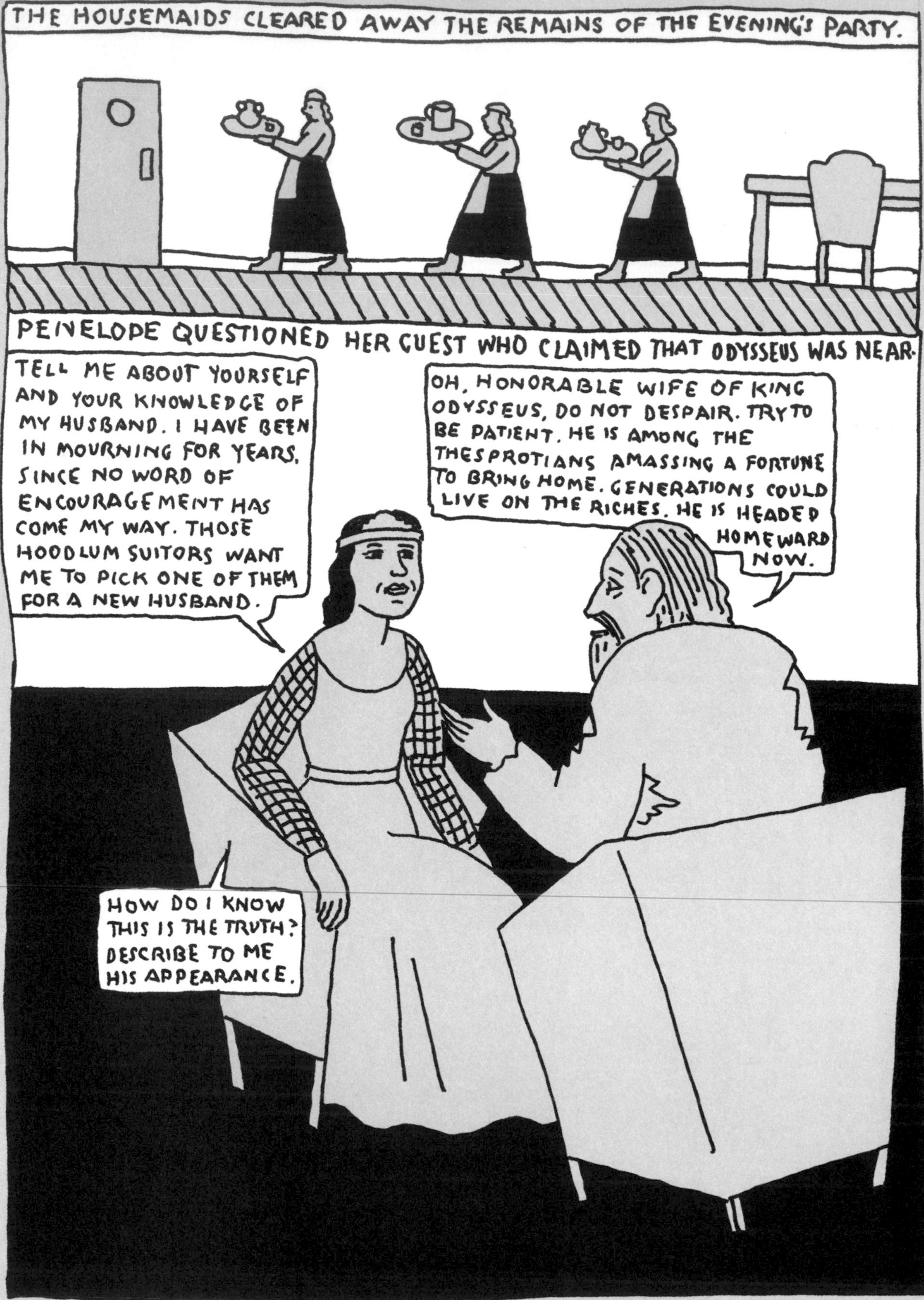
THE HOUSEMAIDS CLEARED AWAY THE REMAINS OF THE EVENING'S PARTY.
PENELOPE QUESTIONED HER GUEST WHO CLAIMED THAT ODYSSEUS WAS NEAR.
TELL ME ABOUT YOURSELF AND YOUR KNOWLEDGE OF MY HUSBAND. I HAVE BEEN IN MOURNING FOR YEARS, SINCE NO WORD OF ENCOURAGEMENT HAS COME MY WAY. THOSE HOODLUM SUITORS WANT ME TO PICK ONE OF THEM FOR A NEW HUSBAND.
OH, HONORABLE WIFE OF KING ODYSSEUS, DO NOT DESPAIR. TRY TO BE PATIENT. HE IS AMONG THE THESPROTIANS AMASSING A FORTUNE TO BRING HOME. GENERATIONS COULD LIVE ON THE RICHES. HE IS HEADED HOMEWARD NOW.
HOW DO I KNOW THIS IS THE TRUTH? DESCRIBE TO ME HIS APPEARANCE.

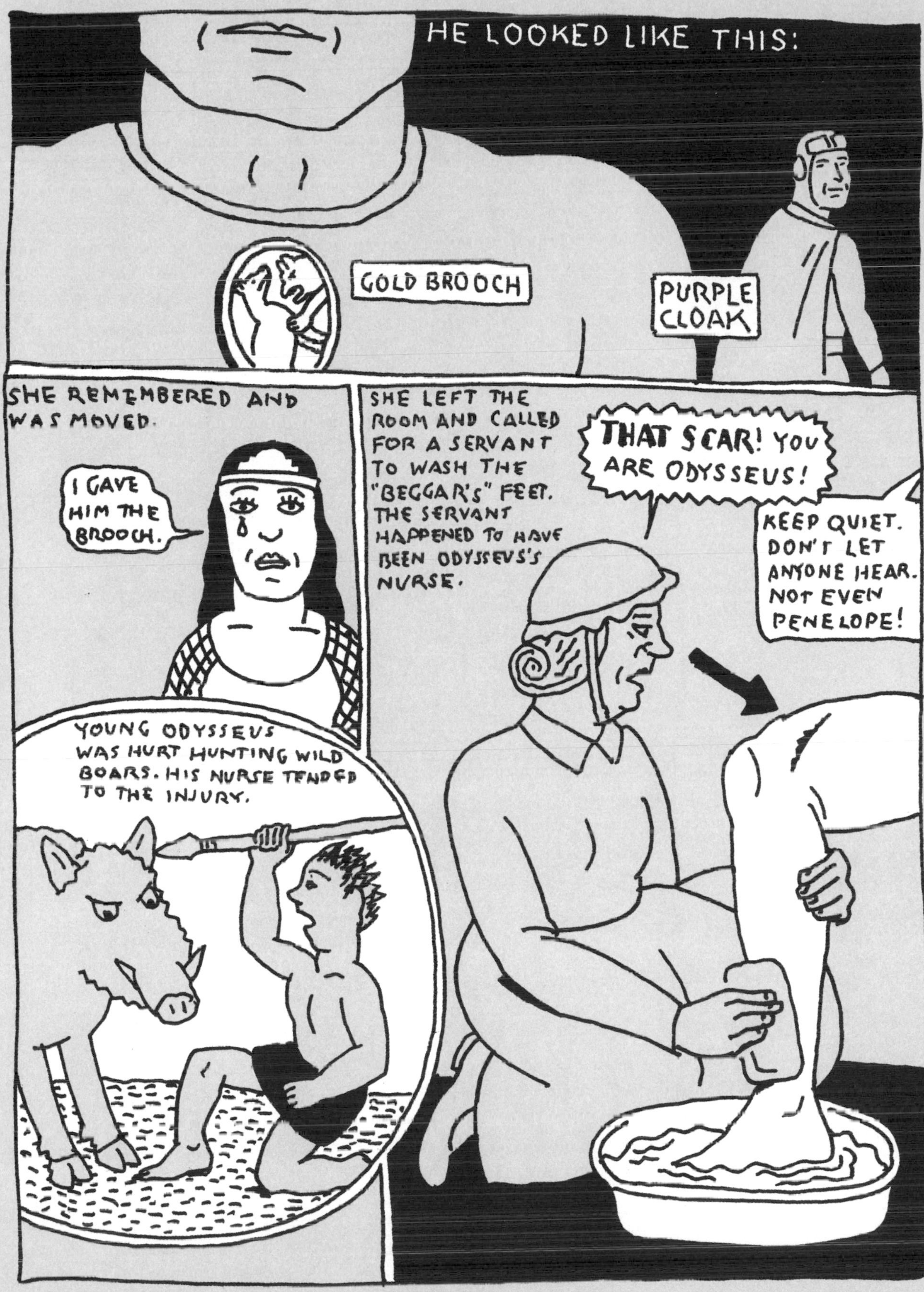
HE LOOKED LIKE THIS:
GOLD BROOCH
PURPLE CLOAK
SHE REMEMBERED AND WAS MOVED.
I GAVE HIM THE BROOCH.
YOUNG ODYSSEUS WAS HURT HUNTING WILD BOARS. HIS NURSE TENDED TO THE INJURY.
SHE LEFT THE ROOM AND CALLED FOR A SERVANT TO WASH THE "BEGGAR'S" FEET. THE SERVANT HAPPENED TO HAVE BEEN ODYSSEUS'S NURSE.
THAT SCAR! YOU ARE ODYSSEUS!
KEEP QUIET. DON'T LET ANYONE HEAR. NOT EVEN PENELOPE!

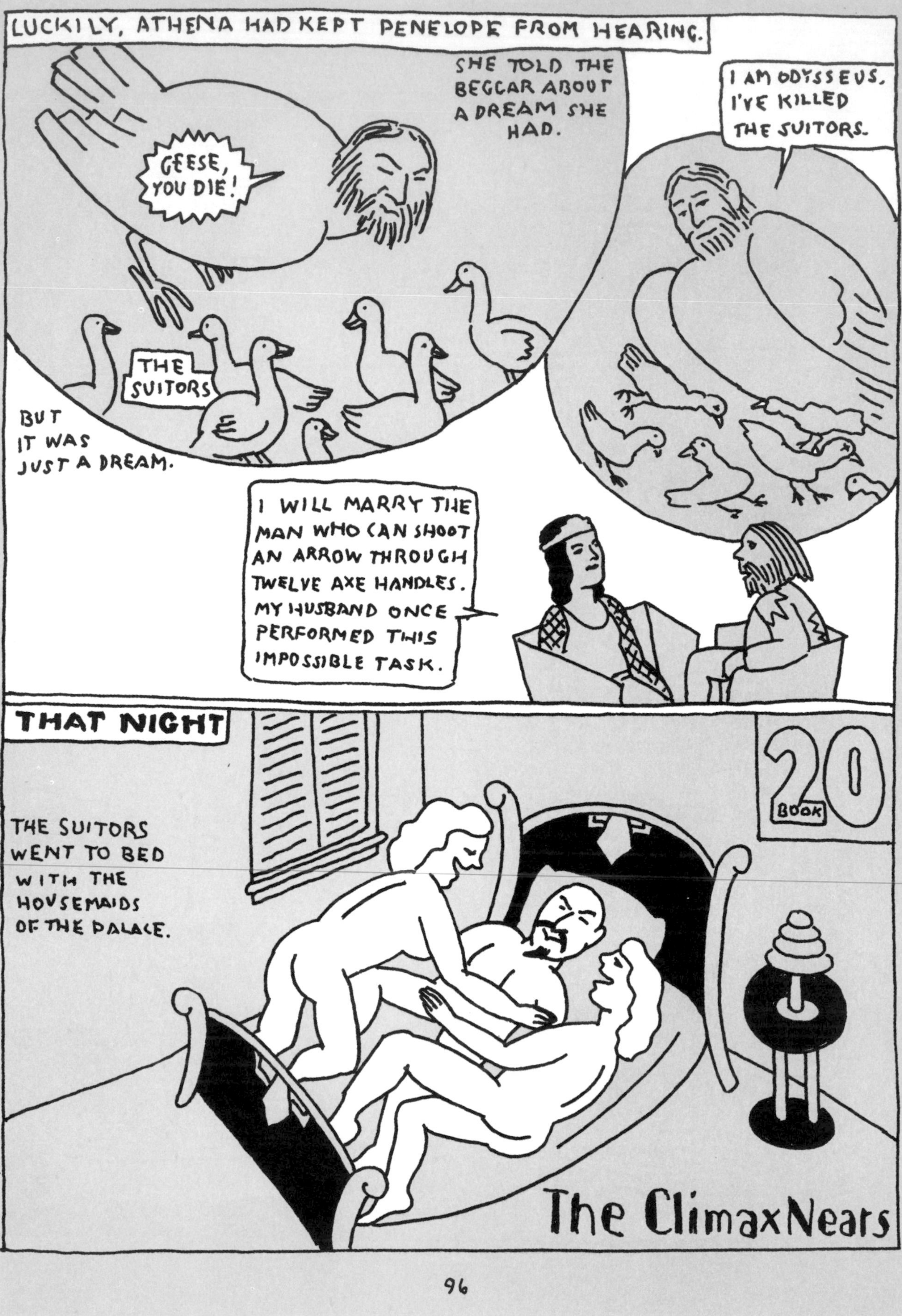
LUCKILY, ATHENA HAD KEPT PENELOPE FROM HEARING.
SHE TOLD THE BEGGAR ABOUT A DREAM SHE HAD.
GEESE, YOU DIE!
THE SUITORS
BUT IT WAS JUST A DREAM.
I AM ODYSSEUS. I'VE KILLED THE SUITORS.
I WILL MARRY THE MAN WHO CAN SHOOT AN ARROW THROUGH TWELVE AXE HANDLES. MY HUSBAND ONCE PERFORMED THIS IMPOSSIBLE TASK.
THAT NIGHT
20 BOOK
THE SUITORS WENT TO BED WITH THE HOUSEMAIDS OF THE PALACE.
The Climax Nears

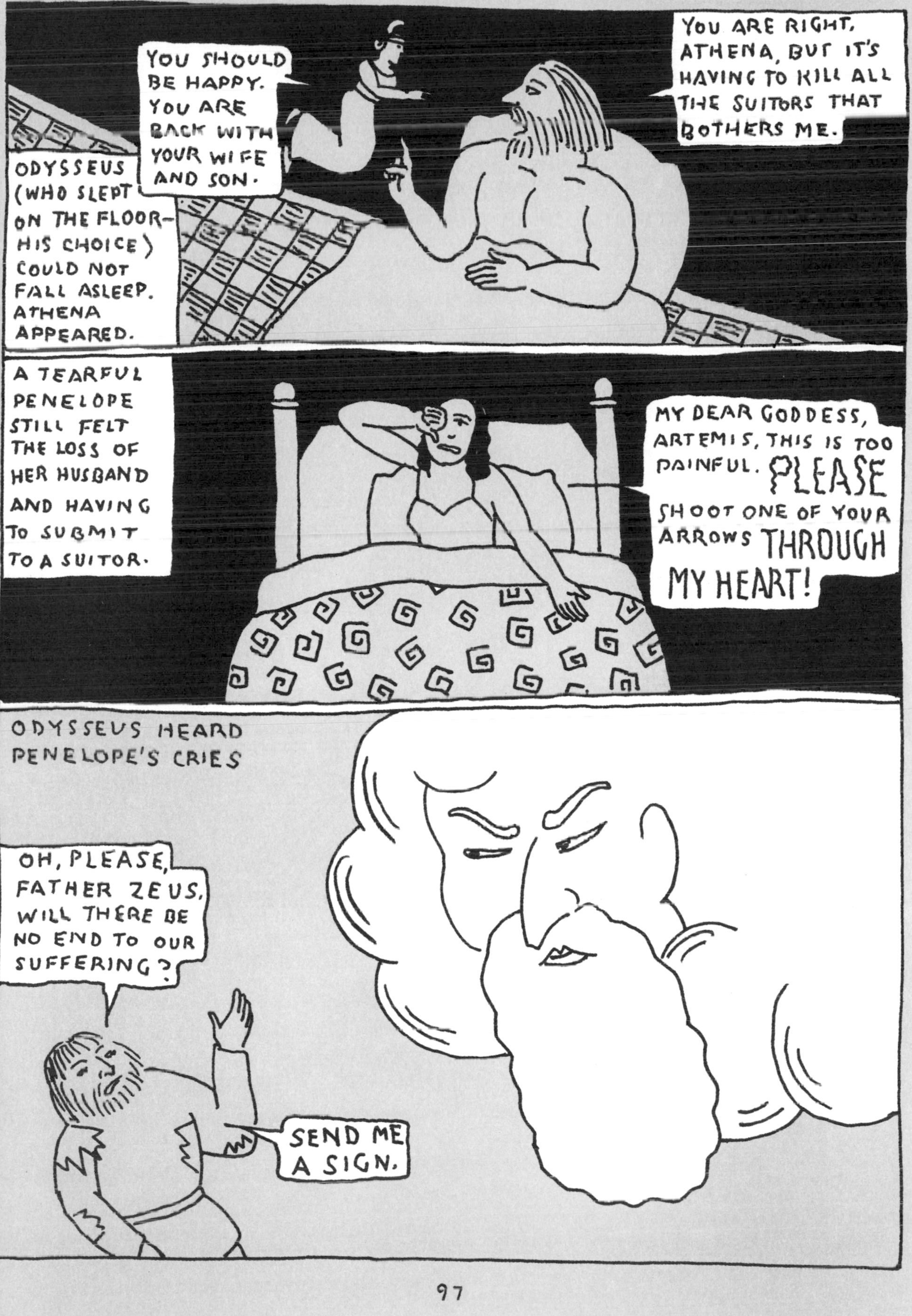
ODYSSEUS (WHO SLEPT ON THE FLOOR- HIS CHOICE) COULD NOT FALL ASLEEP. ATHENA APPEARED.
YOU SHOULD BE HAPPY. YOU ARE BACK WITH YOUR WIFE AND SON.
YOU ARE RIGHT, ATHENA, BUT IT'S HAVING TO KILL ALL THE SUITORS THAT BOTHERS ME.
A TEARFUL PENELOPE STILL FELT THE LOSS OF HER HUSBAND AND HAVING TO SUBMIT TO A SUITOR.
MY DEAR GODDESS, ARTEMIS, THIS IS TOO PAINFUL. PLEASE SHOOT ONE OF YOUR ARROWS THROUGH MY HEART!
ODYSSEUS HEARD PENELOPE'S CRIES
OH, PLEASE, FATHER ZEUS. WILL THERE BE NO END TO OUR SUFFERING?
SEND ME A SIGN.

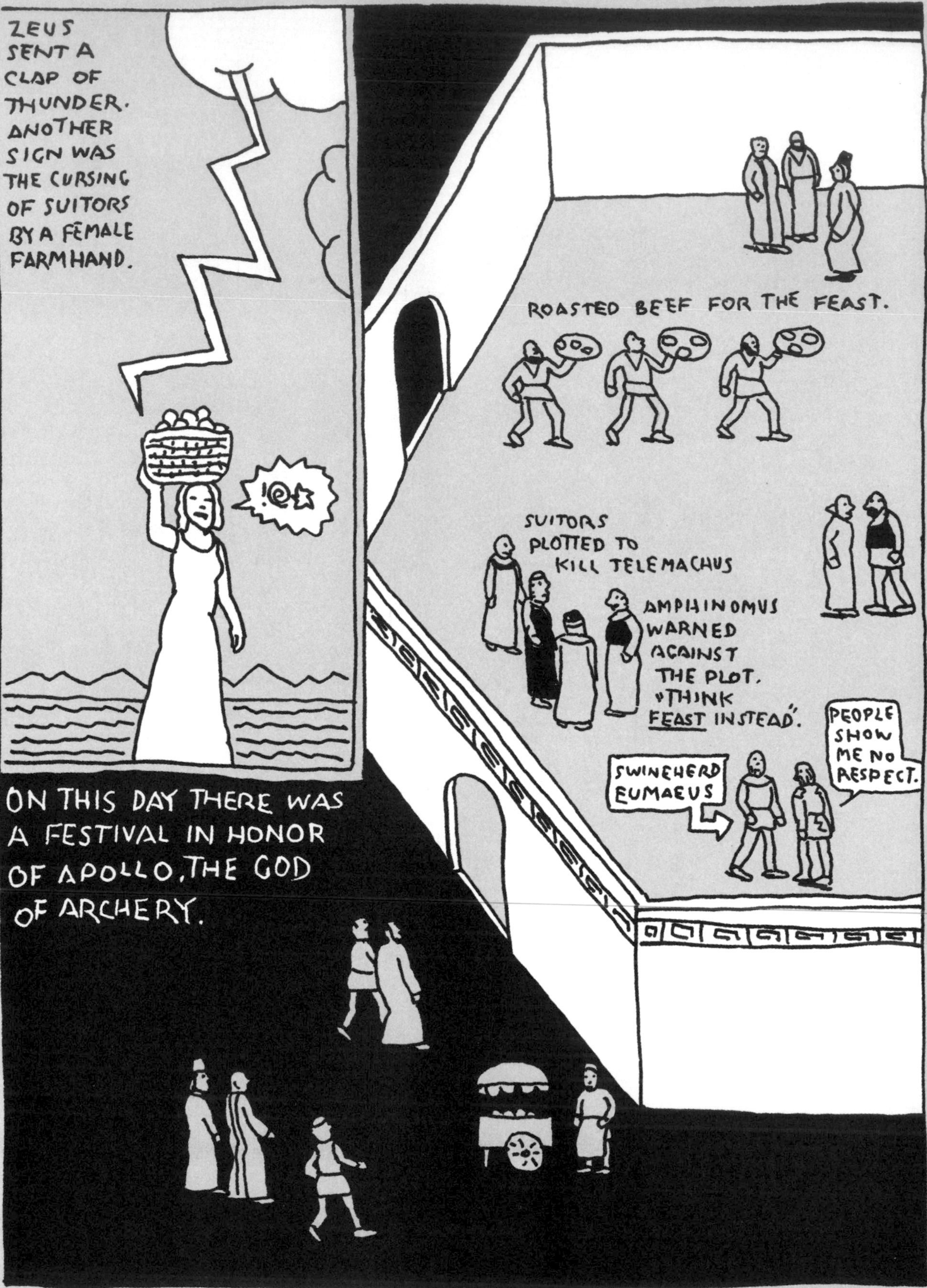
ZEUS SENT A CLAP OF THUNDER. ANOTHER SIGN WAS THE CURSING OF SUITORS BY A FEMALE FARMHAND.
!@*
ROASTED BEEF FOR THE FEAST.
SUITORS PLOTTED TO KILL TELEMACHUS
AMPHINOMUS WARNED AGAINST THE PLOT. "THINK FEAST INSTEAD".
PEOPLE SHOW ME NO RESPECT.
SWINEHERD EUMAEUS
ON THIS DAY THERE WAS A FESTIVAL IN HONOR OF APOLLO, THE GOD OF ARCHERY.

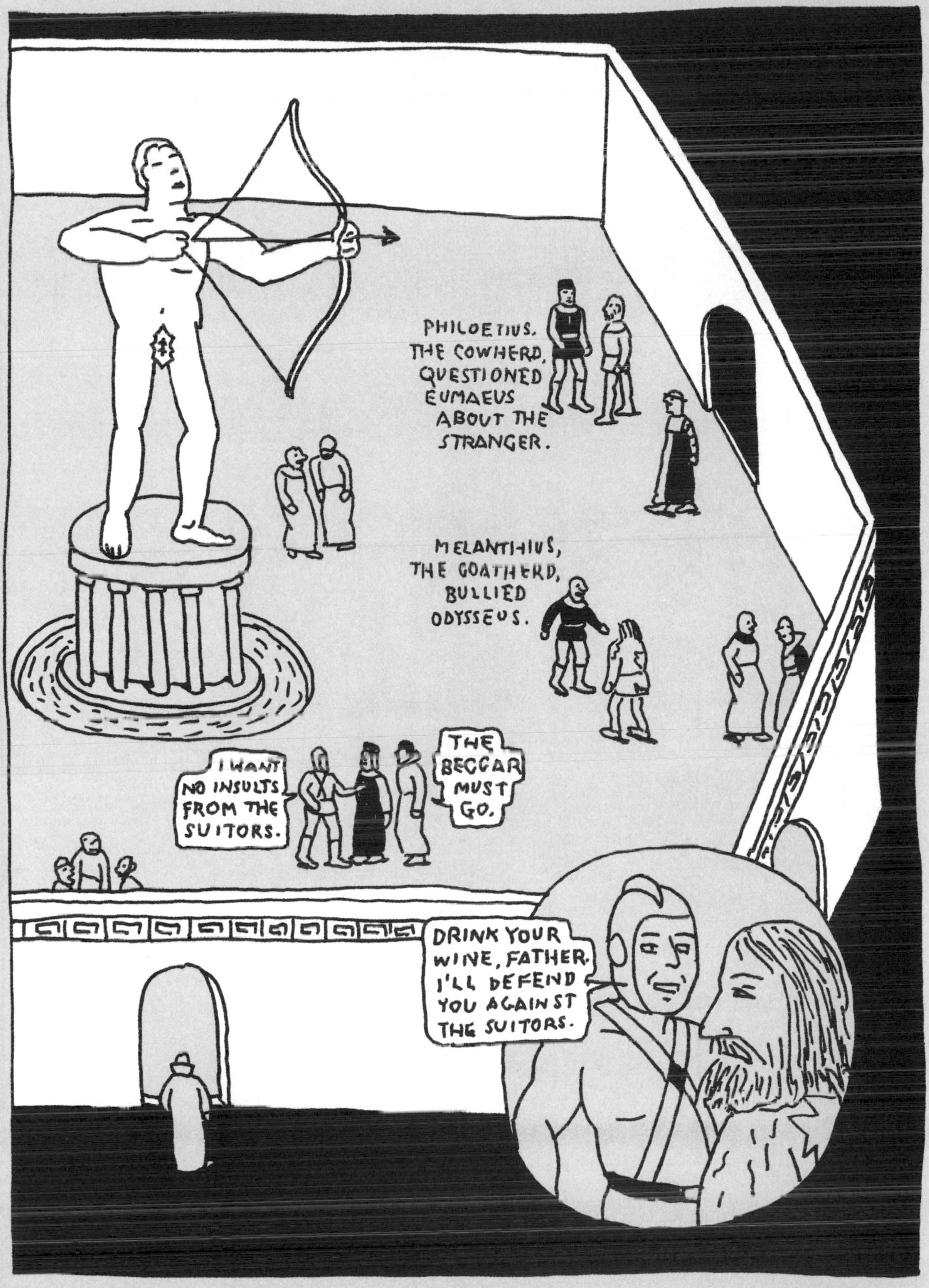
PHILOETIUS, THE COWHERD, QUESTIONED EUMAEUS ABOUT THE STRANGER.
MELANTHIUS, THE GOATHERD, BULLIED ODYSSEUS.
I WANT NO INSULTS FROM THE SUITORS.
THE BEGGAR MUST GO.
DRINK YOUR WINE, FATHER. I'LL DEFEND YOU AGAINST THE SUITORS.

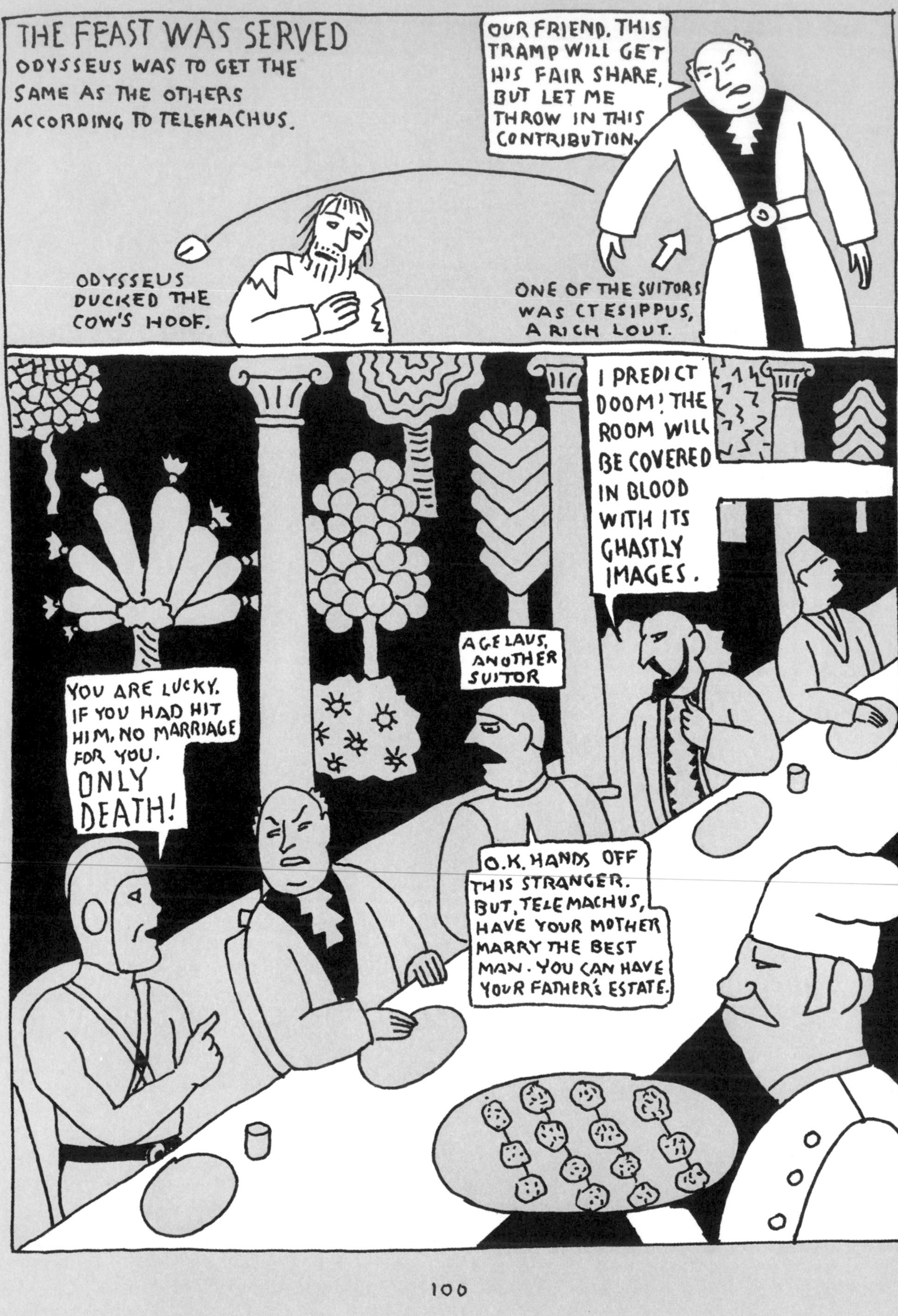
THE FEAST WAS SERVED
ODYSSEUS WAS TO GET THE SAME AS THE OTHERS ACCORDING TO TELEMACHUS.
OUR FRIEND, THIS TRAMP WILL GET HIS FAIR SHARE, BUT LET ME THROW IN THIS CONTRIBUTION.
ODYSSEUS DUCKED THE COW'S HOOF.
ONE OF THE SUITORS WAS CTESIPPUS, A RICH LOUT.
I PREDICT DOOM! THE ROOM WILL BE COVERED IN BLOOD WITH ITS GHASTLY IMAGES.
AGELAUS, ANOTHER SUITOR
YOU ARE LUCKY. IF YOU HAD HIT HIM, NO MARRIAGE FOR YOU. ONLY DEATH!
O.K. HANDS OFF THIS STRANGER. BUT, TELEMACHUS, HAVE YOUR MOTHER MARRY THE BEST MAN. YOU CAN HAVE YOUR FATHER'S ESTATE.

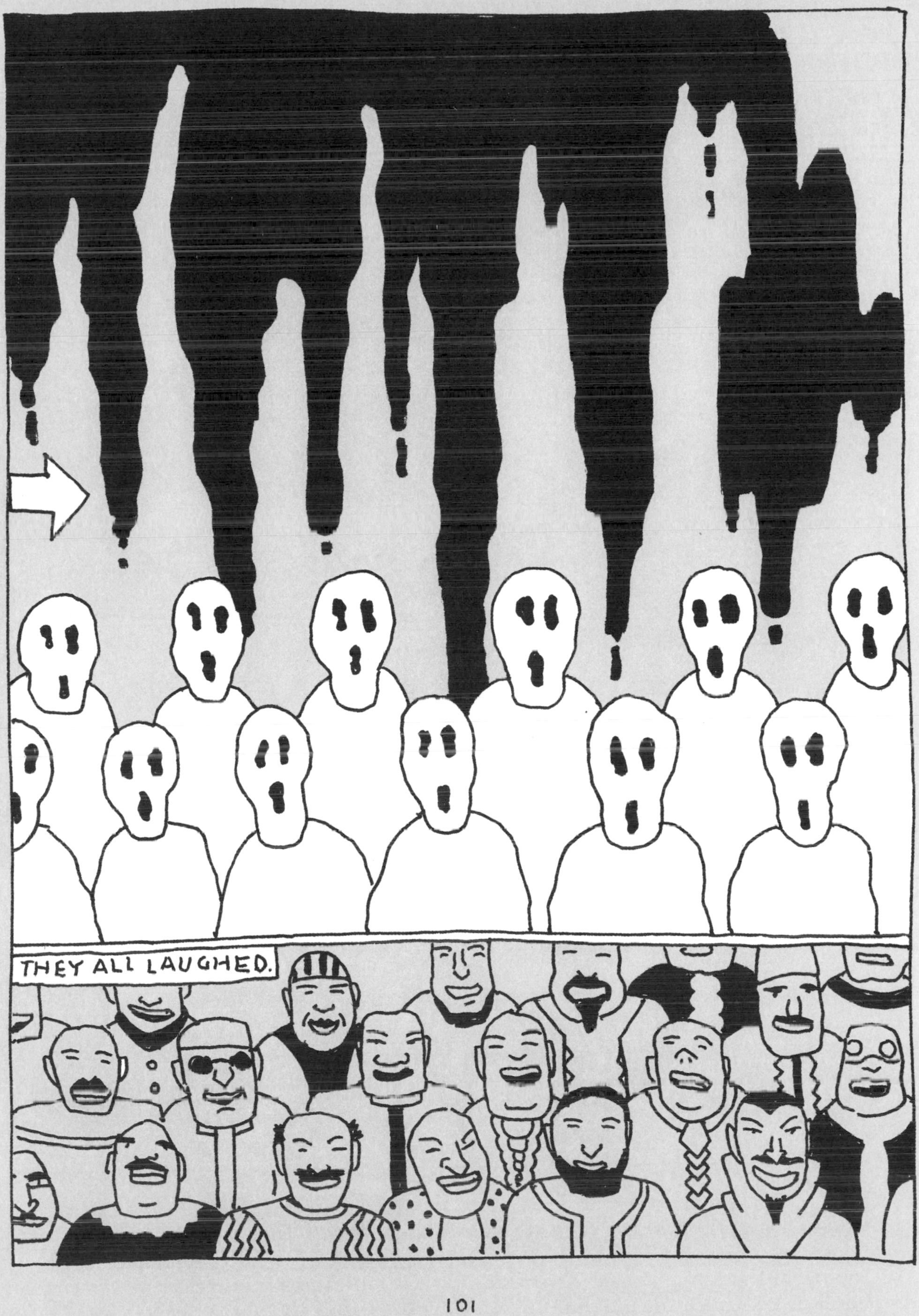
THEY ALL LAUGHED.

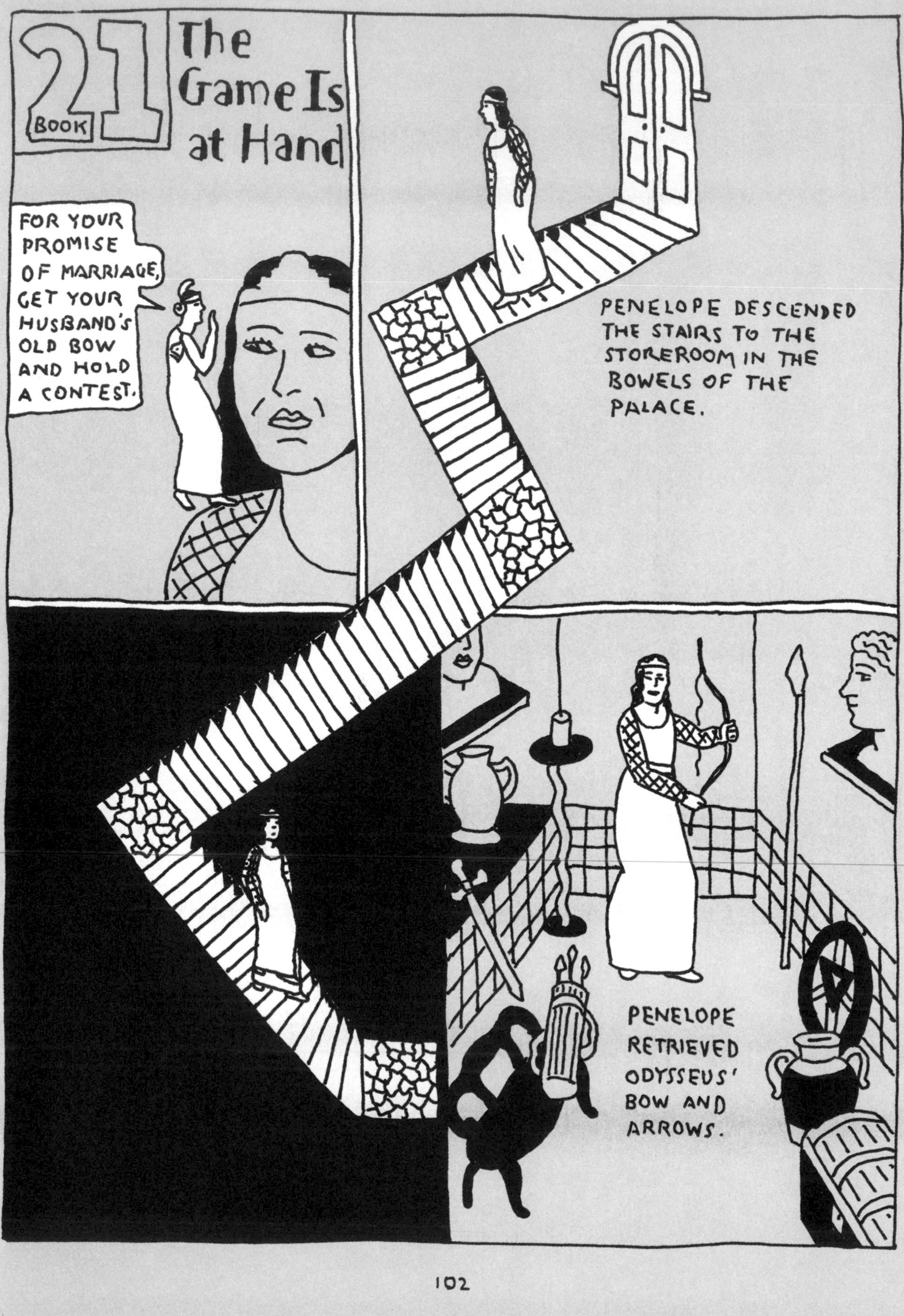
BOOK 21
The Game Is at Hand
FOR YOUR PROMISE OF MARRIAGE, GET YOUR HUSBAND'S OLD BOW AND HOLD A CONTEST.
PENELOPE DESCENDED THE STAIRS TO THE STOREROOM IN THE BOWELS OF THE PALACE.
PENELOPE RETRIEVED ODYSSEUS' BOW AND ARROWS.

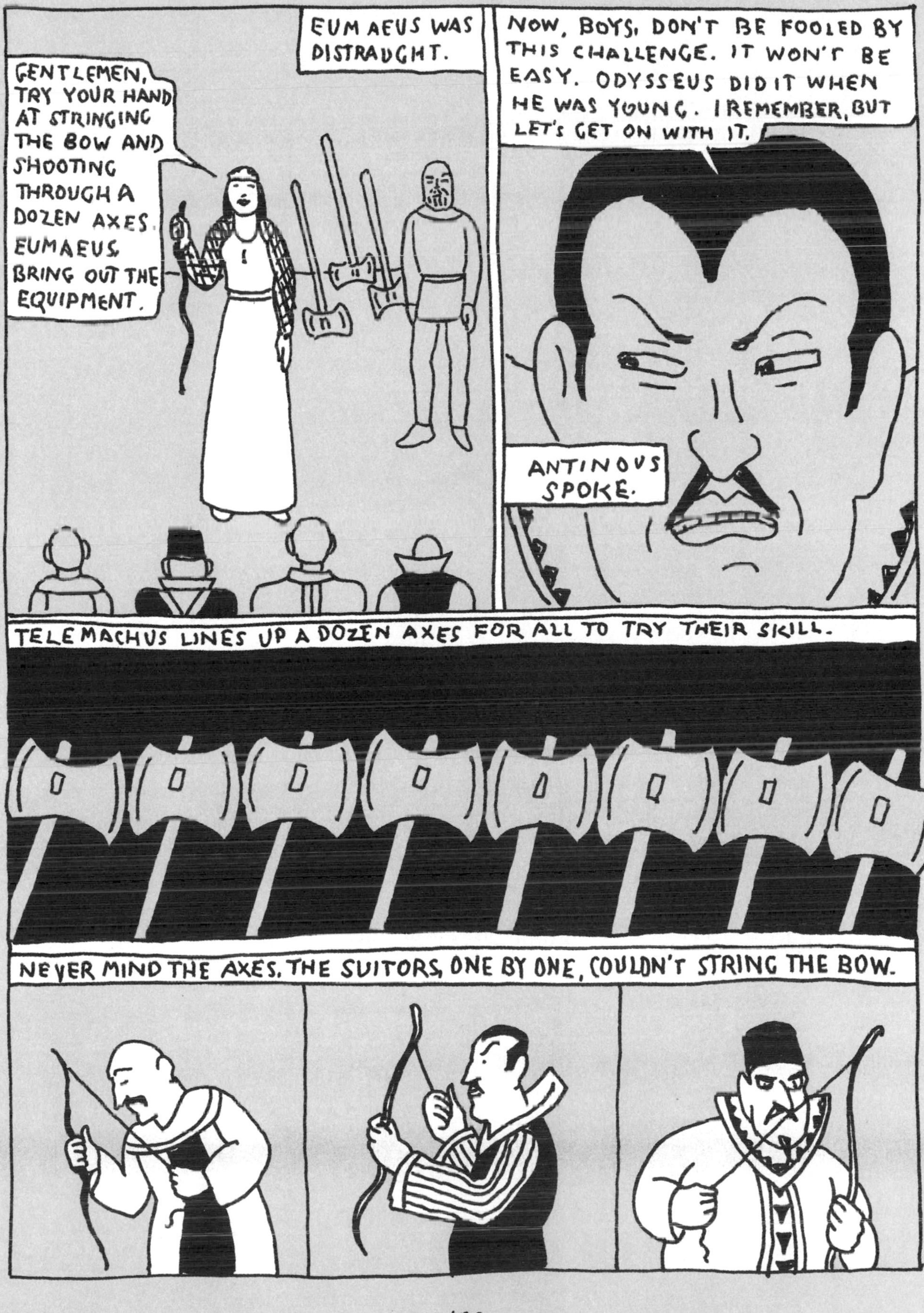
GENTLEMEN, TRY YOUR HAND AT STRINGING THE BOW AND SHOOTING THROUGH A DOZEN AXES. EUMAEUS, BRING OUT THE EQUIPMENT.
EUMAEUS WAS DISTRAUGHT.
NOW, BOYS, DON'T BE FOOLED BY THIS CHALLENGE. IT WON'T BE EASY. ODYSSEUS DID IT WHEN HE WAS YOUNG. I REMEMBER, BUT LET'S GET ON WITH IT.
ANTINOUS SPOKE.
TELEMACHUS LINES UP A DOZEN AXES FOR ALL TO TRY THEIR SKILL.
NEVER MIND THE AXES. THE SUITORS, ONE BY ONE, COULDN'T STRING THE BOW.

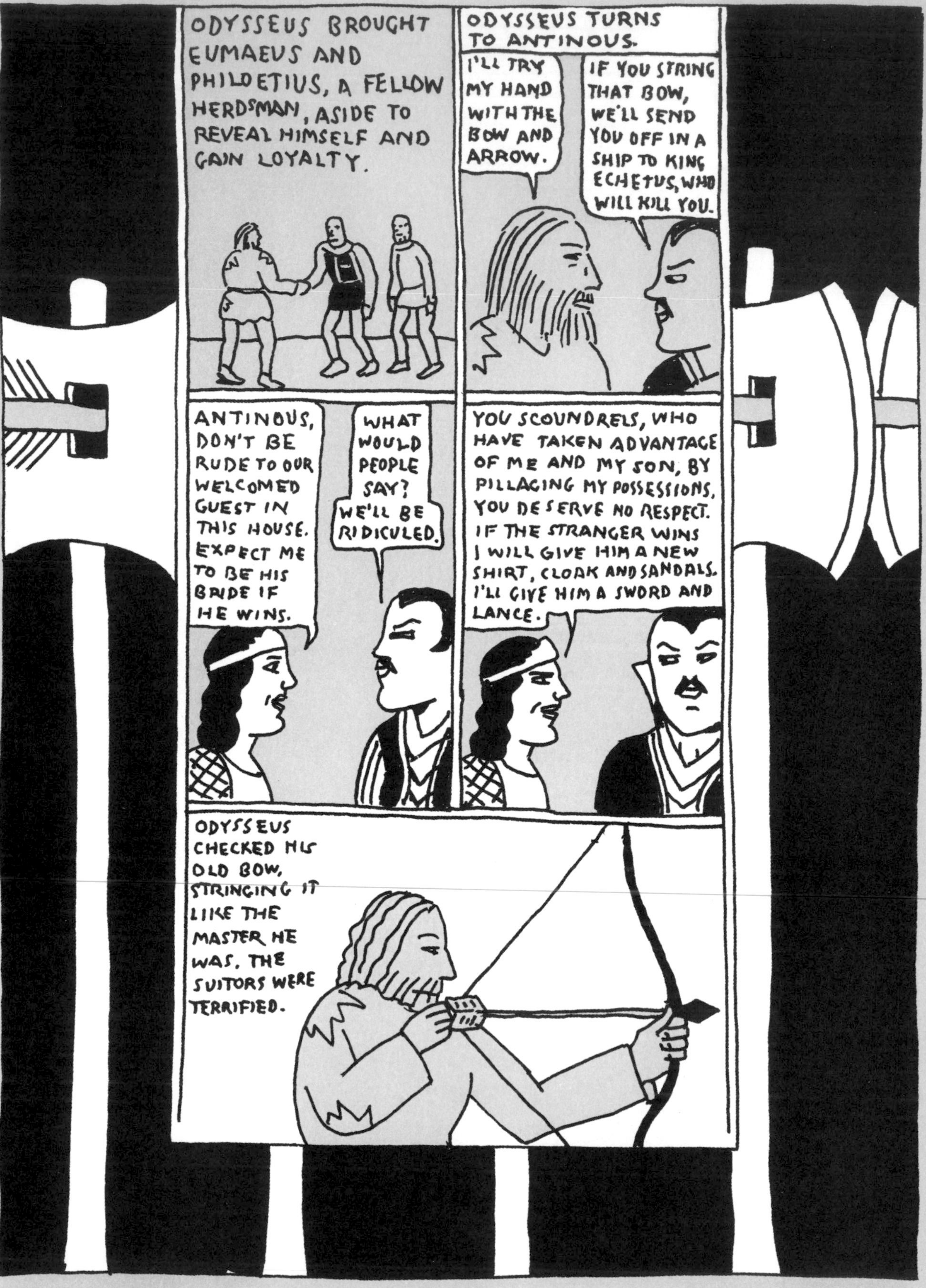
ODYSSEUS BROUGHT EUMAEUS AND PHILOETIUS, A FELLOW HERDSMAN, ASIDE TO REVEAL HIMSELF AND GAIN LOYALTY.
ODYSSEUS TURNS TO ANTINOUS.
I'LL TRY MY HAND WITH THE BOW AND ARROW.
IF YOU STRING THAT BOW, WE'LL SEND YOU OFF IN A SHIP TO KING ECHETUS, WHO WILL KILL YOU.
ANTINOUS, DON'T BE RUDE TO OUR WELCOMED GUEST IN THIS HOUSE. EXPECT ME TO BE HIS BRIDE IF HE WINS.
WHAT WOULD PEOPLE SAY? WE'LL BE RIDICULED.
YOU SCOUNDRELS, WHO HAVE TAKEN ADVANTAGE OF ME AND MY SON, BY PILLAGING MY POSSESSIONS, YOU DESERVE NO RESPECT. IF THE STRANGER WINS I WILL GIVE HIM A NEW SHIRT, CLOAK AND SANDALS. I'LL GIVE HIM A SWORD AND LANCE.
ODYSSEUS CHECKED HIS OLD BOW, STRINGING IT LIKE THE MASTER HE WAS. THE SUITORS WERE TERRIFIED.

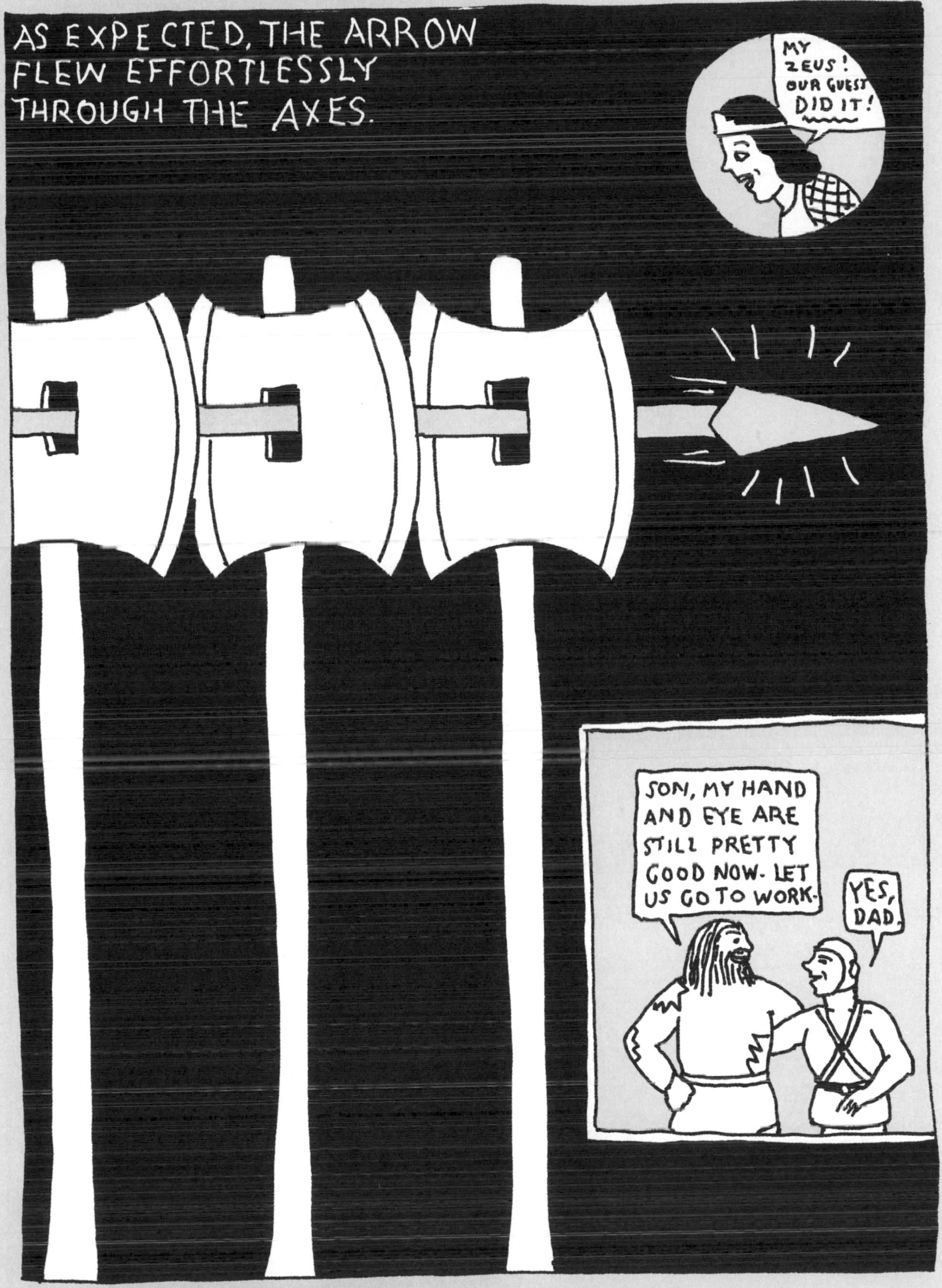
AS EXPECTED, THE ARROW FLEW EFFORTLESSLY THROUGH THE AXES.
MY ZEUS! OUR GUEST DID IT!
SON, MY HAND AND EYE ARE STILL PRETTY GOOD NOW. LET US GO TO WORK.
YES, DAD.

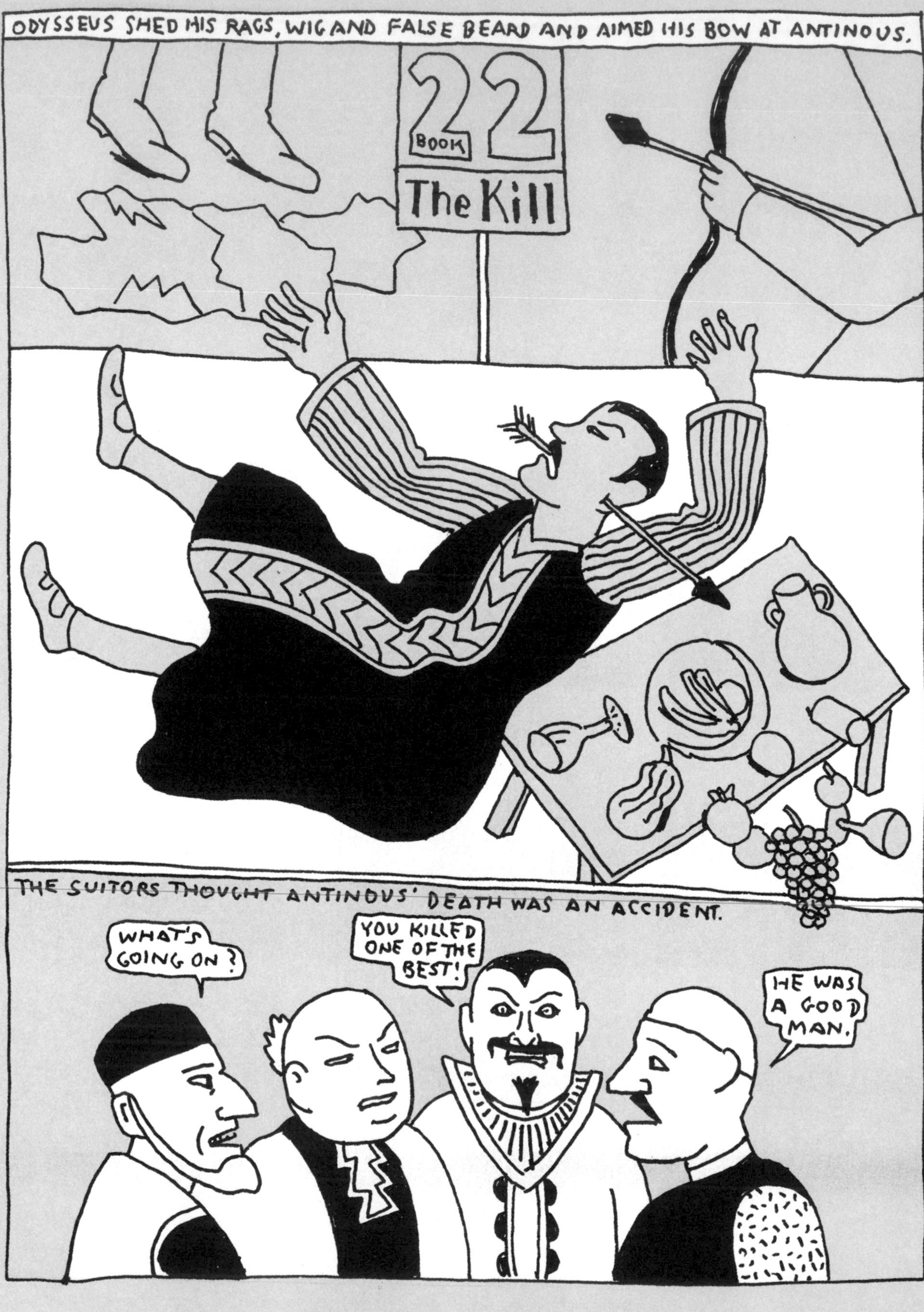

ODYSSEUS SHED HIS RAGS, WIG AND FALSE BEARD AND AIMED HIS BOW AT ANTINOUS.
22 BOOK
The Kill
THE SUITORS THOUGHT ANTINOUS' DEATH WAS AN ACCIDENT.
WHAT'S GOING ON?
YOU KILLED ONE OF THE BEST!
HE WAS A GOOD MAN.

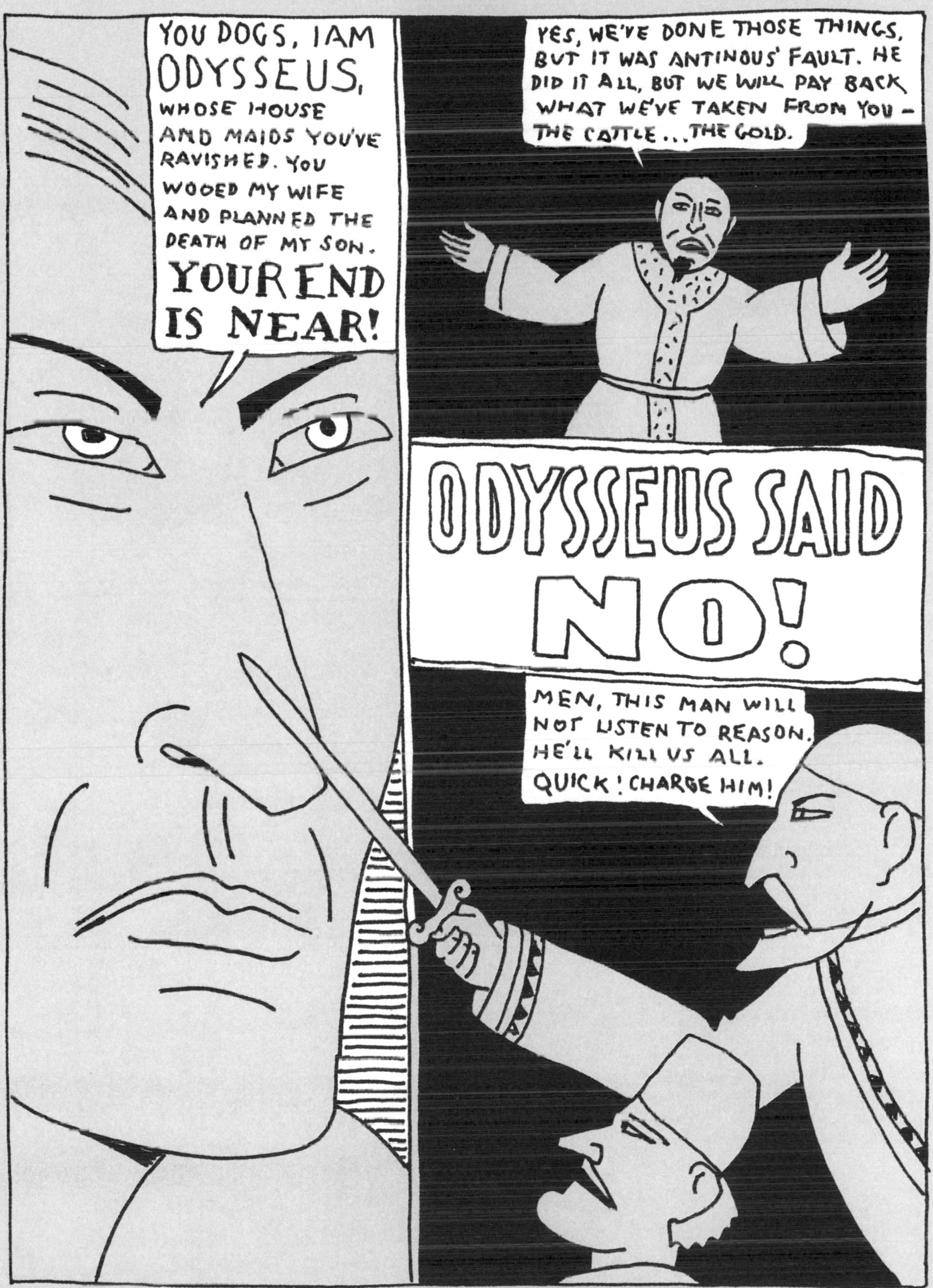
YOU DOGS, I AM ODYSSEUS, WHOSE HOUSE AND MAIDS YOU'VE RAVISHED. YOU WOOED MY WIFE AND PLANNED THE DEATH OF MY SON. YOUR END IS NEAR!
YES, WE'VE DONE THOSE THINGS, BUT IT WAS ANTINOUS' FAULT. HE DID IT ALL, BUT WE WILL PAY BACK WHAT WE'VE TAKEN FROM YOU – THE CATTLE . . . THE GOLD.
ODYSSEUS SAID NO!
MEN, THIS MAN WILL NOT LISTEN TO REASON. HE'LL KILL US ALL. QUICK! CHARGE HIM!

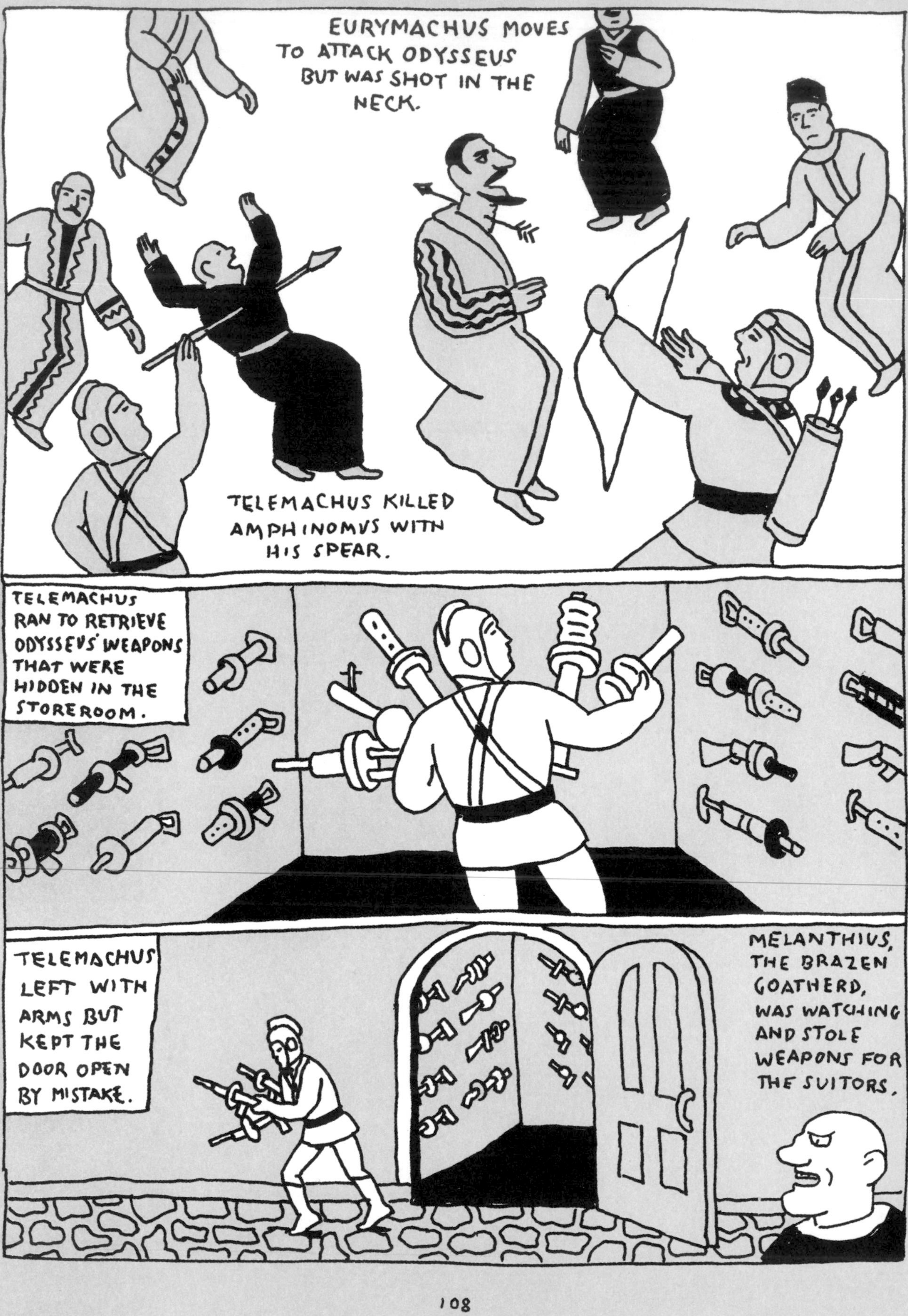
EURYMACHUS MOVES TO ATTACK ODYSSEUS BUT WAS SHOT IN THE NECK.
TELEMACHUS KILLED AMPHINOMUS WITH HIS SPEAR.
TELEMACHUS RAN TO RETRIEVE ODYSSEUS' WEAPONS THAT WERE HIDDEN IN THE STOREROOM.
TELEMACHUS LEFT WITH ARMS BUT KEPT THE DOOR OPEN BY MISTAKE.
MELANTHIUS, THE BRAZEN GOATHERD, WAS WATCHING AND STOLE WEAPONS FOR THE SUITORS.

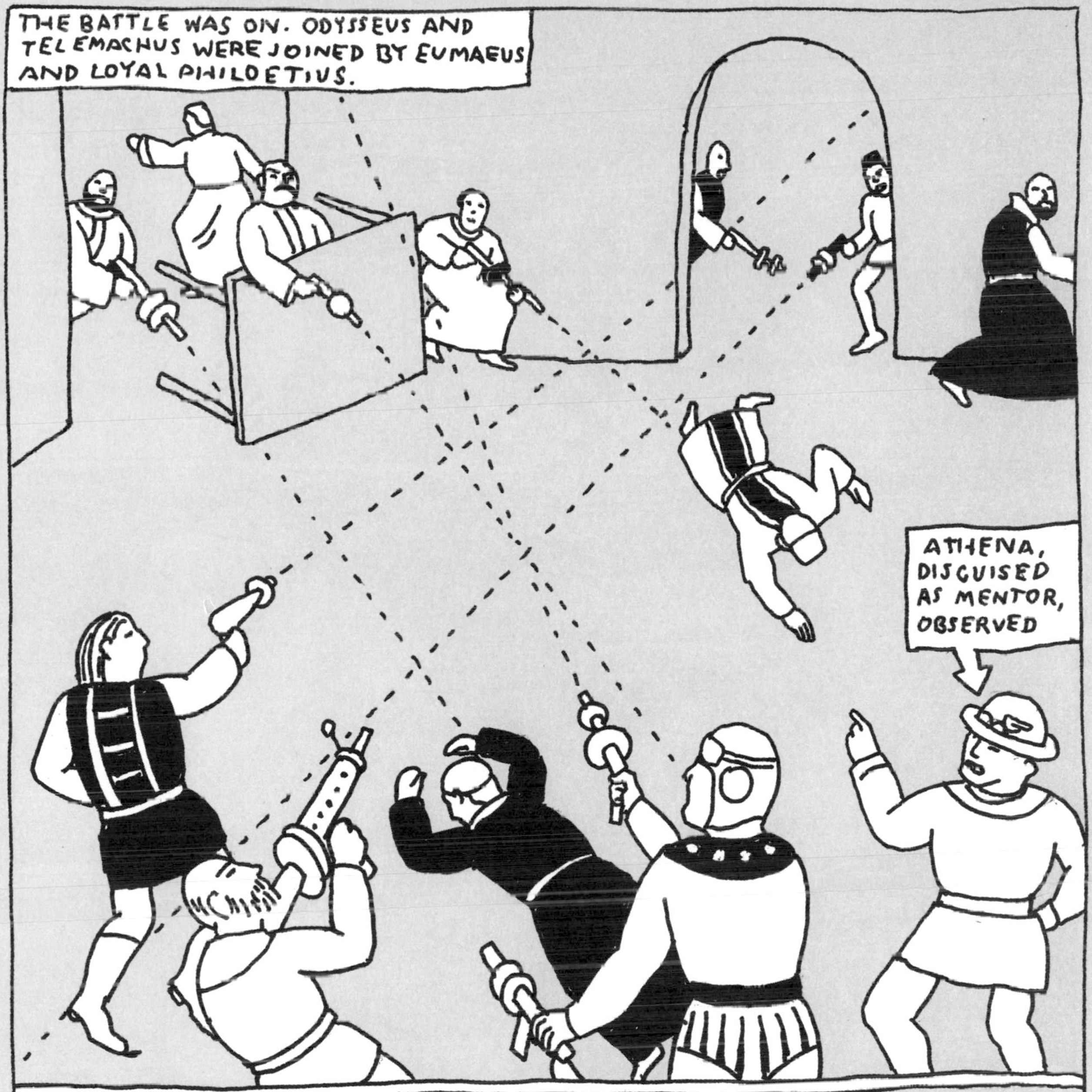
THE BATTLE WAS ON. ODYSSEUS AND TELEMACHUS WERE JOINED BY EUMAEUS AND LOYAL PHILOETIUS.
ATHENA, DISGUISED AS MENTOR, OBSERVED

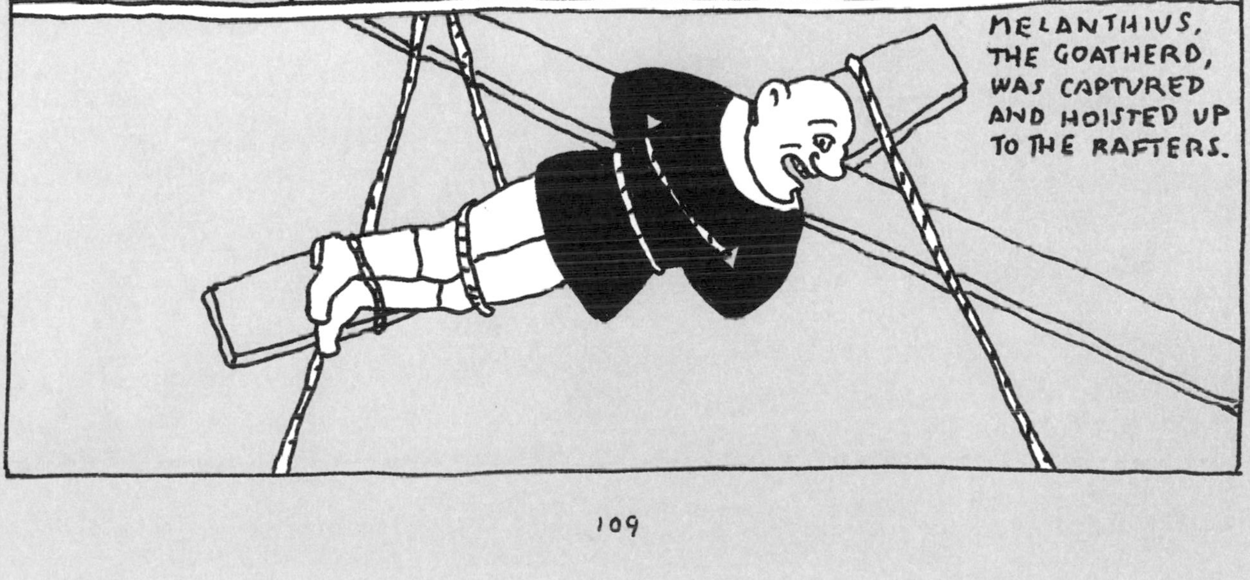
MELANTHIUS, THE GOATHERD, WAS CAPTURED AND HOISTED UP TO THE RAFTERS.

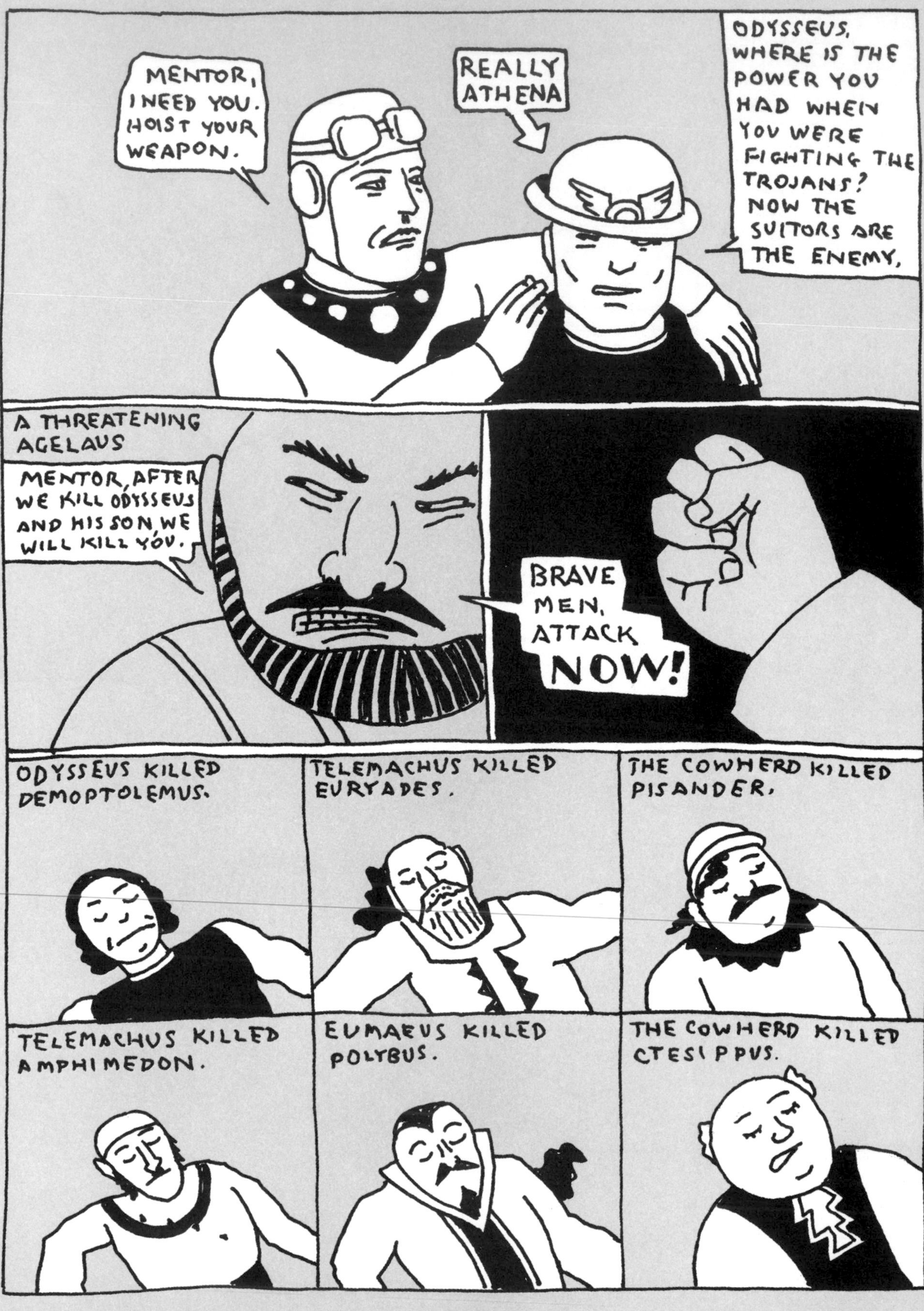
MENTOR, I NEED YOU. HOIST YOUR WEAPON.
REALLY ATHENA
ODYSSEUS, WHERE IS THE POWER YOU HAD WHEN YOU WERE FIGHTING THE TROJANS? NOW THE SUITORS ARE THE ENEMY.
A THREATENING AGELAUS
MENTOR, AFTER WE KILL ODYSSEUS AND HIS SON, WE WILL KILL YOU.
BRAVE MEN, ATTACK NOW!
ODYSSEUS KILLED DEMOPTOLEMUS.
TELEMACHUS KILLED EURYADES.
THE COWHERD KILLED PISANDER.
TELEMACHUS KILLED AMPHIMEDON.
EUMAEUS KILLED POLYBUS.
THE COWHERD KILLED CTESIPPUS.

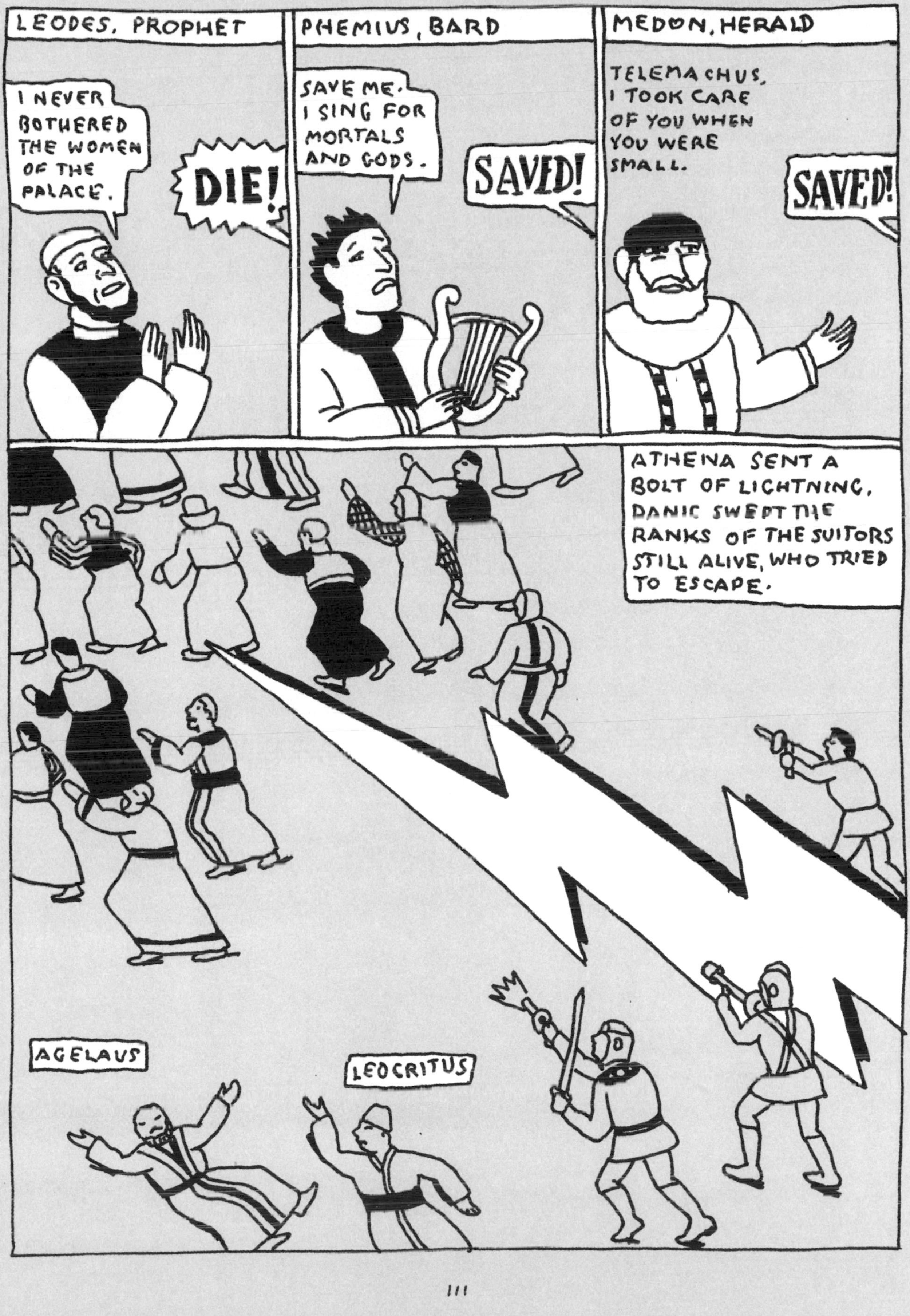
LEODES, PROPHET
I NEVER BOTHERED THE WOMEN OF THE PALACE.
DIE!
PHEMIUS, BARD
SAVE ME. I SING FOR MORTALS AND GODS.
SAVED!
MEDON, HERALD
TELEMACHUS, I TOOK CARE OF YOU WHEN YOU WERE SMALL.
SAVED!
ATHENA SENT A BOLT OF LIGHTNING. PANIC SWEPT THE RANKS OF THE SUITORS STILL ALIVE, WHO TRIED TO ESCAPE.
AGELAUS
LEOCRITUS

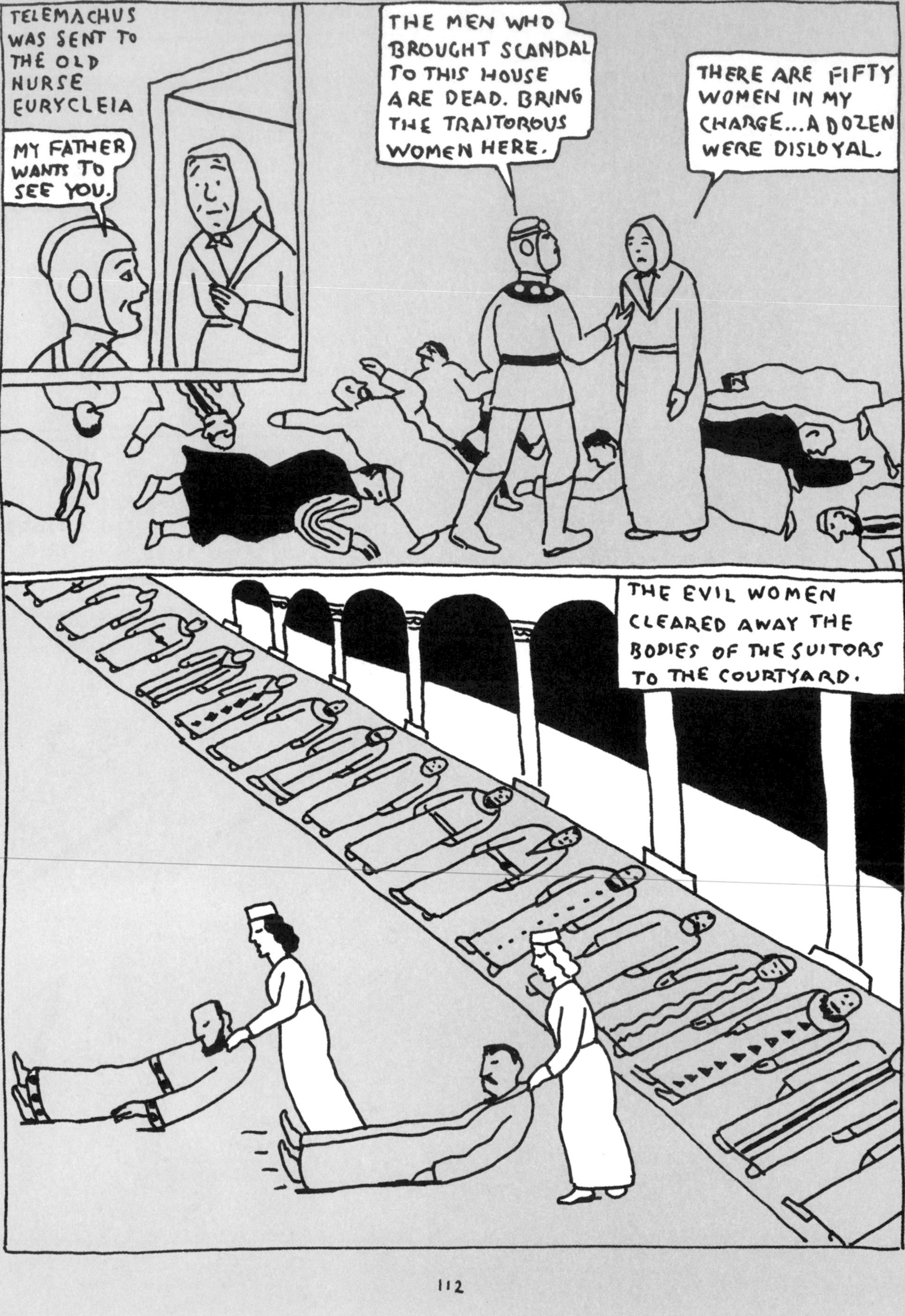
TELEMACHUS WAS SENT TO THE OLD NURSE EURYCLEIA
MY FATHER WANTS TO SEE YOU.
THE MEN WHO BROUGHT SCANDAL TO THIS HOUSE ARE DEAD. BRING THE TRAITOROUS WOMEN HERE.
THERE ARE FIFTY WOMEN IN MY CHARGE...A DOZEN WERE DISLOYAL.
THE EVIL WOMEN CLEARED AWAY THE BODIES OF THE SUITORS TO THE COURTYARD.

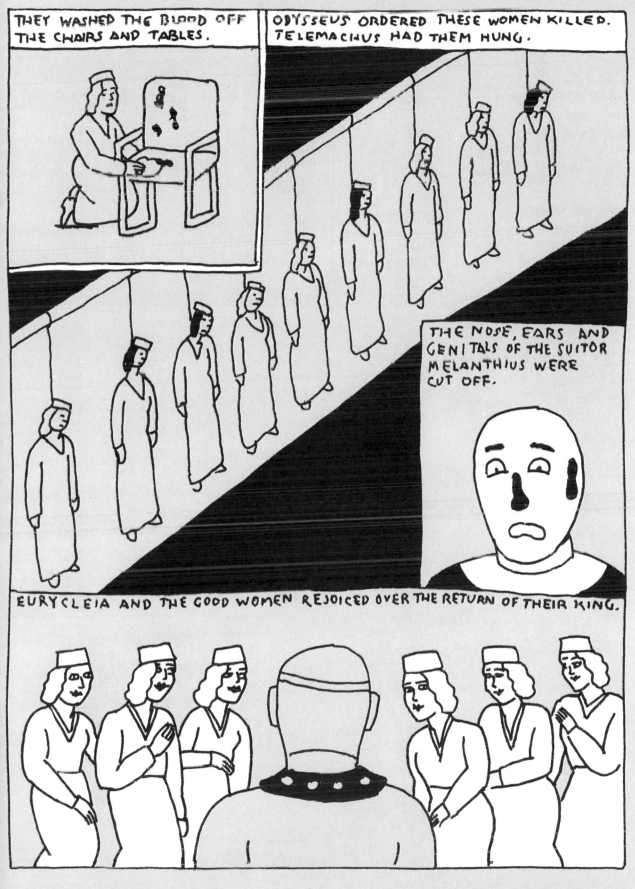

THEY WASHED THE BLOOD OFF THE CHAIRS AND TABLES.

ODYSSEUS ORDERED THESE WOMEN KILLED. TELEMACHUS HAD THEM HUNG.

THE NOSE, EARS AND GENITALS OF THE SUITOR MELANTHIUS WERE CUT OFF.

EURYCLEIA AND THE GOOD WOMEN REJOICED OVER THE RETURN OF THEIR KING.

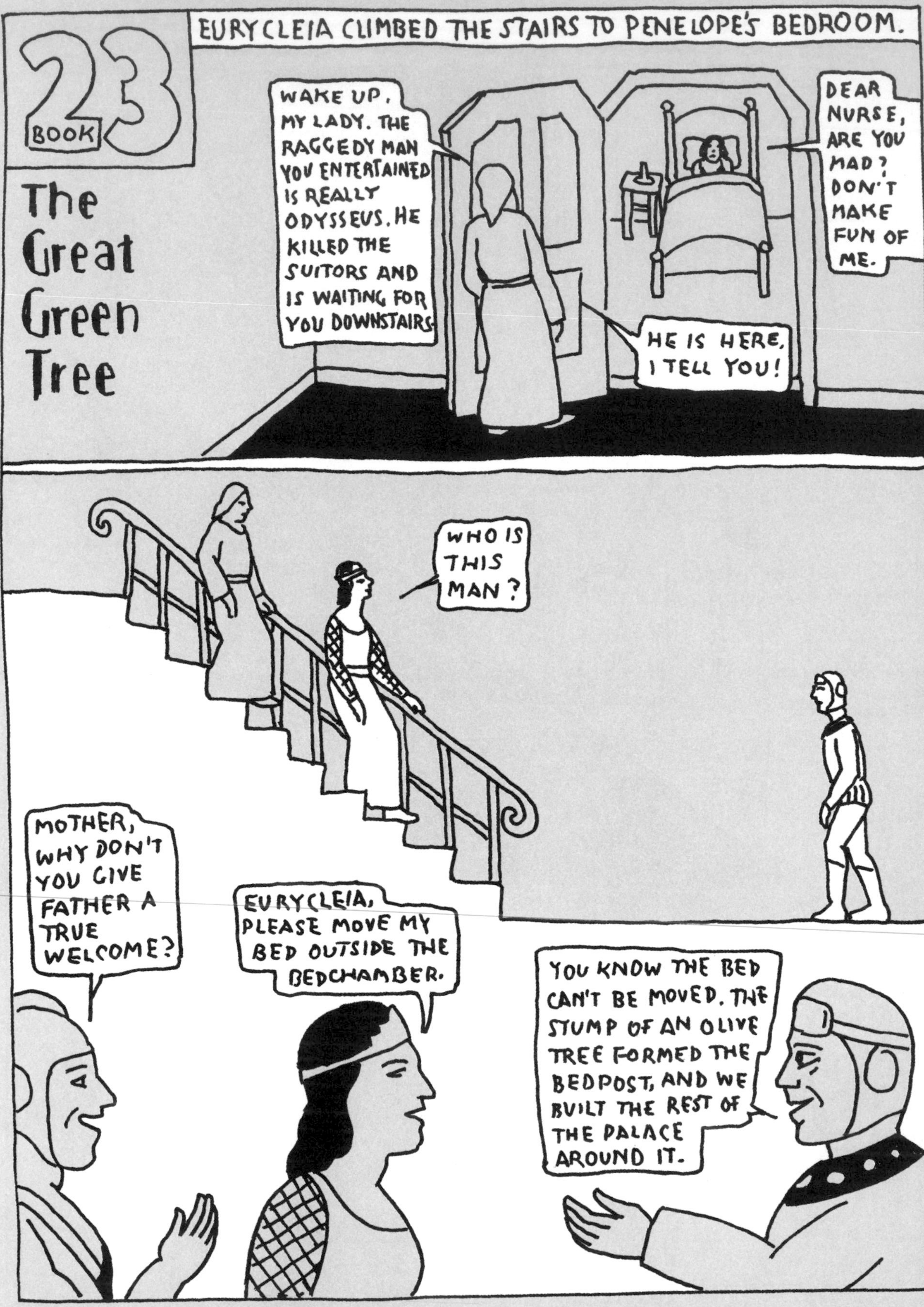
EURYCLEIA CLIMBED THE STAIRS TO PENELOPE'S BEDROOM.
23 BOOK
The Great Green Tree
WAKE UP, MY LADY. THE RAGGEDY MAN YOU ENTERTAINED IS REALLY ODYSSEUS. HE KILLED THE SUITORS AND IS WAITING FOR YOU DOWNSTAIRS.
DEAR NURSE, ARE YOU MAD? DON'T MAKE FUN OF ME.
HE IS HERE, I TELL YOU!
WHO IS THIS MAN?
MOTHER, WHY DON'T YOU GIVE FATHER A TRUE WELCOME?
EURYCLEIA, PLEASE MOVE MY BED OUTSIDE THE BEDCHAMBER.
YOU KNOW THE BED CAN'T BE MOVED. THE STUMP OF AN OLIVE TREE FORMED THE BEDPOST, AND WE BUILT THE REST OF THE PALACE AROUND IT.

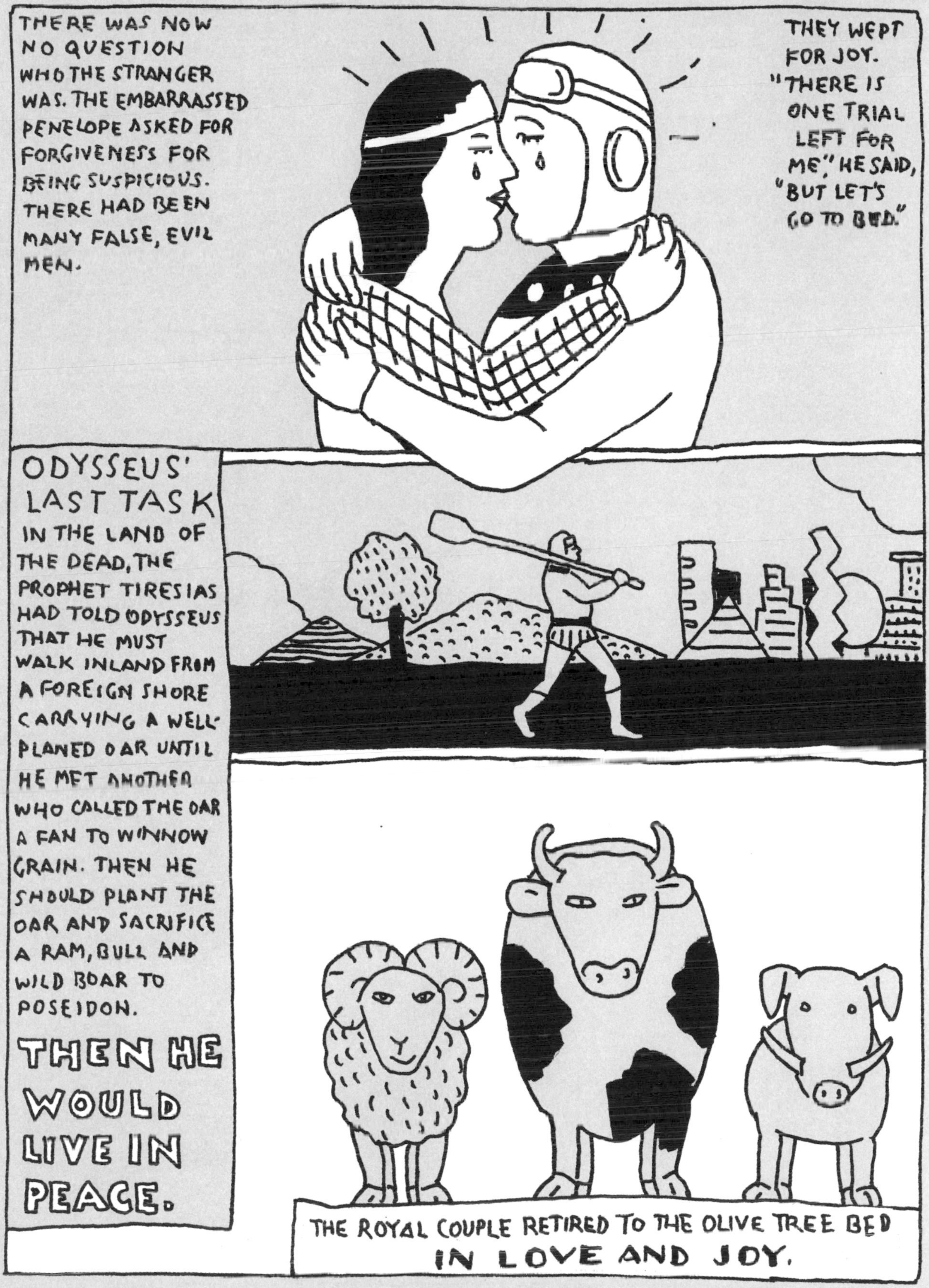
THERE WAS NOW NO QUESTION WHO THE STRANGER WAS. THE EMBARRASSED PENELOPE ASKED FOR FORGIVENESS FOR BEING SUSPICIOUS. THERE HAD BEEN MANY FALSE, EVIL MEN.
THEY WEPT FOR JOY. "THERE IS ONE TRIAL LEFT FOR ME," HE SAID, "BUT LET'S GO TO BED."
ODYSSEUS' LAST TASK
IN THE LAND OF THE DEAD, THE PROPHET TIRESIAS HAD TOLD ODYSSEUS THAT HE MUST WALK INLAND FROM A FOREIGN SHORE CARRYING A WELL-PLANED OAR UNTIL HE MET ANOTHER WHO CALLED THE OAR A FAN TO WINNOW GRAIN. THEN HE SHOULD PLANT THE OAR AND SACRIFICE A RAM, BULL AND WILD BOAR TO POSEIDON.
THEN HE WOULD LIVE IN PEACE.
THE ROYAL COUPLE RETIRED TO THE OLIVE TREE BED IN LOVE AND JOY.

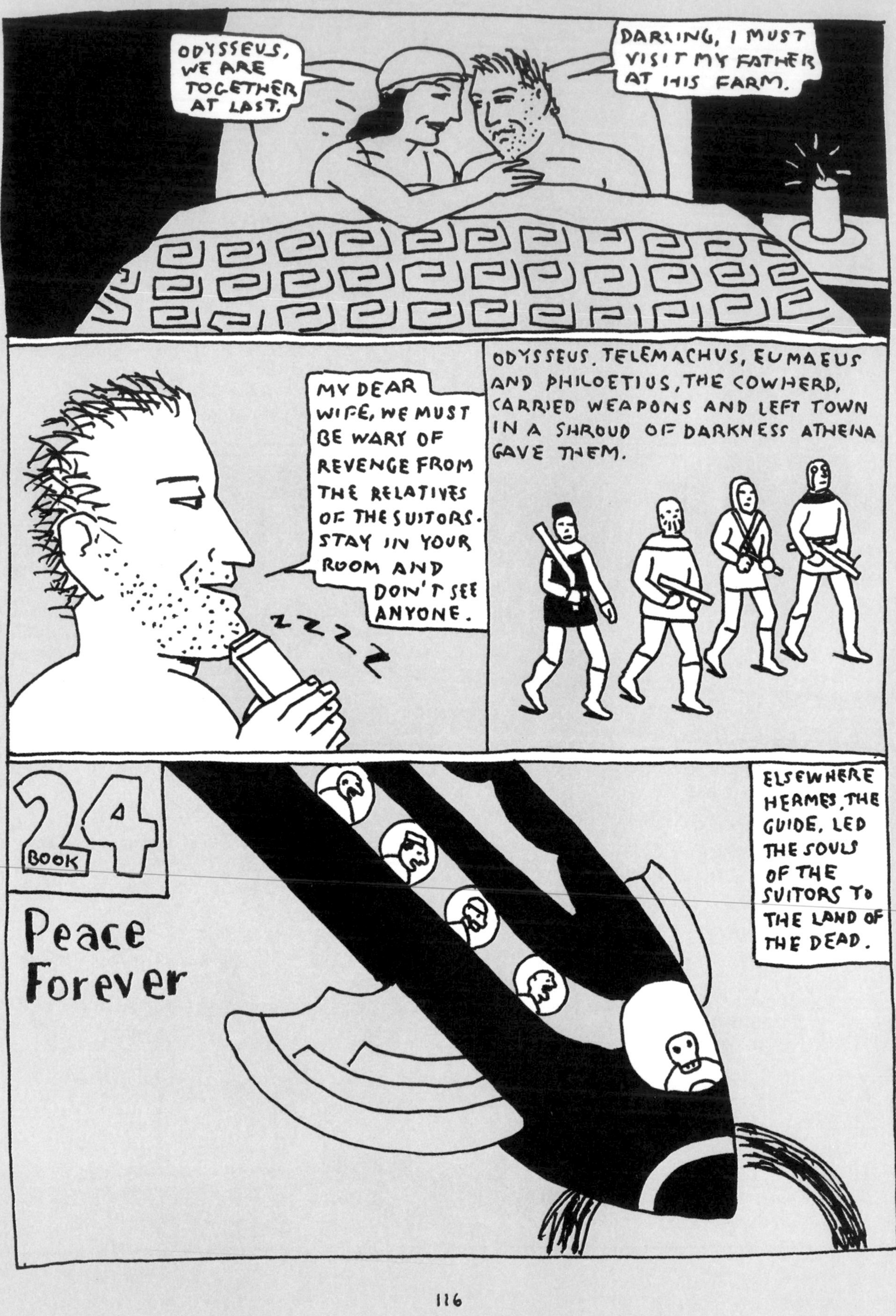
ODYSSEUS, WE ARE TOGETHER AT LAST.
DARLING, I MUST VISIT MY FATHER AT HIS FARM.
MY DEAR WIFE, WE MUST BE WARY OF REVENGE FROM THE RELATIVES OF THE SUITORS. STAY IN YOUR ROOM AND DON'T SEE ANYONE.
ZZZZ
ODYSSEUS, TELEMACHUS, EUMAEUS AND PHILOETIUS, THE COWHERD, CARRIED WEAPONS AND LEFT TOWN IN A SHROUD OF DARKNESS ATHENA GAVE THEM.
BOOK 24
Peace Forever
ELSEWHERE HERMES, THE GUIDE, LED THE SOULS OF THE SUITORS TO THE LAND OF THE DEAD.

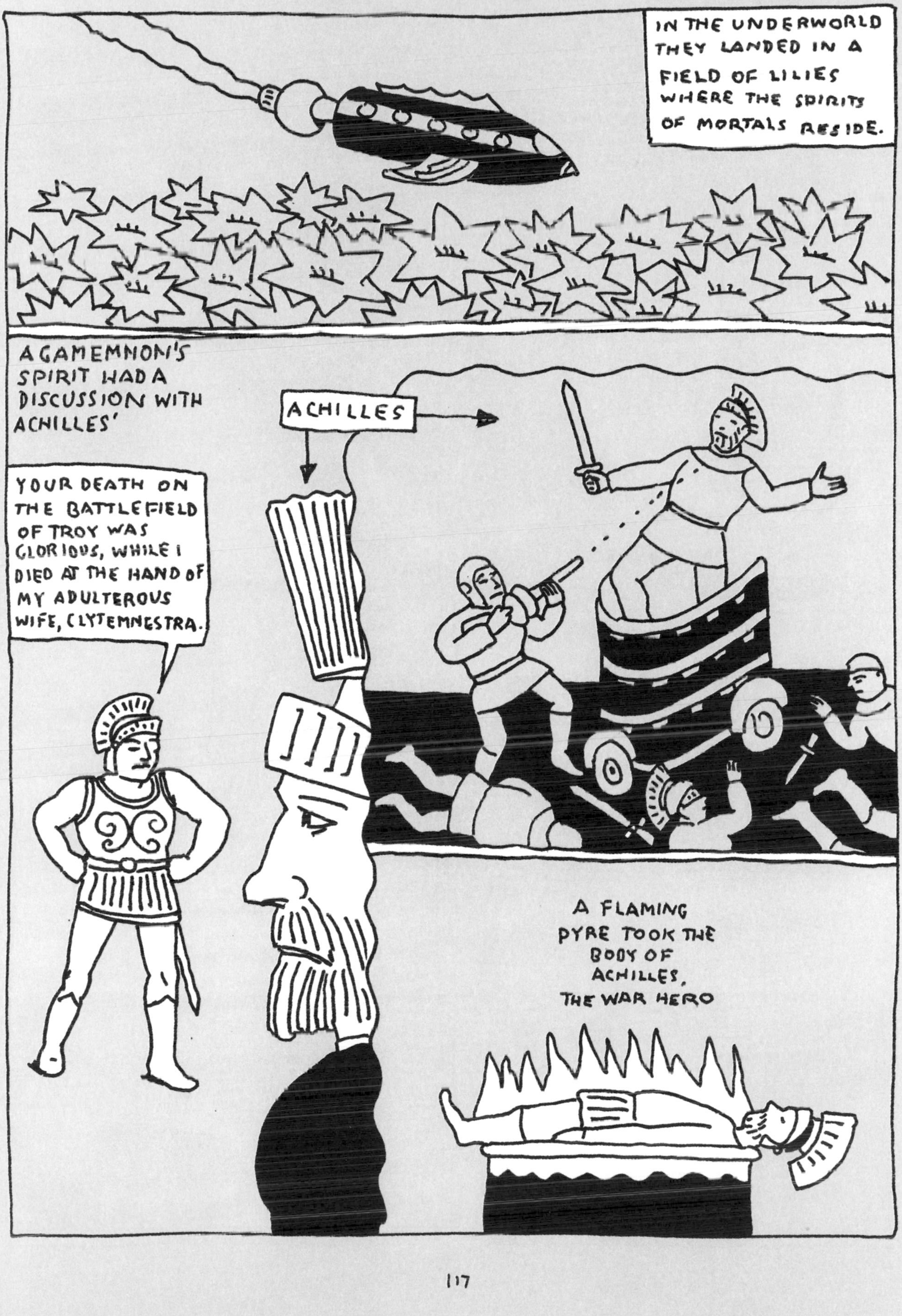
IN THE UNDERWORLD THEY LANDED IN A FIELD OF LILIES WHERE THE SPIRITS OF MORTALS RESIDE.
AGAMEMNON'S SPIRIT HAD A DISCUSSION WITH ACHILLES'
ACHILLES
YOUR DEATH ON THE BATTLEFIELD OF TROY WAS GLORIOUS, WHILE I DIED AT THE HAND OF MY ADULTEROUS WIFE, CLYTEMNESTRA.
A FLAMING PYRE TOOK THE BODY OF ACHILLES, THE WAR HERO

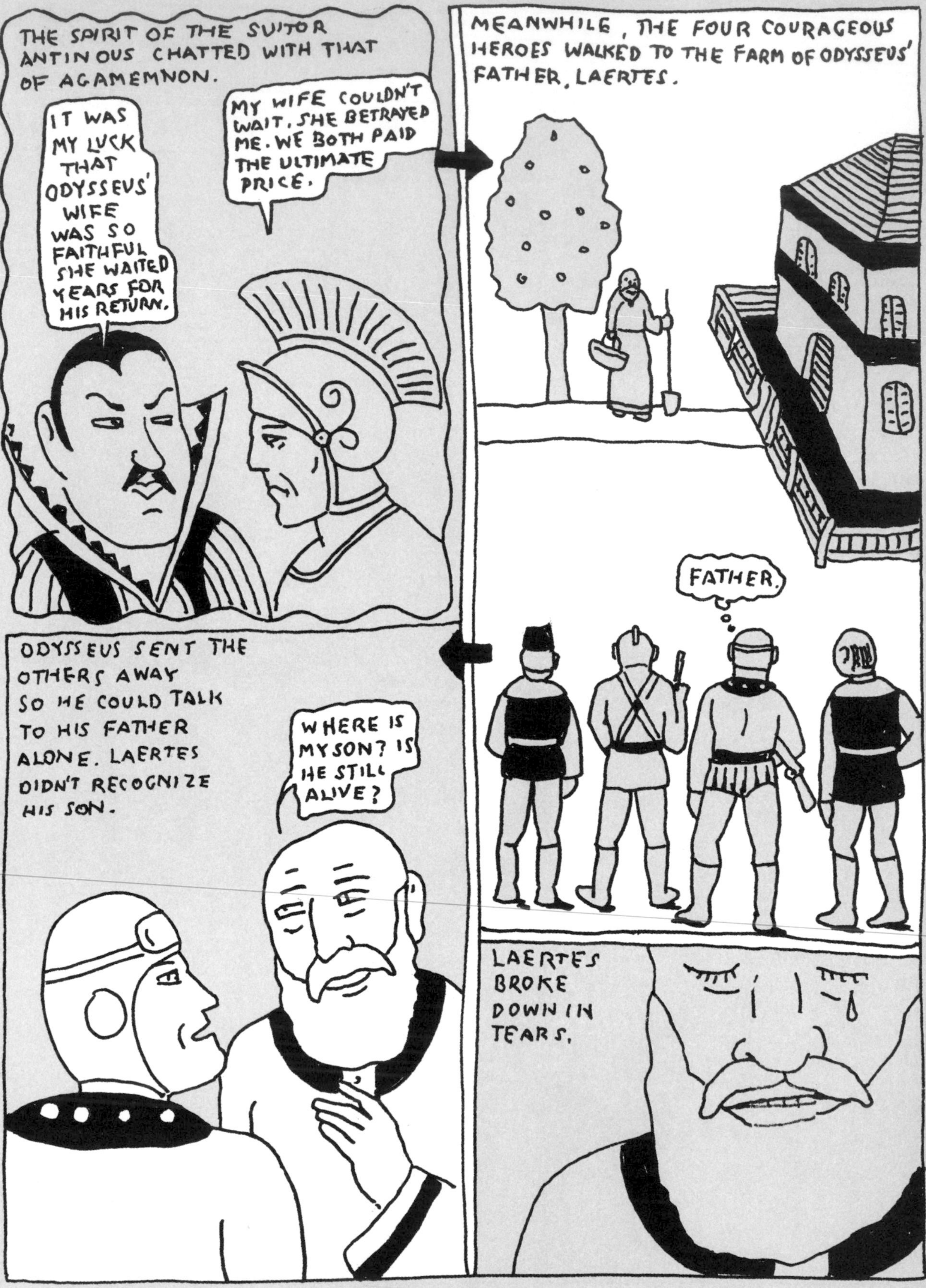
THE SPIRIT OF THE SUITOR ANTINOUS CHATTED WITH THAT OF AGAMEMNON.
IT WAS MY LUCK THAT ODYSSEUS' WIFE WAS SO FAITHFUL SHE WAITED YEARS FOR HIS RETURN.
MY WIFE COULDN'T WAIT. SHE BETRAYED ME. WE BOTH PAID THE ULTIMATE PRICE.
MEANWHILE, THE FOUR COURAGEOUS HEROES WALKED TO THE FARM OF ODYSSEUS' FATHER, LAERTES.
FATHER.
ODYSSEUS SENT THE OTHERS AWAY SO HE COULD TALK TO HIS FATHER ALONE. LAERTES DIDN'T RECOGNIZE HIS SON.
WHERE IS MY SON? IS HE STILL ALIVE?
LAERTES BROKE DOWN IN TEARS.

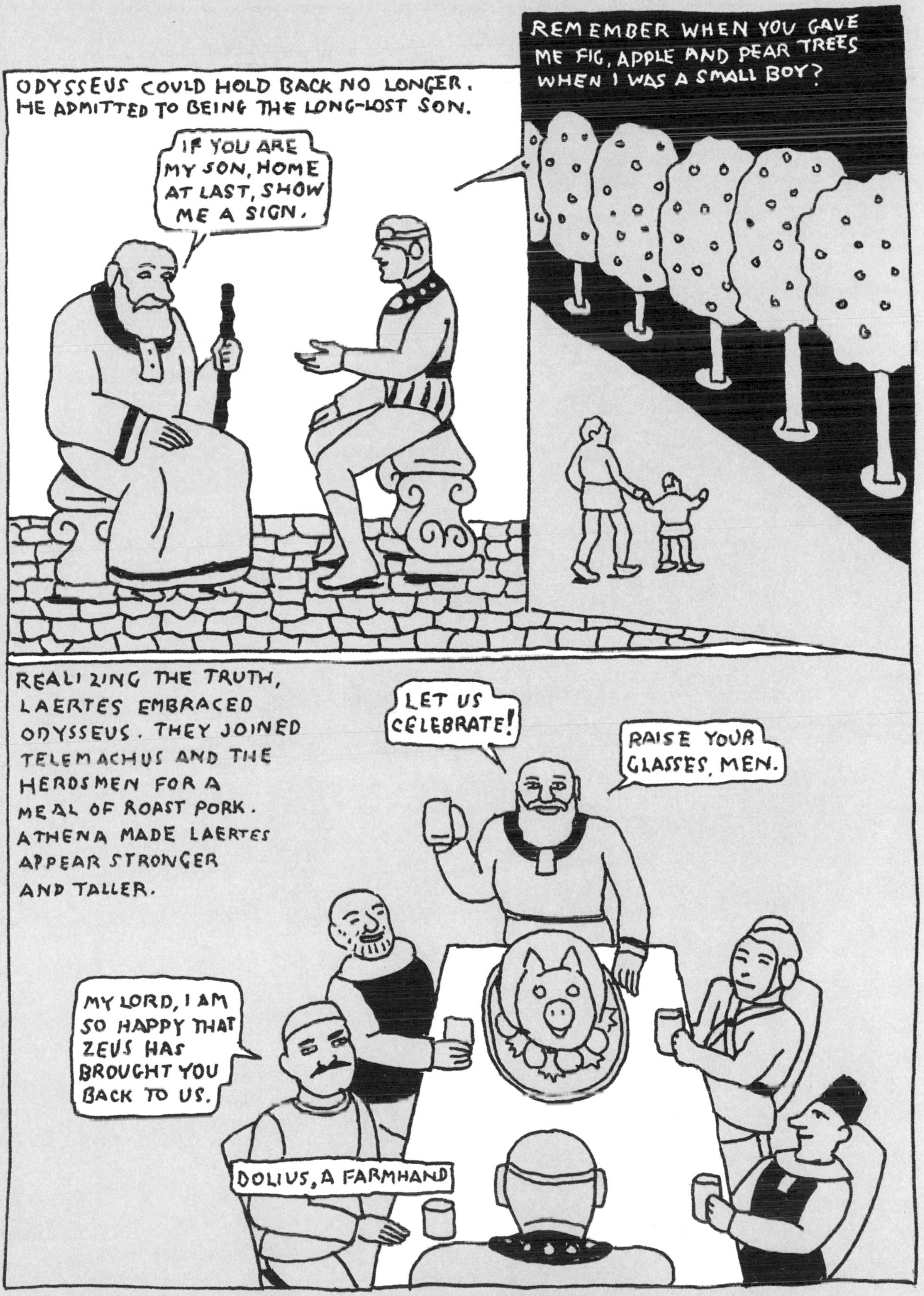
ODYSSEUS COULD HOLD BACK NO LONGER. HE ADMITTED TO BEING THE LONG-LOST SON.
IF YOU ARE MY SON, HOME AT LAST, SHOW ME A SIGN.
REMEMBER WHEN YOU GAVE ME FIG, APPLE AND PEAR TREES WHEN I WAS A SMALL BOY?
REALIZING THE TRUTH, LAERTES EMBRACED ODYSSEUS. THEY JOINED TELEMACHUS AND THE HERDSMEN FOR A MEAL OF ROAST PORK. ATHENA MADE LAERTES APPEAR STRONGER AND TALLER.
LET US CELEBRATE!
RAISE YOUR GLASSES, MEN.
MY LORD, I AM SO HAPPY THAT ZEUS HAS BROUGHT YOU BACK TO US.
DOLIUS, A FARMHAND

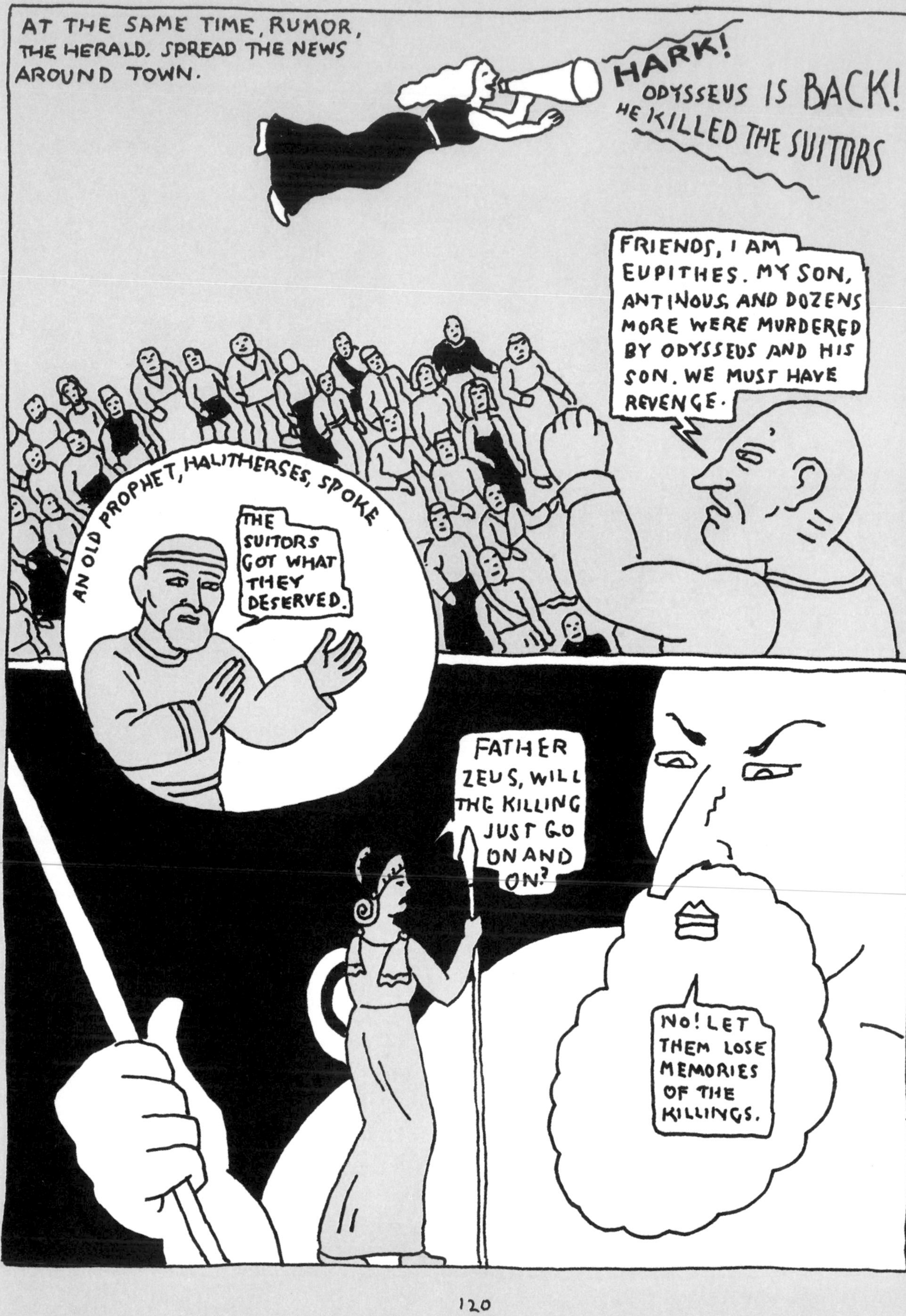
AT THE SAME TIME, RUMOR, THE HERALD. SPREAD THE NEWS AROUND TOWN.
HARK! ODYSSEUS IS BACK! HE KILLED THE SUITORS
FRIENDS, I AM EUPITHES. MY SON, ANTINOUS, AND DOZENS MORE WERE MURDERED BY ODYSSEUS AND HIS SON. WE MUST HAVE REVENGE.
AN OLD PROPHET, HALITHERSES, SPOKE
THE SUITORS GOT WHAT THEY DESERVED.
FATHER ZEUS, WILL THE KILLING JUST GO ON AND ON?
NO! LET THEM LOSE MEMORIES OF THE KILLINGS.

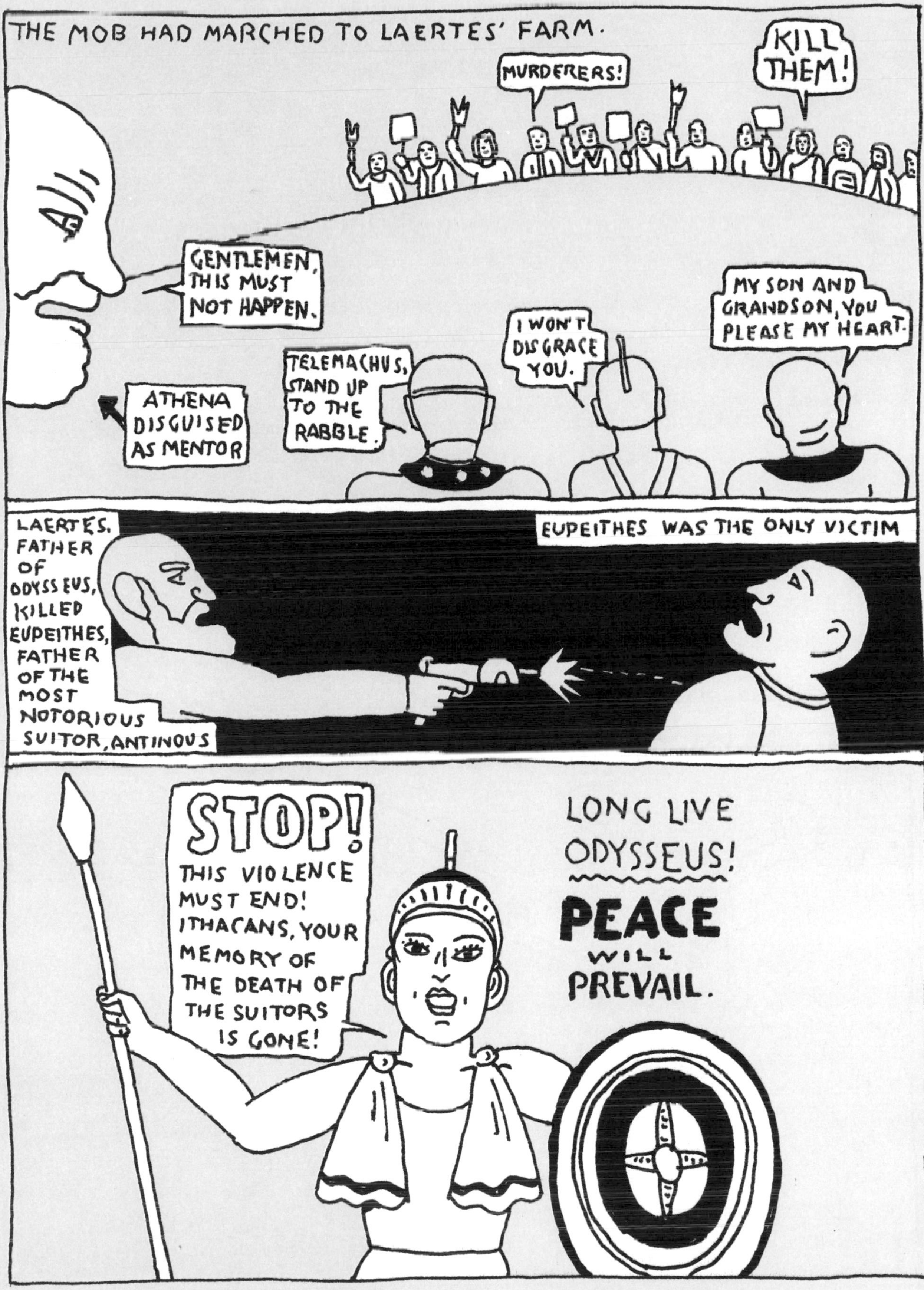
THE MOB HAD MARCHED TO LAERTES' FARM.
MURDERERS!
KILL THEM!
GENTLEMEN, THIS MUST NOT HAPPEN.
ATHENA DISGUISED AS MENTOR
TELEMACHUS, STAND UP TO THE RABBLE.
I WON'T DISGRACE YOU.
MY SON AND GRANDSON, YOU PLEASE MY HEART.
LAERTES, FATHER OF ODYSSEUS, KILLED EUPEITHES, FATHER OF THE MOST NOTORIOUS SUITOR, ANTINOUS
EUPEITHES WAS THE ONLY VICTIM
STOP!
THIS VIOLENCE MUST END! ITHACANS, YOUR MEMORY OF THE DEATH OF THE SUITORS IS GONE!
LONG LIVE ODYSSEUS!
PEACE WILL PREVAIL.

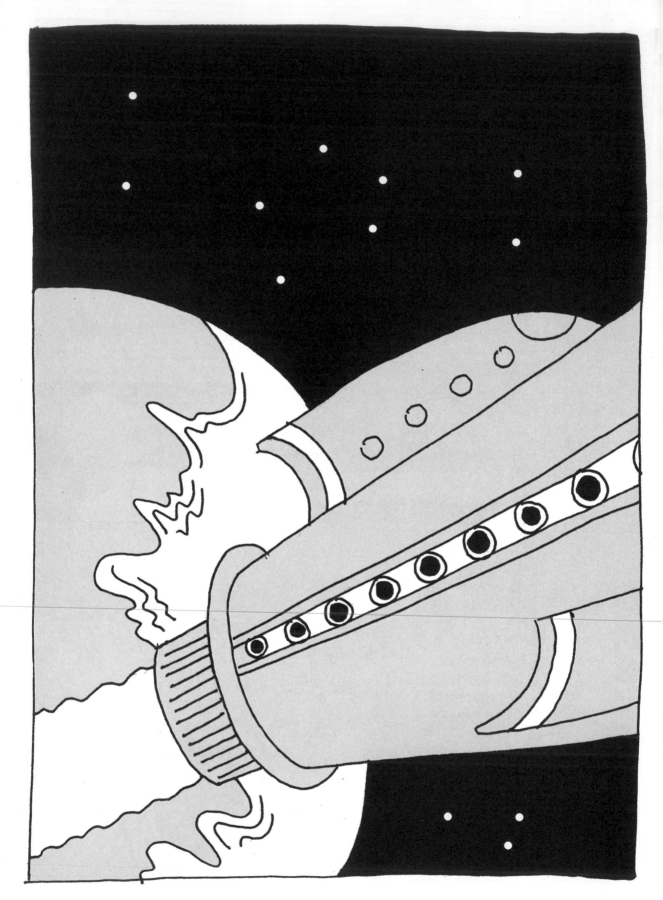

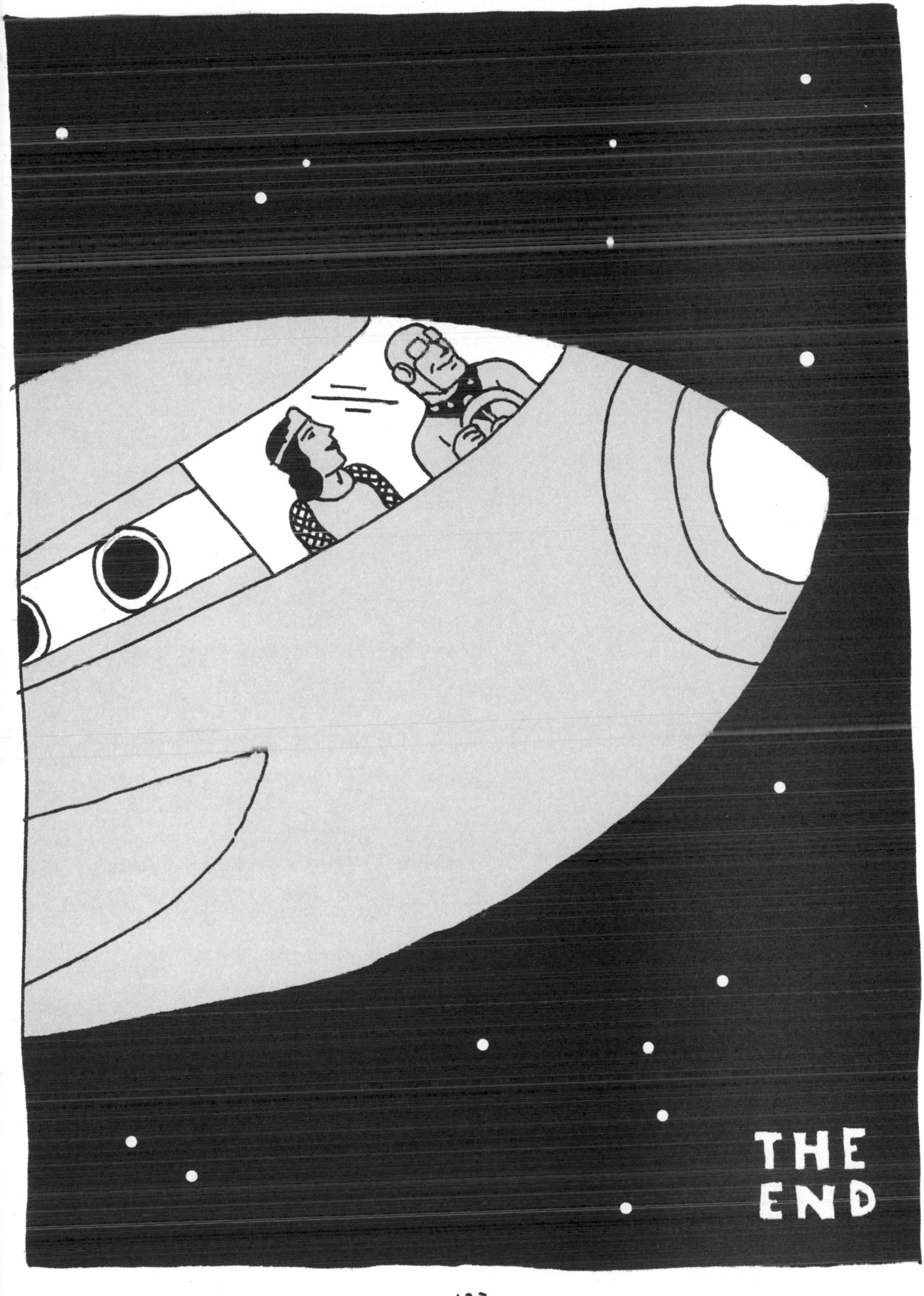
THE
END

EPILOGUE

HOMER SO NOW I'VE TOLD YOU THE STORY OF ODYSSEUS' CUNNING CLEVERNESS, AND HOW IT GOT HIM OUT OF SO MANY SCRAPES AND BACK TO ITHACA.

PRINCE IT'S A GREAT STORY. BUT I NEED YOU TO EXPLAIN ONE THING TO ME: WHY DOES ODYSSEUS ALWAYS DO THINGS THAT GET HIM IN TROUBLE TO BEGIN WITH? DOING THINGS LIKE YELLING HIS NAME TO THE CYCLOPS POLYPHEMUS SO THAT POSEIDON COULD TRACK HIM DOWN DOESN'T SEEM ALL THAT CLEVER TO ME.

HOMER BUT THAT'S WHY WE CARE ABOUT HIM. WHO WOULD CARE ABOUT SOMEONE WHO'S ALWAYS RIGHT? NOW MY TALE IS ENDED AND IT'S TIME FOR ME TO GO. SHALL WE SET OFF ON OUR OWN ADVENTURE?

PRINCE GETTING INTO TROUBLE AND OUT OF IT AGAIN IS REALLY EVERY-ONE'S STORY, ISN'T IT?

HOMER QUITE RIGHT, MY FRIEND, QUITE RIGHT.

A NOTE ON THE AUTHOR

SEYMOUR CHWAST'S AWARD-WINNING WORK HAS INFLUENCED TWO GENERATIONS OF DESIGNERS AND ILLUSTRATORS.

HE COFOUNDED PUSH PIN STUDIOS, WHICH RAPIDLY GAINED AN INTERNATIONAL REPUTATION FOR INNOVATIVE DESIGN AND ILLUSTRATION. PUSH PIN'S VISUAL LANGUAGE (WHICH REFERENCED CULTURE AND LITERATURE) AROSE FROM ITS PASSION FOR HISTORICAL DESIGN MOVEMENTS AND HELPED REVOLUTIONIZE THE WAY PEOPLE LOOK AT DESIGN.

CHWAST IS A RECIPIENT OF THE A.I.G.A. MEDAL, WAS INDUCTED INTO THE ART DIRECTORS HALL OF FAME, AND HAS HONORARY PH.D.S IN FINE ART FROM THE PARSONS SCHOOL OF DESIGN AND THE RHODE ISLAND SCHOOL OF DESIGN. HIS WORK IS IN THE COLLECTIONS OF THE MUSEUM OF MODERN ART AND THE METROPOLITAN MUSEUM OF ART AND HAS BEEN COLLECTED IN THE LEFT-HANDED DESIGNER AND SEYMOUR: THE OBSESSIVE IMAGES OF SEYMOUR CHWAST.

CHWAST'S PREVIOUS GRAPHIC NOVELS ARE DANTE'S DIVINE COMEDY AND THE CANTERBURY TALES.

HE LIVES IN NEW YORK WITH HIS WIFE, THE GRAPHIC DESIGNER AND PAINTER PAULA SCHER.

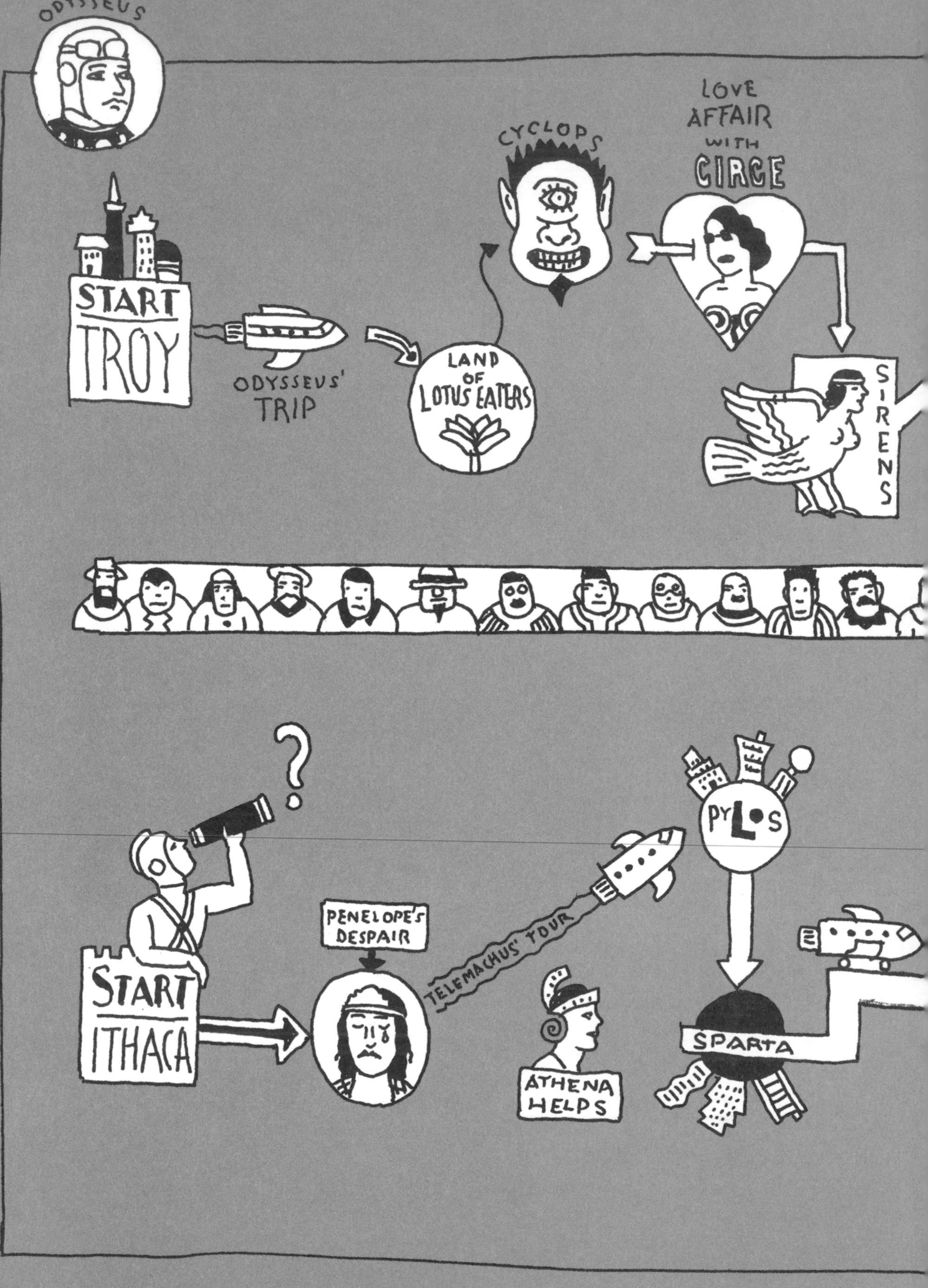
ODYSSEUS
START
TROY
ODYSSEUS' TRIP
LAND OF LOTUS EATERS
CYCLOPS
LOVE AFFAIR WITH CIRCE
SIRENS
START
ITHACA
PENELOPE'S DESPAIR
TELEMACHUS' TOUR
PYLOS
ATHENA HELPS
SPARTA